Telling and Remembering

Telling and Remembering

A Century of American Jewish Poetry

EDITED BY STEVEN J. RUBIN

Beacon Press / Boston

Beacon Press
25 Beacon Street
Boston, Massachusetts 02108–2892

Beacon Press books are published under the auspices of
the Unitarian Universalist Association of Congregations.

02 01 00 99 98 97   8 7 6 5 4 3 2 1

Text design by Christopher Kuntze
Composition by Wilsted & Taylor
Interior art by Amanda Guest

Library of Congress Cataloging-in-Publication Data

Telling and remembering : a century of American Jewish poetry / edited by Steven J. Rubin.
    p. cm.
    Includes indexes.
    ISBN 0-8070-6838-1
    1. American poetry—Jewish authors.   2. Jewish religious poetry, American.
  3. Jews—United States—Poetry.   4. Judaism—Poetry.   5. Jews—Poetry.   I. Rubin, Steven
Joel, 1943– .
    PS591.J4T38   1997
    811′.50808924—dc21   97-19292

Other books by Steven J. Rubin

Meyer Levin

*Writing Our Lives: Autobiographies
of American Jews, 1890–1990* (editor)

To the memory of my father

IRVING H. RUBIN

(1910 – 1996)

Times of counting are times of remembering;
here amidst showers
Of shiny fruits, . . . we can sit facing westward
Toward imminent rich tents, telling and remembering.

—JOHN HOLLANDER, "At the New Year"

Contents

PART II
NEW DAYS FOR OLD, OLD DAYS FOR NEW

PART III
STRUGGLING TO SING WITH ANGELS

Telling and Remembering

Introduction

POETRY HAS ALWAYS BEEN an essential aspect of the Jewish literary experience. Beginning as early as the Bible and the lyrical verses of The Song of Songs, Jewish poetry flourished in the Middle Ages with the great Sephardic poets Solomon ibn Gabirol and Judah Halevi of Spain, thrived in the centers of Yiddish culture in Eastern Europe, and has prospered in post-Holocaust Europe, Israel, and America.

Telling and Remembering recognizes and pays tribute to the rich and varied tradition of Jewish poetry that grew and developed in the United States. It began in the mid-nineteenth century with the religious hymns of Penina Moise (1797–1880), the first recognized American Jewish poet to write in English. Best known for her religious verses, many of which are still included in the *Reform Jewish Hymnal*, she was admired by her Jewish contemporaries but received little national recognition. Yet her influence was felt by several who followed, including another early American Jewish poet of Sephardic descent, Emma Lazarus, whose work begins this collection.

Although American Jewish poetry reaches back to Moise and Lazarus and has continued ever since, it has curiously received little critical or popular attention. And although American Jewish poets have been at the forefront of modern American poetry and have collectively produced a rich body of work on specifically Jewish subjects and themes, there have been few attempts to group them together in collections such as this one. Anthologies and texts of American Jewish literature, of which there are many, have been devoted almost entirely to fiction. Of the very few volumes of Jewish poetry published in the last twenty-five years, none is exclusively American. Similarly, although occasional articles and critical studies of Jewish poetry have been published in the 1990s, American Jewish literary criticism remains overwhelmingly concerned with prose.

This emphasis on fiction is somewhat understandable when one considers the enormous success of such novelists as Saul Bellow, Bernard Malamud, Isaac Bashevis Singer, and Philip Roth. It is less so, however, when one recognizes the achievements of Pulitzer Prize–winning poets Stanley Kunitz, Howard Nemerov, Karl Shapiro, Anthony Hecht, Maxine Kumin, Louise Glück, and Philip Levine, as well as those of other equally accomplished writers such as Louis Zukofsky, Muriel Rukeyser, Denise Levertov, Allen Ginsberg, Adrienne Rich, C. K. Williams, and Robert Pinsky—all important figures in the overall development of modern American poetry.

The poets included in this collection are noteworthy not only as a consequence of their productivity and their prominence in the American literary canon, but also because they have sought to explore enigmatic and meaningful Jewish issues in ways that reach beyond the usual "ethnic" themes of marginality and alienation so often found in American Jewish fiction. Their poetry is distinctive—and distinctively Jewish—in its treatment of such subjects as anti-Semitism, the Holocaust, Israel, ancient and modern Jewish history, the interpretation of sacred and mystical texts, the role of gender in Judaism, the loss of Yiddish language and culture, and the nature of religious faith and belief. Even when these poets write of more universal subjects, such as family relationships, personal memories, daily rituals, love, aging, and death, Jewish beliefs and practices figure prominently in the imagery and symbolism they employ.

This phenomenon can be explained in part by the language of poetry itself, which tends to be more figurative, more transcendent, and less literal than that of prose. "Poetry is the language that tells us," the poet Edwin Arlington Robinson claimed, "something that cannot be said." Free from the constraints of characterization, plot, and setting, poetry is arguably the ideal form to deal with the most metaphysical and ineffable issues. Although Jewish novelists have successfully portrayed Jewish characters and their milieux, Jewish poets have investigated the great Jewish themes in a more personal, emotional, and intense fashion.

Jewish poetry has also served as an effective vehicle for recalling a history that has often been traumatic. Like other Jewish writers and artists, many of the poets represented in this collection have understood that creative activity can play a vital role in the process of remembering, a process that has often been necessary for survival. As the poet Gerald Stern states: "It is the poet's job to remember . . . that is, to keep the past alive." This task is not unique to poets. It is, however, interesting to note that most American Jewish novelists have avoided such subjects as the Holocaust. By contrast, a great many American Jewish poets have sought through their art to imagine and somehow decipher the meaning of the loss of a culture and of six million Jewish lives.

Many of the poets in this collection have succeeded in preserving the past; others have focused their attention on the present moment. All have chosen to write about the experience of being a Jew. And although this volume contains a multitude of poems that bear witness to tragic events, it also includes many others that are joyful, hopeful, and humorous—poems that, in short, give voice to what Muriel Rukeyser refers to as the "whole and fertile spirit" of Jewish existence. It is this poetic rendering of that spirit—in all its diversity—that lies at the heart of this volume.

DIVIDED CHRONOLOGICALLY into four parts, this collection contains 202 poems by fifty-six authors. The first part, "To Be a Jew in the Twentieth Century," takes its title from Part VII of Rukeyser's memorable poem, "Letter to the Front," and includes the work of poets born prior to and just after the turn of the century. It begins with the poetry of Emma Lazarus. Of much greater fame and talent than Penina Moise, Lazarus was the first American Jewish poet whose work reached a wide and diverse audience. Her early poetry, published in the 1860s and 1870s, did not address specifically Jewish themes. Her later work, however, reflected a new commitment to Judaism, and her 1882 collection, *Songs of a Semite*, included many poems about her return to Judaism, Jewish suffering and survival, and her link with world Jewry on the eve of the great wave of Jewish immigration to America.

That migration, which lasted from approximately 1880 to 1920, brought more than three million Eastern European Jews to the United States. They brought with them a rich literary tradition, and several prominent Yiddish-language poets—such as Mani Leib, Chaim Grade, Jacob Glatstein, and Abraham Reisen—continued to succeed in the New World. Their poetry was much admired by their Yiddish-speaking audience, and often dealt with such typical immigrant concerns as assimilation, anti-Semitism, and the difficulties of acculturation. And although *Telling and Remembering* does not include these early Yiddish writers, their influence was felt by many of the English-language poets whose work is included.

One immigrant who did write in his adopted language was Alter Brody. Born in Russia in 1895, he wrote deeply felt poems that expressed his sense of loss and exile, especially his haunting "Kartúsh-kiya-Beróza" and his impressive long poem, "A Family Album." Hyam Plutzik, although born in the United States, spoke only Yiddish until the age of six. As an adult, however, he became quite familiar with contemporary English-language poetry, as is apparent in his delightfully ironic poem, "For T. S. E. Only," addressed to his poetic mentor, T. S. Eliot.

With the exception of Brody and Plutzik, all the poets included in part I were native speakers of English. Two of them, Charles Reznikoff and Louis Zukofsky, quickly moved to the forefront of the American literary scene. Together with George Oppen and Carl Rakosi (two poets not included in this collection), they formed the Objectivist Group, whose poetic manifestos proclaimed the primacy of the poem as an "object," important in and for itself, rather than as a representation of reality. Although Judaism was nowhere discussed in their credos, all the members of the group—with the exception of William Carlos Williams, who was an early, tangential partner—were Jewish. Among them, Reznikoff was the most preoccupied with Jewish themes in his poetry. His perception of himself as a diaspora Jew, alienated from his culture, adrift in the New World, permeates all aspects of his work. Sadly, he viewed the United States as "the noisy world / not mine" and, like many of his generation, failed to find comfort in America.

Other Jewish writers of the time, such as Maxwell Bodenheim, Stanley Kunitz, and Delmore Schwartz, were not as concerned with Jewish subjects in their work. Nevertheless, the Kunitz poems included in part I evoke the poet's sense of himself as an American Jew who has come to understand on the deepest level the difficulties and complexities of that status. "Earth was my home," Kunitz begins his poem, "The Flight of Apollo," "but even there I was a stranger." Similarly, neither Schwartz nor Bodenheim dealt with specific Jewish issues in their work, yet they too often gave voice to the themes of alienation and separation. Occasionally (as in "Abraham," "Jacob," and "Sarah"), Schwartz relied on biblical sources, while Bodenheim at times wrote about anti-Semitism ("Poem to Gentiles") and cultural identity ("Old Age").

Karl Shapiro and David Ignatow, on the other hand, were among the first of their generation to identify themselves clearly as Jewish poets.

All of the poems in Shapiro's *Poems of a Jew* (1958) explore the theme of Jewish identity and the status of the American Jew in relation to mainstream American culture. Similarly, Jewish issues pervade Ignatow's poetry, which contains more than a hint of Yiddish intonations and rhythms. Much of his work concerns Jewish suffering and redemption, as well as his own search for the divine. Like Reznikoff and Allen Ginsberg, Ignatow entitles one of his most moving poems "Kaddish," after the Jewish mourner's prayer for the dead, and uses the occasion to examine his ties both to his mother and to the world.

Rose Drachler, Eve Merriam, and Muriel Rukeyser were among the first poets to explore the "double minority" status of the American Jewish woman. Among them, Rukeyser is the most widely known. A feminist and political activist throughout her career, Rukeyser wrote poetry that resonates with compassion for the oppressed and anger toward the oppressors. As with Kunitz, her work is not always Jewish in content, although she often wrote passionately about Jewish identity ("Traditional Tune"), Jewish history and legend ("Akiba") or, as in her well-known sonnet, "To Be a Jew in the Twentieth Century" (Part VII of "Letter to the Front"), the moral challenge of contemporary Judaism. The work of both Drachler and Merriam is consistently and primarily concerned with Jewi·' ···b:·~~~. Drachler's poems ("The Prophet" and "The Witness," fc   ɔften examine the nature of Jewish religious belief, wherea⸳   ⸻erriam ("Esther" and "Of Dogs and Ostriches") more fre⸻   ⸻ sider the cultural aspects of Judaism and Jewish identity.

Part II of this collection, "⸻   for Old, Old Days for New" (the title of a Philip Levine p   ⸻tains the work of poets born in the 1920s. With the exceptic   nise Levertov, who arrived from England at the age of twent   ⸻ were born in the United States. And although English was theiɪ ɴative language, their poetry often recalls the immigrant experience of their parents and grandparents, as in Ruth Whitman's "Bubba Esther, 1888," Harvey Shapiro's "Death of a Grandmother," Philip Levine's "Zaydee," and Allen Ginsberg's "Visiting Father & Friends." Although these poems present images of the past, they are not merely sentimental portraits. Each of these poets understands the implications of history, the meaning of often-traumatic events, and the importance of the past for both present and future generations.

Among the fifteen poets included in part II, seven are women. While male fiction writers like Malamud, Roth, and Bellow seemed to dominate the Jewish American literary landscape in the 1950s and 1960s, several relatively unknown women poets, including Levertov, Ruth Whitman, Shirley Kaufman, Adrienne Rich, and Maxine Kumin were beginning to publish significant and original poetry, as were Grace Paley and Cynthia Ozick, two writers primarily known for their fiction. Like Rukeyser, Merriam, and Drachler before them, this generation of American Jewish women poets described Jewish experience with particular attention to the concerns of women. Several have offered through their poetry revisionist views of Jewish history, texts, and mythology, thereby redefining the traditional role of women within Judaism.

The poetry of both Whitman and Kaufman is almost exclusively Jewish in subject and theme. Whitman writes of Jewish history from a personal and often feminist perspective ("Cutting the Jewish Bride's Hair" and "Bubba Esther, 1888"). Kaufman, an American poet living in Israel, is inspired by the history and mythology of Israel ("The Western Wall") and intrigued by the psychological bond between America and Israel.

Rich, for the better part of five decades, has written about women's experiences and the situation of women throughout the world. A leftist, a feminist, and a lesbian, Rich addresses subjects ranging from politics and sexuality to Israel and the Holocaust. In the 1980s and 1990s she has identified more strongly with her Jewish heritage and has sought to unite the various strands of her consciousness in her poetry. In "Yom Kippur 1984," for example, set in Israel on the Day of Atonement, Rich sees connections: both the Jew and the lesbian are outcasts; both need their independence but seek a community of like-minded individuals.

Kumin also writes on a variety of subjects. But like Rich, she has demonstrated a renewed interest in Jewish subjects over the past several decades. In many of her more recent poems Kumin investigates such themes as her ties to Israel, the Holocaust, the meaning of her Jewish heritage, and Jewish feminism. "I like to think," Kumin affirms in her 1994 poem, "Getting the Message," "God's talent scouts today / select for covenant without regard / for gender, . . ."

The other poets represented in part II are Howard Nemerov, Anthony Hecht, Allen Ginsberg, Gerald Stern, Harvey Shapiro, Philip

Levine, Irving Feldman, and John Hollander. Nemerov's poems do not address Jewish issues specifically, although the subtle pessimism and sense of alienation that permeate his work are characteristically Jewish in spirit. Hecht is generally considered to be among the best poets of his generation. His work has always included important poems of Jewish content. In the 1980s and 1990s, his poetry has reflected an even stronger identification with and interest in things Jewish, as in "Exile" and "The Book of Yolek."

Like Hecht, both Hollander and Feldman have flourished in academic settings. Their poetry tends to be formal, elegant, and philosophical. Feldman has written poems expressing his identification with the victims of the Holocaust ("To the Six Million" and "The Pripet Marshes"), as well as those exploring his own American Jewish identity. While Hollander's early poetry often investigated the more arcane aspects of Judaism, those poems included here ("At the New Year," "Letter to Jorge Luis Borges," and "Song at the End of a Meal") deal with more familiar facets of Jewish tradition and religion.

Gerald Stern, like Whitman and Kaufman, is one of the more consciously "Jewish" poets of his generation. Through his art, he has struggled to define, in the most profound and personal manner, what it means to be a Jew—ethically and historically—in contemporary America. His range of Jewish subjects is extensive: the Holocaust ("Soap"), the rise and fall of Yiddish culture ("Adler"), religious ritual ("Tashlikh"), and the moral responsibility of Judaism ("Behaving Like a Jew"). His is a major voice in contemporary American Jewish poetry.

Allen Ginsberg is well known for his role as one of the founders of the Beat movement in the 1950s. His early poems, like "Howl" (1956) and "America" (1956), had more to do with his outspoken rebellion against American materialism than his Jewish background. Later his work was influenced by his interest in Buddhism and Eastern philosophy. Yet one of his most famous poems, "Kaddish" (1961), which does not appear in this collection, is dedicated to his immigrant mother and relies on his early Jewish experiences, as does "To Aunt Rose," which is included in part II. Ginsberg's 1994 collection, *Cosmopolitan Greetings*, contains several poems in which he again recalls his family memories and Jewish roots. "I'm Jewish because love my family motzah ball soup," Ginsberg humorously begins his 1991 poem, "Yiddishe Kopf."

Part III of this volume, "Struggling to Sing with Angels," takes its title from David Meltzer's beautiful poem, "Tell Them I'm Struggling to Sing with Angels." It consists of the work of sixteen American Jewish poets born between 1930 and 1944. Growing up in the 1930s and 1940s, they are old enough to have witnessed (albeit from a distance) the most significant events of modern Jewish history: the Holocaust and the establishment of the state of Israel. Yet for the most part they are emotionally removed from the immigrant experience of their parents and grandparents. Their connection to Jewish religion and culture is based less on nostalgia and memory than on ideology and a desire to explore issues and themes that are relevant to their particular Jewish American experience. As a group they have produced an imaginative and eclectic body of work.

Although there are no discernible "schools" among this generation of contemporary American Jewish poets, several do share similar characteristics. Jerome Rothenberg and David Meltzer, for example, both based in California, have a common interest in the apocalyptic. Their poetry frequently explores the more mystical, esoteric aspects and sources of Judaism. Others, like Linda Pastan, Susan Fromberg Schaeffer, and Myra Sklarew, write poems that are more intimate, often based on personal memories and the rituals of home, family, and religion. Deeply felt, yet unsentimental, these poems give voice to the ambiguities and difficulties of being an American Jewish woman in the second half of the twentieth century.

Stephen Berg, C. K. Williams, Alicia Suskin Ostriker, and Louise Glück are important American poets whose sense of Jewish identity does not dominate their work. Nevertheless, all have written meaningfully of various aspects of the Jewish experience. Berg recounts the unusual activities of the poet Robert Desnos at Buchenwald in his long poem, "Desnos Reading the Palms of Men on Their Way to the Gas Chambers." Williams writes of Nazi atrocities with controlled anger, bitterness, and grief in "Spit" and "A Day for Anne Frank." Ostriker's poems included in part III ("The Bride," "A Meditation in Seven Days," "The Opinion of Hagar," and "The Eighth and Thirteenth") reveal her fascination with Jewish history and ceremony, and her willingness to reexamine Jewish ritual from a feminist perspective. Glück, winner of the 1993 Pulitzer Prize, writes about belief ("The Gift"), ancient Jewish history ("Day Without Night"), and—in "Legend"—her immigrant grandfather and his difficult adjustment to the New World:

"In Hungary, a scholar, a man of property. / Then failure: an immigrant / rolling cigars in a cold basement."

Irena Klepfisz is another accomplished American Jewish poet who identifies with many aspects of the Jewish experience. A child survivor of the Holocaust, she writes of Nazi atrocities from personal, often painful memories ("Death Camp" and Dedications from "Bashert"). Her poetry is one of the most successful attempts to bear witness to the events of the Holocaust, which is in part the history of her life as well. Moreover, as one who grew up speaking Yiddish and Polish, she is a writer who—like Cynthia Ozick—has attempted to shape her writing to accommodate her Jewish experience and to keep the language of her ancestors alive. Her poetry contains Yiddish words, phrases, and intonations—as for example in her dual-language titled poem, "*Der mames shabosim* / My Mother's Sabbath Days."

Marvin Bell, like Klepfisz, Feldman, and Williams, has written poems that powerfully depict the Holocaust and its psychological aftermath ("The Extermination of the Jews" and "Getting Lost in Nazi Germany"). Bell's later poetry—especially that which deals with the Holocaust—has become less realistic and more visionary, as for example, his 1997 poem, "The Book of the Dead Man (#58)."

Robert Mezey, Marge Piercy, Eleanor Wilner, Robert Pinsky, and Enid Shomer are also represented in part III. Mezey's poems about Jewish subjects range from serious contemplation ("The Wandering Jew" and "The Silence") to humorous portrayal of his typically Jewish mother ("My Mother"). Piercy is another poet who has explored diverse aspects of her Jewish religion, heritage, and identity. Her commitment to Reconstructionist Judaism, in particular, has inspired her to write liturgical verse; she is, in fact, one of the few contemporary poets to do so. Wilner's poems included in part III ("Miriam's Song," "Sarah's Choice," and "When Asked to Lie Down on the Altar") indicate her interest in reinterpreting Jewish texts and traditions. Like Piercy and Ostriker, she offers an affirming vision for women within traditional Judaism. Pinsky's poems combine past personal experience with a more universal investigation of the meaning of cultural and ethnic identity. Shomer, like Piercy, writes on a variety of Jewish subjects, and her work is frequently motivated by her strong sense of history and religion.

The fourth and last part, "A World Above Suffering," takes its optimistic heading from Albert Goldbarth's 1993 poem of the same title (although the poem refers more to Goldbarth's grandfather's dreams than to present reality). Part IV includes the work of twelve American Jewish poets born since 1945. Much of their work has appeared in the 1980s and 1990s. A few have only recently published their first books of poems. As the work of several of them shows, one of the most striking aspects of contemporary American Jewish poetry is the desire of a significant number of Jewish poets to explore their relationship with religion and the past through their art. While many older Jewish poets, such as Kunitz, Nemerov, Hecht, Rich, and Levertov, have written important poems about Jewish subjects, their work is not exclusively or primarily devoted to Jewish concerns. But poets like Marcia Falk, Mark Rudman, Rodger Kamenetz, and Richard Chess have found that their Jewishness is an integral part of who they are as Americans and as artists. Many have written entire poetic volumes that pertain only to Jewish matters: Falk's *The Book of Blessings*, Rudman's *Rider*, Kamenetz's *The Missing Jew*, and Chess's *Tekiah*, for example. They offer no apologies for the ethnocentric basis of their poetry. Nor do they despair if their audiences are predominately Jewish. Collectively, they comprise one of the most recent and interesting chapters in Jewish American poetry.

Others, such as Philip Schultz, Albert Goldbarth, Edward Hirsch, Alan Shapiro, and Jacqueline Osherow have written extensively about Jewish history, the Holocaust, contemporary American Jewish culture, and their own connections with Judaism. The poems of Schultz and Goldbarth have a distinctly Jewish style that incorporates Yiddish expressions, cadences, and syntax, as well as references to Jewish history and culture. Both Hirsch and Shapiro write personal narratives that tap into their Jewish memories and family roots. In Hirsch's "Ancient Signs" and "My Grandfather's Poems," for example, the poet brings to life and identifies with the immigrant culture of past generations. Shapiro's "Mezuzah" and "A Christmas Story" are personal accounts, written in proselike free verse, of particularly meaningful childhood experiences. Osherow, like Hirsch, identifies with the past, particularly with the victims of the Holocaust, as in "To Eva" and "Song for the Music in the Warsaw Ghetto." She is part of a long tradition of Jewish poets who have felt the need to create in the face of destruction.

For several women poets included in part IV—Robin Becker, Judith Baumel, and Robyn Selman—Jewishness is one of several themes in their poetry, which may also include feminism, lesbianism, environmental issues, and radical politics. Becker and Baumel have both found in their Jewish heritage metaphors to sustain them through personal losses and in their metaphysical quests for meaning and belonging. In similar fashion, Selman employs references to Judaism and to her Jewish upbringing in her poetry as part of her efforts at self-portrayal. Like Shapiro, many of her poems involve personal anecdote and family history, for example, "Descent" and "Work Song." Becker, Baumel, and Selman are part of a larger community of American Jewish women poets, past and present, who have explored in their work the specific aspects of women's experience.

My purpose throughout this collection is to present the best and the most representative work of those writers who can properly be classified as American Jewish poets. I have not included those poets who, although nominally Jewish, do not deal significantly with the American Jewish experience. All the authors represented—male or female, traditionalist or experimental, modernist or postmodernist—share an interest in and a desire to explore those issues surrounding their Jewishness. The results, as the reader will discover, are poems that are as rich and diverse as the experience itself.

Many of the poets included in this volume are well-known figures: Stanley Kunitz, Denise Levertov, Karl Shapiro, Adrienne Rich, Allen Ginsberg, Philip Levine, Robert Pinsky, and Louise Glück. Others—such as Alter Brody, Rose Drachler, Hyam Plutzik, Ruth Whitman, and Irena Klepfisz—are less-recognized poets who have nevertheless produced impressive work and who are deserving of wider audiences. A few, such as Grace Paley, Susan Fromberg Schaeffer, and Cynthia Ozick, are known principally for their fiction, although their poetry is also noteworthy. Still others have distinguished themselves not only as poets but also as translators of ancient and modern Jewish verse—most notably Ruth Whitman and Marcia Falk. The work of a number of poets (Alan Shapiro, Richard Chess, Robyn Selman, and Jacqueline Osherow, among others) has attracted critical attention in the late 1990s and will surely achieve more recognition in coming years. Finally, this collection is not intended to be a comprehensive collection of all that has been written. Several talented poets—such as George Oppen, Allen Grossman, Gil Orlovitz, Ira Sadoff, Carolyn Finkelstein, and Marilyn

Hacker—could have been included had space allowed, and readers are encouraged to discover on their own the work of these and other poets.

Jewish poetry is part of an unbroken tradition that stretches back thirty-five hundred years. It has survived, like the Jewish people, despite enormous odds and through a strong imaginative will. The spirit that has generated that survival is the same spirit that has inspired the poetry contained in this collection. American Jewish poets have given full and imaginative expression to what it is like to be a Jew in twentieth-century America and, in so doing, have added one of the most impressive chapters to the continuing Jewish literary tradition.

Steven J. Rubin
Fall 1996

Editor's Note: All notes appearing in the texts are reprinted from the original poems.

PART I

TO BE A JEW

IN THE

TWENTIETH

CENTURY

Emma Lazarus (1849–1887)

Emma Lazarus, the descendant of Sephardic Jews who came to the United States from Portugal, was born in New York City. Her early poetry, published in the 1860s and 1870s and well received in critical circles, had little to do with Jewish concerns. In the 1880s, however, partly as a reaction to the news of pogroms and widespread persecution of Jews in Russia, and partly as a result of having read George Eliot's *Daniel Deronda*, she turned her attention almost exclusively to Jewish subjects and the translation of Jewish poets. Her 1882 collection, *Songs of a Semite*, from which the selections here are taken, contains several passionate poems about her newfound Jewish identity and her concern for Jewish survival. "The Crowing of the Red Cock" is a vivid portrayal of Jewish suffering, as well as a call for forgiveness. "In the Jewish Synagogue at Newport" recalls Longfellow's famous poem, "The Jewish Synagogue at Newport," and poignantly depicts America's oldest synagogue, now standing strangely empty. She remains best known for her 1883 sonnet "The New Colossus," which is engraved on the base of the Statue of Liberty.

The Crowing of the Red Cock

Across the Eastern sky has glowed
   The flicker of a blood-red dawn,
Once more the clarion cock has crowed,
   Once more the sword of Christ is drawn.
A million burning rooftrees light
The world-wide path of Israel's flight.

Where is the Hebrew's fatherland?
   The folk of Christ is sore bestead;
The Son of Man is bruised and banned,
   Nor finds whereon to lay his head.
His cup is gall, his meat is tears,
His passion lasts a thousand years.

Each crime that wakes in man the beast,
   Is visited upon his kind.
The lust of mobs, the greed of priest,
   The tyranny of kings, combined
To root his seed from earth again,
His record is one cry of pain.

When the long roll of Christian guilt
   Against his sires and kin is known,
The flood of tears, the life-blood spilt,
   The agony of ages shown,
What oceans can the stain remove,
From Christian law and Christian love?

Nay, close the book; not now, not here,
   The hideous tale of sin narrate,

Reechoing in the martyr's ear,
   Even he might nurse revengeful hate,
Even he might turn in wrath sublime,
With blood for blood and crime for crime.

Coward? Not he, who faces death,
   Who singly against worlds has fought,
For what? A name he may not breathe,
   For liberty of prayer and thought.
The angry sword he will not whet,
His nobler task is—to forget.

In the Jewish Synagogue at Newport

Here, where the noises of the busy town,
    The ocean's plunge and roar can enter not,
We stand and gaze around with tearful awe,
    And muse upon the consecrated spot.

No signs of life are here: the very prayers
    Inscribed around are in a language dead;
The light of the "perpetual lamp" is spent
    That an undying radiance was to shed.

What prayers were in this temple offered up,
    Wrung from sad hearts that knew no joy on earth,
By these lone exiles of a thousand years,
    From the fair sunrise land that gave them birth!

Now as we gaze, in this new world of light,
    Upon this relic of the days of old,
The present vanishes, and tropic bloom
    And Eastern towns and temples we behold.

Again we see the patriarch with his flocks,
    The purple seas, the hot blue sky o'erhead,
The slaves of Egypt,—omens, mysteries,—
    Dark fleeing hosts by flaming angels led.

A wondrous light upon a sky-kissed mount,
    A man who reads Jehovah's written law,
'Midst blinding glory and effulgence rare,
    Unto a people prone with reverent awe.

The pride of luxury's barbaric pomp,
　　In the rich court of royal Solomon—
Alas! we wake: one scene alone remains,—
　　The exiles by the streams of Babylon.

Our softened voices send us back again
　　But mournful echoes through the empty hall;
Our footsteps have a strange, unnatural sound,
　　And with unwonted gentleness they fall.

The weary ones, the sad, the suffering,
　　All found their comfort in the holy place,
And children's gladness and men's gratitude
　　Took voice and mingled in the chant of praise.

The funeral and the marriage, now, alas!
　　We know not which is sadder to recall;
For youth and happiness have followed age,
　　And green grass lieth gently over all.

Nathless the sacred shrine is holy yet,
　　With its lone floors where reverent feet once trod.
Take off your shoes as by the burning bush,
　　Before the mystery of death and God.

Maxwell Bodenheim (1892–1954)

Born in Hermanville, Mississippi, Maxwell Bodenheim studied art and law in Chicago, joined the Army, and eventually settled in New York after World War I. He began writing for the Federal Writers' Project in the 1930s, but was dismissed in 1940 for his ties to the Communist Party. He continued to write prodigiously—producing ten volumes of poetry, over a dozen novels, and an autobiography—until his murder (and that of his second wife) in 1954. Although Jewishness was not a persistent theme in his poetry, his later work often expressed his horror of racial hatred in general and anti-Semitism in particular—as, for example, in "Poem to Gentiles," reprinted from *Seven Poets in Search of an Answer* (1944). In an earlier poem, "Old Age," from *Minna and Myself* (1918), Bodenheim creates a series of colorful urban images, suggesting an acceptance of death and the poet's subtle link to the Jewish people.

Old Age

In me is a little painted square
Bordered by old shops with gaudy awnings.
And before the shops sit smoking, open-bloused old men
Drinking sunlight.
The old men are my thoughts;
And I come to them each evening, in a creaking cart,
And quietly unload supplies.
We fill slim pipes and chat
And inhale scents from pale flowers in the center of the square. . . .
Strong men, tinkling women, and dripping, squealing children
Stroll past us, or into the shops.
They greet the shopkeepers and touch their hats or foreheads
     to me. . . .
Some evening I shall not return to my people.

Poem to Gentiles

The butchering must be wholesale and the smell
Of dead Jews must be strong enough to drift,
Like vastly stifled echoes of a yell,
Before the easy, widespread protests lift.
How many of them are sincere?—the tears,
The blades of conscience do not wait, mild, slow,
Until the slaughter-house revolves for years
And business lags because supplies are low.
The little, harried men, depleted, glued
By warm and cumbersome monotonies,
They know quick sympathy, misguided feud,
But they at least hold sharp sincerities.
They are not politicians, mountebanks,
Smooth men who plot the time to cheer or kneel:
And when these Gentiles of the slapped, blurred ranks
Shake hands with Jews, the hard-won touch is real.
They can be poisoned, they have been the prey
Of ranting liars, rumors, kindled lure
For centuries, and yet their creeping day
Of vengeance nears, bruised, wondering, but sure.
The lists of soldier casualties arrive.
The Gentile, Jewish parents finger death.
Some fraction of this nearness must survive
Beyond the sentimental, blundering breath.
The soldiers know hard tolerance roughly snared
From times where bullets strike or barely miss,
For pain and sweat and fear defeated, shared,
Are overwhelming foes of prejudice.
In peace, the slow blend will be selfless deeds,
Hearts naked, problems flattened on the streets.
It will not spring from suave men and their greeds,
Speech-makings, brass-bands, sweet discursive seats.

Charles Reznikoff (1894–1976)

Charles Reznikoff, the son of Russian immigrants, was born in Brooklyn, New York, in 1894. He graduated from the law school of New York University in 1915 and was admitted to the bar the following year. Reznikoff, however, practiced law only briefly, turning instead to writing, editing, and translating. His sense of Jewish identity is central to almost all of his approximately twenty volumes of poetry. His themes and subjects include Jewish ritual and religion, biblical Israel, nineteenth-century Russia, American Jewish culture, anti-Semitism, and details from his own life. In 1976–1977, Black Sparrow Press published an extensive, two-volume collection of his poetry. The first "Kaddish," from Volume I, is a gloss on the "Kaddish de Rabbanan" ("The Rabbi's Kaddish"—one of several forms of the traditional prayer in praise of God). The second poem of the same title, from Volume II, is based on the "Mourner's Kaddish" and realistically describes the death of the poet's mother, as well as his own emotional response.

Kaddish

Upon Israel and upon the Rabbis, and upon their disciples and upon all the disciples of their disciples, and upon all who engage in the study of the Torah in this place and in every place, unto them and unto you be abundant peace, grace, lovingkindness, mercy, long life, ample sustenance and salvation, from their Father who is in Heaven. And say ye Amen.

KADDISH DE RABBANAN, translated by R. Travers Herford

Upon Israel and upon the rabbis
and upon the disciples and upon all the disciples of their
        disciples
and upon all who study the Torah in this place and in every
        place,
to them and to you
peace;

upon Israel and upon all who meet with unfriendly glances,
        sticks and stones and names—
on posters, in newspapers, or in books to last,
chalked on asphalt or in acid on glass,
shouted from a thousand windows by radio;
who are pushed out of class-rooms and rushing trains,
whom the hundred hands of a mob strike,
and whom jailers strike with bunches of keys, with revolver
        butts;
to them and to you
in this place and in every place
safety;

upon Israel and upon all who live
as the sparrows of the streets
under the cornices of the houses of others,
and as rabbits
in the fields of strangers
on the grace of the seasons
and what the gleaners leave in the corners;
you children of the wind—

birds
that feed on the tree of knowledge
in this place and in every place
to them and to you
a living;

upon Israel
and upon their children and upon all the children of their
        children
in this place and in every place,
to them and to you
life.

Kaddish

I

In her last sickness, my mother took my hand in hers
tightly: for the first time I knew
how calloused a hand it was, and how soft was mine.

II

Day after day you vomit the green sap of your life
and, wiping your lips with a paper napkin,
smile at me; and I smile back.
But, sometimes, as I talk calmly to others
I find that I have sighed—irrelevantly.

III

I pay my visit and, when the little we have to say is said,
go about my business and pleasures;
but you are lying these many weeks abed.
The sun comes out; the clouds are gone; the sky is blue;
the stars arise; the moon shines; and the sun shines anew
for me; but you are dying,
wiping the tears from your eyes—
secretly that I may go about my business and pleasures
while the sun shines and the stars rise.

IV

The wind that had been blowing yesterday has fallen;
now it is cold. The sun is shining behind the grove of trees
bare of every leaf (the trees no longer brown
as in autumn, but grayish—dead wood until the spring);
and in the withered grass the brown oak leaves are lying,
gray with frost.

Kaddish—A portion of the ritual of the synagogue recited by mourners.

"I was so sick but now—I think—am better."
Your voice, strangely deep, trembles;
your skin is ashen—
you seem a mother of us both, long dead.

V

The wind is crowding the waves down the river
to add their silver to the shimmering west.
The great work you did seems trifling now,
but you are tired. It is pleasant to close your eyes.
What is a street-light doing
so far from any street? That was the sun,
and now there is only darkness.

VI

Head sunken, eyes closed,
face pallid,
the bruised lips parted;
breathing heavily,
as if you had been climbing flights of stairs,
another flight of stairs—
and the heavy breathing
stopped.
The nurse came into the room silently
at the silence,
and felt your pulse,
and put your hand
beneath the covers,
and drew the covers to your chin,
and put a screen about your bed.
That was all:
you were dead.

VII

Her heavy braids, the long hair of which she had been proud,
cut off, the undertaker's rouge

on her cheeks and lips,
and her cheerful greeting
silenced.

VIII

My mother leaned above me
as when I was a child.
What had she come to tell me
from the grave?
Helpless,
I looked at her anguish;
lifted my hand
to stroke her cheek,
touched it and woke.

IX

STELE

Not, as you were lying, a basin beside your head
into which you kept vomiting; nor, as that afternoon,
when you followed the doctor slowly with hardly the strength
      to stand,
small and shrunken in your black coat;
but, as you half turned to me, before you went through the
      swinging door,
and lifted your head, your face solemn and calm.

X

We looked at the light burning slowly before your picture
and looked away;
we thought of you as we talked but could not bring ourselves
      to speak—
to strangers who do not care, yes,
but not among ourselves.

XI

I know you do not mind
(if you mind at all)

that I do not pray for you
or burn a light
on the day of your death:
we do not need these trifles
between us—
prayers and words and lights.

Meditations on the Fall and Winter Holidays

NEW YEAR'S

The solid houses in the mist
are thin as tissue paper;
the water laps slowly at the rocks;
and the ducks from the north are here
at rest on the grey ripples.

The company in which we went
so free of care, so carelessly,
has scattered. Good-bye,
to you who lie behind in graves,
to you who galloped proudly off!
Pockets and heart are empty.

This is the autumn and our harvest—
such as it is, such as it is—
the beginnings of the end, bare trees and barren ground;
but for us only the beginning:
let the wild goat's horn
and the silver trumpet sound!

Reason upon reason
to be thankful:
for the fruit of the earth,
for the fruit of the tree,
for the light of the fire,
and to have come to this season.

The work of our hearts is dust
to be blown about in the winds
by the God of our dead in the dust

but our Lord delighting in life
(let the wild goat's horn
and the silver trumpet sound!)—
our God Who imprisons in coffin and grave
and unbinds the bound.

You have loved us greatly and given us
Your laws
for an inheritance,
Your sabbaths, holidays, and seasons of gladness,
distinguishing Israel
from other nations—
distinguishing us
above the shoals of men.
And yet why should we be remembered—
if at all—only for peace, if grief
is also for all? Our hopes,
if they blossom, if they blossom at all, the petals
and fruit fall.

You have given us the strength
to serve You,
but we may serve or not
as we please;
not for peace nor for prosperity,
not even for length of life, have we merited
remembrance; remember us
as the servants
You have inherited.

II

DAY OF ATONEMENT

The great Giver has ended His disposing;
the long day
is over and the gates are closing.
How badly all that has been read
was read by us,
how poorly all that should be said.

All wickedness shall go in smoke.
It must, it must!
The just shall see and be glad.
The sentence is sweet and sustaining;
for we, I suppose, are the just;
and we, the remaining.

If only I could write with four pens between five fingers
and with each pen a different sentence at the same time—
but the rabbis say it is a lost art, a lost art.
I well believe it. And at that of the first twenty sins that we
        confess,
five are by speech alone;
little wonder that I must ask the Lord to bless
the words of my mouth and the meditations of my heart.

Now, as from the dead, I revisit the earth and delight
in the sky, and hear again
the noise of the city and see
earth's marvelous creatures—men.
Out of nothing I became a being,
and from a being I shall be
nothing—but until then
I rejoice, a mote in Your world,
a spark in Your seeing.

III

FEAST OF BOOTHS

This was a season of our fathers' joy:
not only when they gathered grapes and the fruit of trees
in Israel, but when, locked in the dark and stony streets,
they held—symbols of a life from which they were banished
but to which they would surely return—
the branches of palm trees and of willows, the twigs of the
        myrtle,
and the bright odorous citrons.

This was the grove of palms with its deep well
in the stony ghetto in the blaze of noon;
this the living stream lined with willows;
and this the thick-leaved myrtles and trees heavy with fruit
in the barren ghetto—a garden
where the unjustly hated were justly safe at last.

In booths this week of holiday
as those who gathered grapes in Israel lived
and also to remember we were cared for
in the wilderness—
I remember how frail my present dwelling is
even if of stones and steel.

I know this is the season of our joy:
we have completed the readings of the Law
and we begin again;
but I remember how slowly I have learnt, how little,
how fast the year went by, the years—how few.

IV

HANUKKAH

The swollen dead fish float on the water;
the dead birds lie in the dust trampled to feathers;
the lights have been out a long time and the quick gentle hands
        that lit them—
rosy in the yellow tapers' glow—
have long ago become merely nails and little bones,
and of the mouths that said the blessing and the minds that
        thought it
only teeth are left and skulls, shards of skulls.
By all means, then, let us have psalms
and days of dedication anew to the old causes.

Penniless, penniless, I have come with less and still less
to this place of my need and the lack of this hour.
That was a comforting word the prophet spoke:

Not by might nor by power but by My spirit, said the Lord;
comforting, indeed, for those who have neither might nor power—
for a blade of grass, for a reed.

The miracle, of course, was not that the oil for the sacred light—
in a little cruse—lasted as long as they say;
but that the courage of the Maccabees lasted to this day:
let that nourish my flickering spirit.

Go swiftly in your chariot, my fellow Jew,
you who are blessed with horses;
and I will follow as best I can afoot,
bringing with me perhaps a word or two.
Speak your learned and witty discourses
and I will utter my word or two—
not by might nor by power
but by Your spirit, Lord.

Alter Brody (b. 1895)

Alter Brody was born in the village of Kartúshkiya-Beróza in Russia (the subject of one of the poems included here) and came to New York in 1903. He wrote in obscurity most of his life and expressed a deep sense of loss and alienation in almost all his poems. "Kartúshkiya-Beróza" combines a feeling of longing and nostalgia for Brody's past life in Russia with the knowledge of the town's ultimate destruction. In "Times Square" the poet poignantly juxtaposes his boyhood memories with his present New York reality. The memorable long poem, "A Family Album," recalls Brody's family history and his sad, lonely life in the New World. Brody disappeared from the literary scene after World War II, and it has not been possible to determine what became of him.

Kartúshkiya-Beróza

It is twelve years since I have been there—
I was born there,
In the little town, by the river—
It all comes back to me now
Reading in the newspaper:
"The Germans have seized the bridge-head at Kartúshkiya-Beróza;
The Russians are retreating in good order across the marshes.
The town is in flames."

Kartúshkiya-Beróza!
Sweet-sounding, time-scented name—
Smelling of wide-extending marshes of hay;
Smelling of cornfields;
Smelling of apple-orchards;
Smelling of cherry-trees in full blossom;
Smelling of all the pleasant recollections of my childhood—
Smelling of Grandmother's kitchen,
Grandmother's freshly-baked dainties,
Grandmother's plum-pudding—
Kartúshkiya-Beróza!
I see before me a lane running between two rows of straggling
    cottages—
I cannot remember the name of the lane;
I do not know whether it has any name at all;
But I remember it was broad and unpaven and shaded with wide-
    branching chestnuts
And enters the market-place
Just a few houses after my Grandfather's—
Kartúshkiya-Beróza!
I can see it even now
My Grandfather's house—
On the lane, to the right, as you come from the market-place;

A big, hospitable frame building—
Big as my Grandfather's own heart,
And hospitable as Grandmother's smile.
I can see it even now,
With the white-pillared porch in the center and the sharp-gabled roof
Pierced with little windows;
And the great quadrangular garden behind it;
And the tall fence surrounding the garden;
And the old well in the corner of the garden;
With the bucket-lift
Rising over the fence—
Kartúshkiya-Beróza!
I can see him even now,
My Grandfather—
Bending over me, tall and sad-eyed and thoughtful—
Lifting me up and seating me on his knees
Lovingly,
And listening to all my childish questions and confessions;
Pardoning, admonishing, remonstrating—
Satisfying my interrogative soul with good-humored indulgence.
And my Grandmother,
Dear little woman!
I can never dissociate her from plum-pudding and apple-dumplings,
And raisin-cakes and almond-cakes and crisp potato-pancakes
And the smell of fish frying on the fire.
And then there is my cousin, Miriam,
Who lived in the yellow house across the lane—
A freckle-faced, cherry-eyed little girl with a puckered-up nose—
I was very romantic about her.
And then there is my curse, my rival at school, my archenemy—
Jacob,
The synagogue sexton's boy,
On whom I was always warring—
God knows on what battlefield he must be lying now!
And then there is Nathan and Joseph and Berel and Solomon
And Ephraim, the baker's boy,
And Baruch and Gershen and Mendel

And long-legged, sandy-haired Emanuel who fell into the pond with
    me that time,
While we were skating on the ice—
Kartúshkiya-Beróza!
I can see myself even now
In the lane on a summer's day,
Cap in hand, chasing after dragon-flies—
Suddenly, nearby, sounds the noise of drums and bugles—
I know what that means!
Breathlessly I dash up the lane.
It is the regiment quartered in the barracks at the end of the town, in
    its annual parade on the highway—
How I would wish to be one of those gray-coated heroes!
I watch them eager-eyed—
And run after them until they reach the Gentile Quarter—
And then I turn back.
Kartúshkiya-Beróza!
I am in the market-place—
At a Fair;
The market-place is a heaving mass of carts and horses and oxen;
The oxen are lowing, the horses are neighing, the peasants are
    cursing in a dozen different dialects.
I am in Grandfather's store,
On the lower end of the market-place, right opposite the public well—
The store is full of peasants and peasant women, bargaining at the top
    of their voices;
The peasants are clad in rough sheepskin coats and fur caps;
The peasant women are gay in bright-colored cottons and wear red
    kerchiefs around their heads;
My Grandfather is standing behind the counter measuring out rope to
    some peasants;
Grandmother is cutting a strip of linen for a peasant woman,
    chaffering with another one at the same time about the price of a
    pair of sandals—
And I am sitting there, behind the counter, on a sack of flour,
Playing with my black-eyed little cousin. . . .

Kartúshkiya-Beróza!
Kartúshkiya-Beróza!
It comes back to me suddenly—
That I am sitting here, with a newspaper in my hand
Reading:
"The Germans have seized the bridge-head at Kartúshkiya-Beróza;
The Russians are retreating in good order across the marshes.
The town is in flames!"

Times Square

An August day,
The eddying roar of the Square—
Crowds, stores, theatres, tall buildings
Assaulting the senses together—
And suddenly,
The taste of an apple between my teeth
Suffuses my mouth. . . .
Where did it come from?—
Strong and sharp and deliciously sour,
The taste in my mouth—
Where?

I cross the street
And suddenly,
Crowds, stores, theatres, tall buildings,
The blare and the glare of the day
Fade. . . .
October blows through the market-place
In a town of faraway Russia—
The booths are laden with fruit. . . .
A little boy,
Snub-nosed, freckle-faced, plump,
Dressed in a newly-washed jacket,
Stolidly strolls by the booths
Clutching a coin in his fingers—

I know him,
That freckle-faced boy;
I know him.
Proudly he passes the stores of the Row,
Ignoring them all—
Until he reaches at last

The booth of the widow Rebecca:
"What do you want, little darling?"
"Here is a penny;
I want this apple."
"Take it."
The tense little fingers unclose to surrender the penny
And close on a big red apple.
And suddenly,
The taste of an apple between my teeth,
Strong and sharp and deliciously sour,
Suffuses my mouth. . . .

The toot of an automobile,
Insistent, shrill,
Jars me back to the Square.

Ghetto Twilight

An infinite weariness comes into the faces of the old tenements,
As they stand massed together on the block,
Tall and thoughtfully silent,
In the enveloping twilight.
Pensively,
They eye each other across the street,
Through their dim windows—
With a sad recognizing stare,
Watching the red glow fading in the distance,
At the end of the street,
Behind the black church spires;
Watching the vague sky lowering overhead,
Purple with clouds of colored smoke
From the extinguished sunset;
Watching the tired faces coming home from work,
Like dry-breasted hags
Welcoming their children to their withered arms.

A Family Album

I

Worn and torn by many fingers
It stands on the bedroom dresser,
Resting back against its single cardboard buttress,
(There were two),
The gilt clasp that bound it, loose and broken,
The beautiful Madonna on its cover, faded and pencil-marked,
And the coarse wood of its back showing through its velvet lining.

II

I remember the time that my sister Pauline bought it for the house
(300 Cherry Street, fourth floor, right-hand side, front)
Thirteen years ago,
With the proceeds of her first week at the factory.
It was beautiful then,
The golden-haired, grave-eyed Madonna that adorned it.
Her blue eyes were ever so much bluer and clearer, and so sweetly
    pensive,
Her golden hair fell forward over her bare breast,
Brighter and yellower than gold,
And there were no black pencil marks across the pure white of her
    brow
Or the delicate pink of her cheeks.
She was beautiful . . .
And my father,
I remember my father didn't like that album,
And murmured against the open-bosomed female on its cover,
"It is sinful to have such a picture in a Jewish home!"
But I,
I loved that album because of its glorious, golden-haired Madonna.
And when I was left alone in the house
I would stand in the parlor for hours
And gaze into her ecstatic face

Half reverently, half tenderly.
And sometimes,
When I was doubly certain of being alone,
I would drag a chair up to the mantelpiece
And get on top of it,
And, timidly extending my hand,
Touch with my trembling fingers the yellow threads of her hair as
    they lay across her breast,
Or the soft slope of her breast into her loose robe.
And once, I remember,
Ashamed of my feelings, yet unable to repress them,
I drew the picture closer to my face.
And pressed my lips passionately on that white bosom—
My first kiss . . .

III

Somehow I never cared to open the gilt clasp of the album
And look through the photographs that were collecting there:
Photographs brought here from Russia,
Photographs taken here at various times,
Grandfathers, grandmothers, aunts, uncles, cousins,
Sisters and sisters-in-law, brothers and brothers-in-law;
Photographs of some of the many boarders that always occupied our
    bedrooms
(The family usually slept on folding beds in the kitchen and parlor
Together with some other boarders);
Boarders-in-law; sweethearts, wives, husbands of the boarders;
Group pictures: family pictures, shop pictures, school pictures.
Somehow I never cared to open the gilt clasp of the album
And look through that strange kaleidoscope of Life.
But now,
As I find myself turning its heavy cardboard pages,
Turning them meditatively back and forth,
My brain loosens like the gilt clasp of the album,
Unburdening itself of its locked memories,
Page after page, picture after picture,
Until the miscellaneous photographs take to themselves color and
    meaning,

Standing forth out of their places like a series of paintings;
As if a Master-Artist had gone over them with his brush,
Revealing in them things I did not see in the originals,
Solving in Art that which baffled me in Life.
And all the while as I go through the album, supporting the cover
    with my hand,
The yellow-haired Madonna gazes at me from under my fingers.
Sadly, reproachfully.

IV

Poor, warm-hearted, soft-headed, hard-fisted Uncle Isaac
In his jaunty coat and flannel shirt,
Stiff and handsome and mustached,
Standing as if he were in evening dress—
His head thrown backward, his eyes fixed forward;
Conscious of the cleanliness of his face and hands,
Fresh washed from a day's grime at the coal cellar.
When I look at his bold, blank face
My mind tears through the dense years,
Along the crazy alley of his life,
Back to a Lithuanian village on a twig of the Vistula.
Kartúshkiya-Beróza (what a sweet name—
Beróza is the Russian for birch trees)
And from a background of a dusty road meandering between high,
    green banks of foliage
I feel two black eyes looking at me strangely,
Two black passion-pregnant eyes
Nestling in a little dark face.

V

Every Saturday afternoon in the summertime
When the town was like a green bazaar
With the houses half-hidden under leaves and the lanes drifting
    blindly between the dense shade trees
After the many-coursed Sabbath dinner and the long synagogue
    services that preceded it
Mother took the four of us over to Grandpa's

A few houses up the lane
Where the aunts and the uncles and the cousins and the nephews
    and the nieces
In silk and in flannel and in satin and in linen,
Every face shining with a Sabbath newness,
Gathered on the porch for the family promenade:
Up to the lane and across the Gentile quarter and around the
    Bishop's orchard;
Through the Polish Road past the Tombs of the Rebels to the
    haunted red chapel at the crossroads—
And back again by cross cuts through the cornfields,
With the level yellow plain mellowing mystically around us in the
    soft sunshine,
And the sunset fading behind us like the Sabbath,
At twilight—just before the evening service—
Every Saturday afternoon, in summertime.

VI

They rise in my brain with mysterious insistence
The blurred images of those Sabbath walks—
Poignantly, painfully, vaguely beautiful,
Half obliterated under the cavalcade of the years,
They lurk in the wayside of my mind and ambush me unawares—
Like little children they steal behind me unawares and blindfold me
    with intangible fingers
Asking me to guess who it is:
Across a wide city street a patch of pavement like a slab of gold;
A flash of sunlight on a flying wheel—
And I am left wondering, wondering where I have seen sunlight
    before?
By a holiday-thronged park walk, a trio of huge trees thrust their
    great, brown arms through uplifted hillocks of green leaves—
And I stand staring at them penetratively;
Trying to assure myself that they were real,
And not something that had swum up in my mind
From a summer that has withered years ago—
In the beeches by the wayside on the Polish Road,

Isled among the birch woods,

As you come out of Kartúshkiya-Beróza.

On my bed, within the padded prison-walls of sleep, lurching
through a night of dreams;

I am awakened by a shrill wide-spreading triumphant outburst of
incessant twittering—

Under my window in the park,

Catching like fire from tree to tree, from throat to throat

Until the whole green square seems ablaze with joy,

As if each growing leaf had suddenly found tongue—

And I raise myself in my bed, dreamily, on my elbows

Listening with startled attentiveness to a sweet, clear twittering in
my brain

As of a hundred populous treetops vying with the pebble-tuned
waters of a brook

Gurgling timidly across a wide road.

In a hallway among a party of girls and young men tripping
downstairs for an outing on a Sunday morning,

The coarse, keen pungency of satin from some girl's new shirtwaist,

Through my nose into my brain pierces like a rapier—

And suddenly I am standing on a sunny country porch with
whitewashed wooden columns,

All dressed up for a Sabbath walk,

In a red satin blouse with a lacquered, black belt

With my mother in her blue silk Sabbath dress and grandmother
with a black lace shawl around her head

With my sisters and my brother and portly Uncle Zalman with his
fat, red-bearded face

And my grandfather stooping in his shining black capote with his
grizzled beard and earlocks and thoughtful, tiny eyes

And poor Aunt Bunya who died of her first childbirth, with her
roguish-eyed young husband

And smooth-shaven, mustached Uncle Isaac half-leaning, half-
sitting on the banister with his little girl clamped playfully
between his knees

And his wife Rebecca, with black eyes and pursed up scornful lips
standing haughtily aloof

And my cousins Basha and Miriam and little Nachman clutching at
  Uncle Zalman's trousers
And their mother, smiling, big-hearted, big-bosomed Aunt Golda,
  offering me a piece of tart
As I am staring absently sideways
Into the little dark face rimmed lovingly between Uncle Isaac's
  coarse hands.

Louis Zukofsky (1904–1978)

Louis Zukofsky was born on Manhattan's Lower East Side to newly arrived Lithuanian parents whose only language was Yiddish. A brilliant student, Zukofsky entered Columbia University at the age of sixteen and, already a published writer, graduated at nineteen. Although he was one of the leaders and founders of Objectivism, a major poetic movement of the 1930s, his work received little recognition outside literary circles. His poetry tended to be obscure, experimental, and intellectual. In spite of his parents' cultural and deeply religious background, Zukofsky turned away from formal religion early in his life. Nevertheless, several of his poems contain moving descriptions of his parents' life in Lithuania, while others explore his own ambiguous identity as a first-generation American Jew. "Autobiography" is the fifth movement of his long impressionistic poem, "Poem Beginning 'The.'" It combines a variety of literary allusions (Robert Herrick, William Shakespeare, and Heinrich Heine) with fragments of Jewish folk songs, Yiddish expressions, and contemporary American slang. Similarly, "A Song for the Year's End" blends disparate themes and images in a stream-of-consciousness style.

A Song for the Year's End

1

Daughter of music
and her sweet son
so that none rule
the dew to his own hurt
with the year's last sigh
awake
the starry sky and bird.

2

I shall go back to my mother's grave after this war
Because there are those who'll still speak of loyalty
In the outskirts of Baltimore
Or wherever Jews are not the right sort of people,
And say to her one of the dead I speak to—
There are less Jews left in the world,
While they were killed
I did not see you in a dream to tell you,
And that I now have a wife and son.

Then I shall go and write of my country,
Have a job all my life
Seldom write with grace again, be part of the world,
See every man in forced labor,
Dawn only where suburbs are *restricted*
To people who take trains every morning,
Never the gentleness that can be,
The hope of the common man, the eyes that love leaves
Any shade, thought or thing that makes all man uncommon,

But always the depraved bark
Fight or work,
Dawn the red poster, the advertiser's cock crow,

Sunset a lack of wonder, the lone winged foot of Mercury in
    tie with a tire,
The fashion model
Her train stopped in the railroad cut
Looking up to a billboard of herself
As she goes home to her small son asleep,

So early and so late in the fortunes that followed
    me from my mother's grave
A lovely air follows her
And the dead President who is worth it:
'Dear death, like peace, I end not speaking,
The chitchat has died
And the last smile is unwilled
I am dead, I can't talk
To blossoms or spring in the world.'

3

"Because he was crying
I like him most of all," says my son
"Because he was crying,"—the red fox
With three porcupine quills in his paw—
Who brings tears to the eyes,
    button nose against shambles,
Valentines all day, all night, tomorrow
The simplest the keyboard can play,
'Pony gay, on your way,' love's hair
With two gray, Papa Bear's Song
    new to renew,
'Who's been sitting in my chair?'

Poem Beginning "The"

FIFTH MOVEMENT: AUTOBIOGRAPHY

Speaking about epics, mother,
How long ago is it since you gathered
       mushrooms,
Gathered mushrooms while you mayed.
Is it your mate, my father, boating.
A stove burns like a full moon in a desert night.
Un in hoyze is kalt. You think of a new
       grave,
In the fields, flowers.

Night on the bladed grass, bayonets dewed.
Is it your mate, my father, boating.
Speaking about epics, mother—
Down here among the gastanks, ruts,
       cemetery-tenements—
It is your Russia that is free.
And I here, can I say only—
       "So then an egoist can never embrace
         a party
       Or take up with a party?
       Oh, yes, only he cannot let himself
       Be embraced or taken up by the party."
It is your Russia that is free, mother.
Tell me, mother.

Winged wild geese, where lies the passage,
In far away lands lies the passage.
Winged wild geese, who knows the pathway?
Of the winds, asking, we shall say:
Wind of the South and wind of the North

Where has our sun gone forth?
Naked, twisted, scraggly branches,
And dark, gray patches through the branches,
Ducks with puffed-up, fluttering feathers
On a cobalt stream.
And faded grass that's slowly swaying.
A barefoot shepherd boy
Striding in the mire:
Swishing indifferently a peeled branch
On jaded sheep.
An old horse strewn with yellow leaves
By the edge of the meadow
Draws weakly with humid nostrils
The moisture of the clouds.
Horses that pass through inappreciable
       woodland,
Leaves in their manes tangled, mist, autumn
       green,
Lord, why not give these bright brutes—
       your good land—
Turf for their feet always, years for their mien.
See how each peer lifts his head, others follow,
Mate paired with mate, flanks coming full
       they crowd,
Reared in your sun, Lord, escaping each hollow
Where life-struck we stand, utter their praise
       aloud.
Very much Chance, Lord, as when you first
       made us,
You might forget them, Lord, preferring what
Being less lovely where sadly we fuss?
Weed out these horses as tho they were not?
Never alive in brute delicate trembling
Song to your sun, against autumn assembling.

If horses could but sing Bach, mother,—
Remember how I wished it once—
Now I kiss you who could never sing Bach,
        never read Shakespeare.

In Manhattan here the Chinamen are yellow
        in the face, mother,
Up and down, up and down our streets they
        go yellow in the face,
And why is it the representatives of your,
        my, race are always hankering for
        food, mother?
We, on the other hand, eat so little.
Dawn't you think Trawtsky rawthaw a
        darrling,
I ask our immigrant cousin querulously.
Naw! I think hay is awlmawst a Tchekoff.
But she has more color in her cheeks than
        the Angles—Angels—mother,—
They have enough, though. We should
        get some more color, mother.
If I am like them in the rest, I should
        resemble them in that, mother,
Assimilation is not hard,
And once the Faith's askew
I might as well look Shagetz just as much
        as Jew.

I'll read their Donne as mine,
And leopard in their spots
I'll do what says their Coleridge,
Twist red hot pokers into knots.
The villainy they teach me I will execute
And it shall go hard with them,
For I'll better the instruction,
Having learned, so to speak, in their
        colleges.
    It is engendered in the eyes

With gazing fed, and fancy dies
In the cradle where it lies
In the cradle where it lies
I, Senora, am the Son of the Respected
        Rabbi,
Israel of Saragossa,
Not that the Rabbis give a damn,
Keine Kadish wird man sagen.

Stanley Kunitz (b. 1905)

Since the 1950s, Stanley Kunitz has been one of the most prominent figures in American poetry, having published more than fifteen volumes of poetry, essays, and translations. He received the Pulitzer Prize in 1959 for *Selected Poems 1928–1958*, and the National Book Award in 1995 (at the age of ninety) for *Passing Through: The Later Poems New and Selected*. His poems are frequently personal ("Father and Son"), more spiritual than specifically religious ("The Flight of Apollo"), and often inspired by his own sense of alienation and loneliness as both poet and Jew ("An Old Cracked Tune" and "The Quarrel"). Kunitz was born in Worcester, Massachusetts, brought up in New England, and attended Harvard University. He has served on the faculty of numerous universities, including Brandeis, Columbia, Yale, and the New School for Social Research.

The Quarrel

The word I spoke in anger
weighs less than a parsley seed,
but a road runs through it
that leads to my grave,
that bought-and-paid-for lot
on a salt-sprayed hill in Truro
where the scrub pines
overlook the bay.
Half-way I'm dead enough,
strayed from my own nature
and my fierce hold on life.
If I could cry, I'd cry,
but I'm too old to be
anybody's child.
Liebchen,
with whom should I quarrel
except in the hiss of love,
that harsh, irregular flame?

The Flight of Apollo

Earth was my home, but even there I was a stranger. This mineral crust.
I walk like a swimmer. What titanic bombardments in those old astral
wars! I know what I know: I shall never escape from strangeness or
complete my journey. Think of me as nostalgic, afraid, exalted. I am
your man on the moon, a speck of megalomania, restless for the leap to-
ward island universes pulsing beyond where the constellations set. In-
finite space overwhelms the human heart, but in the middle of nowhere
life inexorably calls to life. Forward my mail to Mars. What news from
the Great Spiral Nebula in Andromeda and the Magellanic Clouds?

2

I was a stranger on earth.
Stepping on the moon, I begin
the gay pilgrimage to new
Jerusalems
in foreign galaxies.
Heat. Cold. Craters of silence.
The Sea of Tranquillity
rolling on the shores of entropy.
And, beyond,
the intelligence of the stars.

An Old Cracked Tune

My name is Solomon Levi,
the desert is my home,
my mother's breast was thorny,
and father I had none.

The sands whispered, *Be separate*,
the stones taught me, *Be hard*.
I dance, for the joy of surviving,
on the edge of the road.

Father and Son

Now in the suburbs and the falling light
I followed him, and now down sandy road
Whiter than bone-dust, through the sweet
Curdle of fields, where the plums
Dropped with their load of ripeness, one by one.
Mile after mile I followed, with skimming feet,
After the secret master of my blood,
Him, steeped in the odor of ponds, whose indomitable love
Kept me in chains. Strode years; stretched into bird;
Raced through the sleeping country where I was young,
The silence unrolling before me as I came,
The night nailed like an orange to my brow.

How should I tell him my fable and the fears,
How bridge the chasm in a casual tone,
Saying, "The house, the stucco one you built,
We lost. Sister married and went from home,
And nothing comes back, it's strange, from where she goes.
I lived on a hill that had too many rooms:
Light we could make, but not enough of warmth,
And when the light failed, I climbed under the hill.
The papers are delivered every day;
I am alone and never shed a tear."

At the water's edge, where the smothering ferns lifted
Their arms, "Father!" I cried, "Return! You know
The way. I'll wipe the mudstains from your clothes;
No trace, I promise, will remain. Instruct
Your son, whirling between two wars,
In the Gemara of your gentleness,
For I would be a child to those who mourn

And brother to the foundlings of the field
And friend of innocence and all bright eyes.
O teach me how to work and keep me kind."

Among the turtles and the lilies he turned to me
The white ignorant hollow of his face.

Hyam Plutzik (1911–1962)

Born in Brooklyn, New York, to Russian immigrants, Hyam Plutzik was raised on a farm in New England, where he spoke no English until he entered public school. He eventually attended Trinity College in Connecticut, received an M.A. degree from Yale, and taught literature and creative writing for most of his career at the University of Rochester. He is the author of four volumes of poetry, almost all of which reflect his Jewish background and his interest in Jewish history and texts. In one of his better-known poems, "For T. S. E. Only," originally published in *Apples from Shinar* (1959), Plutzik admonishes T. S. Eliot, his literary idol, for the poet's many anti-Semitic references. "Portrait" is an equally ironic view of an assimilated "casual" Jew. "Commentary," an imaginative glimpse into the mind of God, strikes a more contemplative, solemn tone.

Commentary

Once, when I entered the Holy of Holies to burn the incense, I saw
the Lord of all Hosts sitting on a high and exalted throne, and He
said to me: "Ishmael, my son, bless me."   —THE TALMUD

I

He is lonely then within the pale of the palace—
The Enthroned Will, whose fingers must ever shore
The pitiful islands against the destroyer of all.

To guard the breath of the violet for its time,
And Helen's face, and the gay moment the sun
Touches the street in the town where children play.

To shape and reshape forever the crumbling substance
Yet see the ruin so quickly, the figurines
Wasting in air, the brush-strokes graying like ash.

If only once out of the flow, the river,
To make the lasting, the perfect—O to create
What will endure for all the creator's time.

II

Lonely, lonely in the pale of the palace.
Once there were others, rivals, Ammon or Zeus.
Brother or foe, to bring the blood to the face,

Or who fashioned himself a mate out of the ground,
For eternity, his paltry thousand years.
But to shape and reshape forever the dust, the dust.

III

And the desperate tricks, the man or the nation beloved.
The disguises: dream or fire or a cloak by the gate
Of an unknown city, beyond the candlelight's friendship,

Where the guard cries out who goes, and sees no thing
But the darkening sand and a desert bird wheeling
With the cry that a gull makes on an empty coast.

O he is lonely in the pale of the palace—
The Enthroned Will, whose fingers must ever shore
The pitiful islands against the destroyer of all.

For T. S. E. Only

You called me a name on such and such a day—
Do you remember?—you were speaking of Bleistein our brother,
The barbarian with the black cigar, and the pockets
Ringing with cash, and the eyes seeking Jerusalem,
Knowing they have been tricked. Come, brother Thomas,
We three must weep together for our exile.

I see the hunted look, the protestation,
The desperate seeking, the reticence and the brashness
Of the giver of laws to the worshippers of calves.
At times you speak as if the words were walls,
But your walls fell with mine to the torch of a Titus.
Come, let us weep together for our exile.

We two, no doubt, could accommodate ourselves:
We've both read Dante and we both dislike Chicago,
And both, you see, can be brutal—but you must bow down
To our brother Bleistein here, with the unaesthetic
Cigar and the somber look. Come, do so quickly,
For we must weep together for our exile.

O you may enwomb yourself in words or the Word
(The Word is a good refuge for people too proud
To swallow the milk of the mild Jesus' teaching),
Or a garden in Hampshire with a magic bird, or an old
Quotation from the Reverend Andrewes, yet someone or something
(Let us pause to weep together for our exile)

Will stick a needle in your balloon, Thomas.
Is it the shape that you saw upon the stair?
The four knights clanking toward the altar? the hidden

Card in the deck? the sinister man from Nippon?
The hordes on the eastern horizon? Come, brother Burbank,
And let us weep together for our exile.

In the time of sweet sighing you wept bitterly,
And now in the time of weeping you cannot weep.
Will you wait for the peace of the sailor with pearly bones?
Where is the refuge you thought you would find on the island
Where each man lives in his castle? O brother Thomas,
Come let us weep together for our exile.

You drew us first by your scorn, first by your wit;
Later for your own eloquent suffering.
We loved you first for the wicked things you wrote
Of those you acknowledged infinitely gentle.
Wit is the sin that you must expiate.
Bow down to them, and let us weep for our exile.

I see your words wrung out in pain, but never
The true compassion for creatures with you, that Dante
Knew in his nine hells. O eagle! master!
The eagle's ways of pride and scorn will not save
Though the voice cries loud in humility. Thomas, Thomas,
Come, let us pray together for our exile.

You, hypocrite lecteur! mon semblable! mon frère!

Portrait

Notice with what careful nonchalance
He tries to be a Jew casually,
To ignore the monster, the mountain—
A few thousand years of history.

Of course he personally remembers nothing,
And the world has forgotten the older objections—
The new ones not being socially acceptable:
Hangdogs, hiding in the privies and alleys of the mind.

It is agreed
That he of all men has gained the right to his soul
(Though like the others he no longer believes in one).
He lives in his own house under his oak.
He stands by his car, shod in decently-grained leather.
He is smiling. His hair is peacefully in place.
His suit is carefully pressed; his cravat harmonious.

Whose father, it is whispered, stubbornly cried old clothes
    and bric-a-brac,
He of all men might yet be master of self, all self-possession,
Were it not (how gauche and incredible!) for the one
    ill-fitting garment—
The historical oversight in the antique wardrobe—
The shirt, the borrowed shirt,
The Greek shirt.

Notice how even when at ease he is somehow anxious,
Like a horse who whiffs smoke somewhere nearby faintly.
Notice with what nonchalance,
The magazine in his hand and the casual cigarette to his lips,
He wears a shirt by Nessus.

Rose Drachler (1911–1982)

Born in Brooklyn, New York, Rose Drachler attended Hunter College, Columbia University, and the New School for Social Research. For more than thirty years she was a teacher in the New York City public school system. Although not as widely recognized as several of her contemporaries, Drachler nevertheless produced an impressive body of poetry—one that was distinctly Jewish in both theme and subject. Her poems reveal her religious background (her father was an Orthodox Rabbi and she an Orthodox Jew), her interest in all aspects of Jewish culture and history, her feminism, and her own, particular messianic vision. In "The Prophet," "The Witness," and "Athens and Jerusalem" Drachler explores the human response to the divine and to the possibility of a Messiah. "As I Am My Father's" expresses both a feminist and a religious point of view.

As I Am My Father's

I am my own
My opinions and feelings
Are my own

I do not conceal
Or deny what I am
What you put there

In the end
At the end of days
You will be just

Like Balaam
Who beat his ass
For seeing

What was there
You beat us
These many times

But in the end
You will see the angel too
Since you put this angel

In our way
You will be just
Since justice is your name

I do not speak of mercy
Which is your name too

The Prophet

The prophet works hard at dreaming
He allows his dreams to take over

He was not born a prophet
He was born able to become one

As the lammergeyer comes out of its egg
Bald and weak but with soaring

Coded in its cells for the future
Able to learn to seek far below it

The gift of prophecy comes out in sad times
To the proper one who has prepared himself

By persistent practice to be able
To be strongwinged and wise for soaring

To follow the prediction of his dreams
Far down on the ground where his kin

Lie helpless and dying of cold
Like lambs to the lamb-vulture in spring

The Witness

Not a prophet, he says of himself
But a witness, like Nicodemus
Standing foursquare, close to the ground
Reaches his arm way out and points
To what was there all the time

The young men crowd around
For a taste of the crumbs
From his full mouth. They listen
They repeat. *"Agapae," he said, "not Eros."*
Explaining what was there plainly

His square grey beard, his rooted feet
His open eyes, looking through
Looking right into them
Their wavering meaning, meeting it
Plain as a board, to themselves now too

Making straight to the spiral
Thinking of the theologists
The historians full of praise
Praise unwelcome to him, he says
Simple, breathing loud like a

Small horse delighted to be
Trotting on grass, breathing fresh air
He is "freed from the belief
That there is no freedom
Therefore he is free."

Athens and Jerusalem

I

Tipping down from above the clouds at Athens
we saw the roots of the islands growing out
of the old Greek soil. The sea in separate
layers of frothy white, winedark and pale
cerulean blue around the immodest roots
of the old-tooth islands. The air here was
good as in Jerusalem, dry smelling of
grey rosemary and thyme, but it did not tremble.
The gold light was quiet and calmly still.
The girls were Greek, from Greece a long time and dressed
reasonably in the reasonable, measured
light of the old, culpable gods. "No one is
coming. We are here. We wear plain woolens to
keep warm as we did two thousand years ago.
We are not waiting for anyone. They were here.
But it is not that important. We are here
in the light and the dry, clear air of our past,
of our daily past and our daily future."

II

Well, if the waters rise up
to the east and the west here
on this street where the bus runs
and the gaudy copies of
Persian rugs hang over the balconies to sun and where
the pudding-breasted houris
from Marrakesh lean over
the window sills, Jews, what will
the Messiah look like on
that Day? Here in the light that
is much more than light, in the
singing sweetness of golden

motes, in the honeyed breath of
the Shechina, the Messiah
will wear an Italian silk
suit cut in the latest mode
and drive a fine, white sports car.
Its roar and take-off will bring
all the curly wives out of
the recesses of their
one room flats to lean their full
breasts on the sills with garish
machine made pillows to OH
at the Man as beautiful
as the latest movie star
in a white car the like of
which has not until this Day
been seen in Jerusalem

Delmore Schwartz (1913–1966)

The son of immigrant parents, Delmore Schwartz was born in Brooklyn, New York. He attended the University of Wisconsin for a year, received a B.A. degree from New York University, and did graduate work at Harvard. Schwartz's first book, *In Dreams Begin Responsibilities*—a combination of short fiction and poetry—was published to great critical acclaim in 1937, when he was only twenty-four. In spite of his descent—especially in the last decade of his life—into alcoholism, depression, and psychosis, and his early death at the age of fifty-three, Schwartz produced an important body of poetry, fiction, and criticism. His poetry, like his fiction, often revolves around the central themes of alienation and separation, although not necessarily from a specifically Jewish point of view. The poems that follow, from *Selected Poems: Summer Knowledge*, are dramatic monologues which expound on the biblical stories of Abraham, Jacob, and Sarah.

Abraham

To J. M. Kaplan

I was a mere boy in a stone-cutter's shop
When, early one evening, my raised hand
Was halted and the soundless voice said:
"Depart from your father and your country
And the things to which you are accustomed.
Go now into a country unknown and strange
I will make of your children a great nation,
Your generations will haunt every generation of all the nations,
They will be like the stars at midnight, like the sand of the sea."
Then I looked up at the infinite sky,
Star-pointing and silent, and it was then, on that evening, that I
Became a man: that evening of my manhood's birthday.

I went then to Egypt, the greatest of nations.
There I encountered the Pharaoh who built the tombs,
Great public buildings, many theatres, and seashore villas:
And my wife's beauty was such that, fearing his power and lust,
I called her my sister, a girl neither for him nor for me.
And soon was fugitive, a nomad again.
Living alone with my sister, becoming very rich
In all but children, in herds, in possessions, the herds continually
Increased my possessions through prodigies of progeny.

From time to time, in the afternoon's revery
In the late sunlight or the cool of the evening
I called to mind the protracted vanity of that promise
Which had called me forth from my father's house unwillingly
Into the last strangeness of Egypt and the childless desert.
Then Sarah gave me her handmaid, a young girl
That I might at least at last have children by another
And later, when a great deal else had occurred,
I put away Hagar, with the utmost remorse
Because the child was the cause of so much rivalry and jealousy.

At last when all this had passed or when
The promise seemed the parts of dream,
When we were worn out and patient in all things
The stranger came, suave and elegant,
A messenger who renewed the promise, making Sarah
Burst out laughing hysterically!

But the boy was born and grew and I saw
What I had known, I knew what I had seen, for he
Possessed his mother's beauty and his father's humility,
And was not marked and marred by her sour irony and my endless
    anxiety.

Then the angel returned, asking that I surrender
My son as a lamb to show that humility
Still lived in me, and was not altered by age and prosperity.

I said nothing, shocked and passive. Then I said but to myself alone:
"This was to be expected. These promises
Are never unequivocal or unambiguous, in this
As in all things which are desired the most:
I have had great riches and great beauty.
I cannot expect the perfection of every wish
And if I deny the command, who knows what will happen?"

But his life was forgiven and given back to me:
His children and their children are an endless nation:
Dispersed on every coast. And I am not gratified
Nor astonished. It has never been otherwise:
Exiled, wandering, dumbfounded by riches,
Estranged among strangers, dismayed by the infinite sky,
An alien to myself until at last the caste of the last alienation
The angel of death comes to make the alienated and indestructible
    one a part of his famous society.

Jacob

All was as it is, before the beginning began, before
We were bared to the cold air, before
Pride. Fullness of bread. Abundance of idleness.
No one has ever told me what now I know:
Love is unjust, justice is loveless.

So, as it was to become, it was, in the black womb's ignorance
Coiled and bound, under the mother's heart.
There in the womb we wrestled, and writhed, hurt
Each other long before each was other and apart,
Before we breathed: who then committed greed,
Impersonation, usurpation? So, in the coming forth,
In the noose and torment of birth, Esau went first,
He was red all over. I followed him, clutching his heel,
And we were named: Esau, the one of the vivid coat,
Jacob, the one who clutches the heel of the one
Who has a vivid coat. The names were true
As the deceptive reality into which we were thrown.
For I did not know what clutching was, nor had I known
Would I have known whose heel I clutched, my brother's or my own!

So, the world we entered then and thus was one
In which the second must be second that the first may be first.
The world of precedence, order, other, under and above,
The darkness, sweetness, confusion and unity of love!
How the truth of our names became, as we grew, more true,
Growing like truth. How could it be otherwise? For truth abides
Hidden in the future, in the ambush of the marvellous,
Unknown and monstrous, at the very heart of surprise.

The gift was mind. The gift was eminence. The gift
Like every gift, was guilt. The guilt began

In the darkness and dark mystery where all begins.
The mystery of the perpetual invisible fires whence flow
The very beasts and woods where—
                              with what happiness!
                              what innocence!—
Esau my brother hunted, cantering like the horses of summer,
And sleeping, when he returned, the sleep of winter farms,
Spontaneous and blessed, like energy itself, sleeping or awake.
Until the hour when the angel struck!

So it was: so:
O angel of the unspeakable,
Why must a gift be guilt and hurt the gifted one?
O angel of the unspeakable, power of powers,
Locking my reins, my arms, my heart all night
So that my body was burdened as with the load of all stones
Does thou remember what, in the darkness, I cried,
During the desperation in which I died
The last death of hope and the little deaths of the heart
Wrestling and writhing between two rivers—on one bank,
Esau, awaiting me, like a river slept—beneath me once more.
"Hast thou not seen," I cried aloud, to the unspeakable,
"Esau my brother: his handsome hunting heart upon a horse?"
How should it seem so strange that I should win,
Since victory was my gift? Unjust, like every gift,
A something neither deserved, nor gained by toil . . .
How else could it be gift and given?
Favor: favored: favorite:
Gold hair: great strength: Esau was very tall,
Possessed by the supple grace of the sea's waves, breaking.

Now Joseph is, as I was: in Egypt's pit,
In that accustomed depth and isolated height
The solitude of eminence, the exiled intelligence,
Which separated me even as it created me:
Estranged and unloved, gifted and detested,
Denied the love of the servants and the dogs.
Joseph a stranger in Egypt may only know

What I have known: my gifts, my victory, my guilt.
For Egypt is a country like a gift.

The gift is loved but not the gifted one.
The coat of many colors is much admired
By everyone, but he who wears the coat
Is not made warm. Why should the gift be the cause of pain,
O thou unspeakable? Must the vivid coat
Of eminence elect the favored favorite
As scapegoat or turncoat, exile or fugitive,
The loved of mother and God, and by all others
Shunned in fear or contempt?
                                    I knew what it was,
When Joseph became my favorite: knew the sympathy
Of the long experience of the unasked-for gift:
Knew the nature of love: how many colors
Can a coat have? What should we wish, if
We could choose? What should I desire
—Not to have loved my son, the best of sons?
Rejected the choice of love? Should I have hidden
My love of him? Or should he have concealed the self
I loved, above all others, wearing the coat
Which is customary, the coats his brothers wore?
To how many coats can a color give vividness?
How can the heart know love, and not love one the more?
Love is unjust: justice is loveless.

Sarah

The angel said to me: "Why are you laughing?"
"Laughing! Not me. Who was laughing? I did not laugh. It was
A cough. I was coughing. Only hyenas laugh.
It was the cold I caught nine minutes after
Abraham married me: when I saw
How I was slender and beautiful, more and more
Slender and beautiful.
                              I was also
Clearing my throat; something inside of me
is continually telling me something
I do not wish to hear: A joke: A big joke:
But the joke is always just on me.
He said: you will have more children than the sky's stars
And the seashore's sands, if you just wait patiently.
Wait: patiently: ninety years? You see
The joke's on me!"

Muriel Rukeyser (1913–1980)

Muriel Rukeyser was born in New York City to American Jewish parents. She attended Vassar College and Columbia University. Her first book of poems, *Theory of Flight* (1935), published when she was only twenty-one, won the Yale Younger Poets Prize. In her lifetime, Rukeyser published sixteen volumes of poetry, as well as dozens of books of fiction, nonfiction, criticism, and children's literature. Her poetry is imbued with her passionate quest for social justice (she was a political activist all her life) and her pride in Jewish identity. Part VII of "Letter to the Front" ("To Be a Jew in the Twentieth Century") declares Rukeyser's view of Judaism as both a challenge and a "gift." Similarly, in "Bubble of Air," she affirms her heritage as "Woman, American, and Jew," while "Traditional Tune" merges her lifelong concern with both Judaism and the struggle against oppression. "Akiba" is a poetic rendering of the story of the legendary second-century Jewish martyr, an ignorant shepherd who eventually became one of the great scholars of his time before being tortured and killed by the Romans. "For My Son" is a more personal treatment of the theme of heritage.

Letter to the Front

VII

To be a Jew in the twentieth century
Is to be offered a gift.   If you refuse,
Wishing to be invisible, you choose
Death of the spirit, the stone insanity.
Accepting, take full life.   Full agonies:
Your evening deep in labyrinthine blood
Of those who resist, fail, and resist; and God
Reduced to a hostage among hostages.

The gift is torment.   Not alone the still
Torture, isolation; or torture of the flesh.
That may come also.   But the accepting wish,
The whole and fertile spirit as guarantee
For every human freedom, suffering to be free,
Daring to live for the impossible.

Traditional Tune

After the revolution came the Fuehrer;
And after the resurrection, the Christian Era.
Not yet simple and not yet free.

Just after the Exodus, in the divided sea
The chariots drowned, and then the tempering
By forty sandy years of misery.

And after the King of the Jews came Godfrey King;
Kneedeep in blood the children wandering,
Holy Holy Holy hear the children sing.

Now mouthdeep nosedeep the fires reach our eye.
Teach us from torment to fly and not to fly.
Not yet safe, not ready to die.

Illumination and night cast on the eyes of those
Believing and fighting, playing the Worldly Fool,
Fool of Thy Word, who feel the century

Rule, under whose deep wave explosion waits;
We know the dead power of Thy Allied States.
Not yet simple and not yet free.

Sailing, remembering the rock and the child,
Sailing remember the sand, the city, the wild
Holy songs.   Deaths!   Pillar of cloud and sun,

Remember us and remember them and all
Not safe, not free sailing again upon
The sacred dangerous harbor, Jerusalem.

Bubble of Air

The bubbles in the blood sprang free,
crying from roots, from Darwin's beard.
The angel of the century
stood on the night and would be heard;
turned to my dream of tears and sang:
Woman, American, and Jew,
three guardians watch over you,
three lions of heritage
resist the evil of your age:
life, freedom, and memory.
And all the dreams cried from the camps
and all the steel of torture rang.
The angel of the century
stood on the night and cried the great
notes Give Create and Fight—
while war
runs through your veins, while life
a bubble of air stands in your throat,
answer the silence of the weak:
Speak!

Akiba

THE WAY OUT

The night is covered with signs. The body and face of man,
with signs, and his journeys.   Where the rock is split
and speaks to the water;   the flame speaks to the cloud;
the red splatter, abstraction, on the door
speaks to the angel and the constellations.
The grains of sand on the sea-floor speak at last to the noon.
And the loud hammering of the land behind
speaks ringing up the bones of our thighs, the hoofs,
we hear the hoofs over the seethe of the sea.

All night down the centuries, have heard, music of passage.

Music of one child carried into the desert;
firstborn forbidden by law of the pyramid.
Drawn through the water with the water-drawn people
led by the water-drawn man to the smoke mountain.
The voice of the world speaking, the world covered by signs,
the burning, the loving, the speaking, the opening.
Strong throat of sound from the smoking mountain.
Still flame, the spoken singing of a young child.
The meaning beginning to move, which is the song.

Music of those who have walked out of slavery.

Akiba is the Jewish shepherd-scholar of the first and second century, identified with The Song of
Songs and with the insurrection against Hadrian's Rome, led in A.D. 132 by Bar Cochba (Son of
the Star). After this lightning war, Jerusalem captured, the Romans driven out of the south, Rome
increased its military machine; by 135, the last defenses fell, Bar Cochba was killed, Akiba was tor-
tured to death at the command of his friend, the Roman Rufus, and a harrow was drawn over the
ground where Jerusalem had stood, leaving only a corner of wall. The story in my mother's family
is that we are descended from Akiba—unverifiable, but a great gift to a child.

Into that journey where all things speak to all things
refusing to accept the curse, and taking
for signs the signs of all things, the world, the body
which is part of the soul, and speaks to the world,
all creation being created in one image, creation.
This is not the past walking into the future,
the walk is painful, into the present, the dance
not visible as dance until much later.
These dancers are discoverers of God.

We knew we had all crossed over when we heard the song.

Out of a life of building lack on lack:
the slaves refusing slavery, escaping into faith:
an army who came to the ocean: the walkers
who walked through the opposites, from I to opened Thou,
city and cleave of the sea. Those at flaming Nauvoo,
the ice on the great river: the escaping Negroes,
swamp and wild city: the shivering children of Paris
and the glass black hearses; those on the Long March:
all those who together are the frontier, forehead of man.

Where the wilderness enters, the world, the song of the world.

Akiba rescued, secretly, in the clothes of death
by his disciples carried from Jerusalem
in blackness journeying to find his journey
to whatever he was loving with his life.
The wilderness journey through which we move
under the whirlwind truth into the new,
the only accurate. A cluster of lights at night:
faces before the pillar of fire. A child watching
while the sea breaks open. This night. The way in.

Barbarian music, a new song.

Acknowledging opened water, possibility:
open like a woman to this meaning.
In a time of building statues of the stars,
valuing certain partial ferocious skills
while past us the chill and immense wilderness
spreads its one-color wings until we know
rock, water, flame, cloud, or the floor of the sea,
the world is a sign, a way of speaking. To find.
What shall we find? Energies, rhythms, journey.

Ways to discover. The song of the way in.

FOR THE SONG OF SONGS

However the voices rise
They are the shepherd, the king,
The woman; dreams,
Holy desire.

Whether the voices
Be many the dance around
Or body led by one body
Whose bed is green,

I defend the desire
Lightning and poetry
Alone in the dark city
Or breast to breast.

Champion of light I am
The wounded holy light,
The woman in her dreams
And the man answering.

You who answer their dreams
Are the ruler of wine
Emperor of clouds
And the riches of men.

This song
Is the creation
The day of this song
The day of the birth of the world.

Whether a thousand years
Forget this woman, this king,
Whether two thousand years
Forget the shepherd of dreams.

If none remember
Who is lover, who the beloved,
Whether the poet be
Woman or man,

The desire will make
A way through the wilderness
The leopard mountains
And the lips of the sleepers.

Holy way of desire,
King, lion, the mouth of the poet,
The woman who dreams
And the answerer of dreams.

In these delights
Is eternity of seed,
The verge of life,
Body of dreaming.

THE BONDS

In the wine country, poverty, they drink no wine—
In the endless night of love he lies, apart from love—
In the landscape of the Word he stares, he has no word.

He hates and hungers for his immense need.

He is young. This is a shepherd who rages at learning,
Having no words. Looks past green grass and sees a woman.
She, Rachel, who is come to recognize.
In the huge wordless shepherd she finds Akiba.

To find the burning Word. To learn to speak.

The body of Rachel says, the marriage says,
The eyes of Rachel say, and water upon rock
Cutting its groove all year says All things learn.
He learns with his new son whose eyes are wine.

To sing continually, to find the word.

He comes to teaching, greater than the deed
Because it begets the deed, he comes to the stone
Of long ordeal, and suddenly knows the brook
Offering water, the citron fragrance, the light of candles.

All given, and always the giver loses nothing.

In giving, praising, we move beneath clouds of honor,
In giving, in praise, we take gifts that are given,
The spark from one to the other leaping, a bond
Of light, and we come to recognize the rock;

We are the rock acknowledging water, and water
Fire, and woman man, all brought through wilderness;
And Rachel finding in the wordless shepherd
Akiba who can now come to his power and speak:
The need to give having found the need to become:

More than the calf wants to suck, the cow wants to give suck.

When his death confronted him, it had the face of his friend
Rufus the Roman general with his claws of pain,
His executioner. This was an old man under iron rakes
Tearing through to the bone. He made no cry.

After the failure of all missions. At ninety, going
To Hadrian in Egypt, the silver-helmed,
Named for a sea. To intercede. Do not build in the rebuilt
    Temple.

Your statue, do not make it a shrine to you.
Antinous smiling. Interpreters. This is an old man, pleading.
Incense of fans. The emperor does not understand.

He accepts his harvest, failures. He accepts faithlessness,
Madness of friends, a failed life; and now the face of storm.

Does the old man during uprising speak for compromise?
In all but the last things. Not in the study itself.
For this religion is a system of knowledge;
Points may be one by one abandoned, but not the study.
Does he preach passion and non-violence?
Yes, and trees, crops, children honestly taught. He says:
Prepare yourselves for suffering.

Now the rule closes in, the last things are forbidden.
There is no real survival without these.
Now it is time for prison and the unknown.
The old man flowers into spiritual fire.

Streaking of agony across the sky.
Torn black. Red racing on blackness. Dawn.
Rufus looks at him over the rakes of death
Asking, "What is it?
Have you magic powers? Or do you feel no pain?"

The old man answers, "No. But there is a commandment
    saying
Thou shalt love the Lord thy God with all thy heart, with all
    thy soul and with all thy might.
I knew that I loved him with all my heart and might.
Now I know that I love him with all my life."

The look of delight of the martyr
Among the colors of pain, at last knowing his own response
Total and unified.
To love God with all the heart, all passion,
Every desire called evil, turned toward unity,
All the opposites, all in the dialogue.
All the dark and light of the heart, of life made whole.

Surpassing the known life, day and ideas.
My hope, my life, my burst of consciousness:
To confirm my life in the time of confrontation.

The old man saying Shema.
The death of Akiba.

THE WITNESS

Who is the witness? What voice moves across time,
Speaks for the life and death as witness voice?
Moving tonight on this city, this river, my winter street?

He saw it, the one witness. Tonight the life as legend
Goes building a meeting for me in the veins of night
Adding its scenes and its songs. Here is the man transformed,

The tall shepherd, the law, the false messiah, all;
You who come after me far from tonight finding
These lives that ask you always Who is the witness—

Take from us acts of encounter we at night
Wake to attempt, as signs, seeds of beginning,
Given from darkness and remembering darkness,

Take from our light given to you our meetings.
Time tells us men and women, tells us You
The witness, your moment covered with signs, your self.

Tells us this moment, saying You are the meeting.
You are made of signs, your eyes and your song.
Your dance the dance, the walk into the present.

All this we are and accept, being made of signs, speaking
To you, in time not yet born.
                              The witness is myself.
                                          And you,
The signs, the journeys of the night, survive.

For My Son

You come from poets, kings, bankrupts, preachers,
   attempted bankrupts, builders of cities, salesmen,
the great rabbis, the kings of Ireland, failed drygoods
   storekeepers, beautiful women of the songs,
great horsemen, tyrannical fathers at the shore of ocean, the
   western mothers looking west beyond from their
      windows,
the families escaping over the sea hurriedly and by night—
the roundtowers of the Celtic violet sunset,
the diseased, the radiant, fliers, men thrown out of town, the
      man bribed by his cousins to stay out of town, teachers,
         the cantor on Friday evening, the lurid newspapers,
strong women gracefully holding relationship, the Jewish girl
      going to parochial school, the boys racing their iceboats
         on the Lakes,
the woman still before the diamond in the velvet window, saying
      "Wonder of nature."
Like all men,
you come from singers, the ghettoes, the famines, wars and
      refusal of wars, men who built villages
that grew to our solar cities, students, revolutionists, the
      pouring of buildings, the market newspapers.
a poor tailor in a darkening room,
a wilderness man, the hero of mines, the astronomer, a white-
      faced woman hour on hour teaching piano and her
         crippled wrist,
like all men,
you have not seen your father's face

but he is known to you forever in song, the coast of the skies,
  in dream, wherever you find man play playing his part
    as father, father among our light, among our darkness,
and in your self made whole, whole with yourself and whole
  with others,
the stars your ancestors.

Karl Shapiro (b. 1913)

Born in Baltimore, Maryland, Karl Shapiro was educated at the University of Virginia and Johns Hopkins University. While still serving in the Armed Forces, Shapiro published his first volume of poetry, *Person, Place, and Thing* (1942). His second book, *V-Letter and Other Poems* (1945), received the Pulitzer Prize, and at the age of thirty-two Shapiro became a nationally recognized poet. To date, he has produced over a dozen volumes of poetry and several collections of critical essays. Shapiro's "Jewish consciousness" (to use his term) is most evident in his early poetry, especially in *Poems of a Jew* (1958). The poems in that collection follow traditional metric patterns and cover a wide range of Jewish subjects and themes, including a portrait of the poet's immigrant grandmother ("My Grandmother"), a history of his developing sense of himself as an American, a Jew, and a writer ("Recapitulations"), a commentary on the 151st Psalm ("The 151st Psalm"), and a symbolic contrast of gentile and Jewish modes of existence ("The Alphabet"). "My Father's Funeral" (1976) is typical of Shapiro's later poetry, with its open-ended lines and free verse.

My Grandmother

My grandmother moves to my mind in context of sorrow
And, as if apprehensive of near death, in black;
Whether erect in chair, her dry and corded throat harangued
       by grief,
Or at ragged book bent in Hebrew prayer,
Or gentle, submissive, and in tears to strangers;
Whether in sunny parlor or back of drawn blinds.

Though time and tongue made any love disparate,
On daguerreotype with classic perspective
Beauty I sigh and soften at is hers.
I pity her life of deaths, the agony of her own,
But most that history moved her through
Stranger lands and many houses,
Taking her exile for granted, confusing
The tongues and tasks of her children's children.

Recapitulations

I

I was born downtown on a wintry day
    And under the roof when Poe expired;
Tended by nuns my mother lay
    Dark-haired and beautiful and tired.

Doctors and cousins paid their call,
    The rabbi and my father helped.
A crucifix burned on the wall
    Of the bright room where I was whelped.

At one week all my family prayed,
    Stuffed wine and cotton in my craw;
The rabbi blessed me with a blade
    According to the Mosaic Law.

The white steps blazed in Baltimore
    And cannas and white statuary.
I went home voluble and sore
    Influenced by Abraham and Mary.

II

At one the Apocalypse had spoken,
Von Moltke fell, I was housebroken.

At two how could I understand
The murder of Archduke Ferdinand?

France was involved with history,
I with my thumbs when I was three.

A sister came, we neared a war,
Paris was shelled when I was four.

I joined in our peach-kernel drive
For poison gas when I was five.

At six I cheered the big parade,
Burned sparklers and drank lemonade.

At seven I passed at school though I
Was far too young to say *Versailles.*

At eight the boom began to tire,
I tried to set our house on fire.

The Bolsheviks had drawn the line,
Lenin was stricken, I was nine.

—What evils do not retrograde
To my first odious decade?

III

Saints by whose pages I would swear,
⠀⠀My Zarathustra, Edward Lear,
Ulysses, Werther, fierce Flaubert,
⠀⠀Where are my books of yesteryear?

Sixteen and sixty are a pair;
⠀⠀We twice live by philosophies;
My marginalia of the hair,
⠀⠀Are you at one with Socrates?

Thirty subsides yet does not dare,
⠀⠀Sixteen and sixty bang their fists.
How is it that I no longer care
⠀⠀For Kant and the Transcendentalists?

Public libraries lead to prayer,
⠀⠀EN APXH ἦν ὁ λόγος—still
Eliot and John are always there
⠀⠀To tempt our admirari nil.

IV

I lived in a house of panels,
    Victorian, darkly made;
A virgin in bronze and marble
    Leered from the balustrade.

The street was a tomb of virtues,
    Autumnal for dreams and haunts;
I gazed from the polished windows
    Toward a neighborhood of aunts.

Mornings I practiced piano,
    Wrote elegies and sighed;
The evenings were conversations
    Of poetry and suicide.

Weltschmerz and mysticism,
    What tortures we undergo!
I loved with the love of Heinrich
    And the poison of Edgar Poe.

V

My first small book was nourished in the dark,
Secretly written, published, and inscribed.
Bound in wine-red, it made no brilliant mark.
Rather impossible relatives subscribed.

The best review was one I wrote myself
Under the name of a then-dearest friend.
Two hundred volumes stood upon my shelf
Saying my golden name from end to end.

I was not proud but seriously stirred;
Sorrow was song and money poetry's maid!
Sorrow I had in many a ponderous word,
But were the piper and the printer paid?

VI

The third-floor thoughts of discontented youth
Once saw the city, hardened against truth,
Get set for war. He coupled a last rime
And waited for the summons to end time.

It came. The box-like porch where he had sat,
The four bright boxes of a medium flat,
Chair he had sat in, glider where he lay
Reading the poets and prophets of his day,

He assigned abstractly to his dearest friend,
Glanced at the little street hooked at the end,
The line of poplars lately touched with spring,
Lovely as Laura, breathless, beckoning.

Mother was calm, until he left the door;
The trolley passed his sweetheart's house before
She was awake. The Armory was cold,
But naked, shivering, shocked he was enrolled.

It was the death he never quite forgot
Through the four years of death, and like as not
The true death of the best of all of us
Whose present life is largely posthumous.

VII

We waged a war within a war,
    A cause within a cause;
The glory of it was withheld
    In keeping with the laws
Whereby the public need not know
The pitfalls of the status quo.

Love was the reason for the blood:
    The black men of our land

Were seen to walk with pure white girls
    Laughing and hand in hand.
This most unreasonable state
No feeling White would tolerate.

We threw each other from the trams,
    We carried knives and pipes,
We sacrificed in self-defense
    Some of the baser types,
But though a certain number died
You would not call it fratricide.

The women with indignant tears
    Professed to love the Blacks,
And dark and wooly heads still met
    With heads of English flax.
Only the cockney could conceive
Of any marriage so naïve.

Yet scarcely fifty years before
    Their fathers rode to shoot
The undressed aborigines,
    Though not to persecute.
A fine distinction lies in that
They have no others to combat.

By order of the high command
    The black men were removed
To the interior and north;
    The crisis thus improved,
Even the women could detect
Their awful fall from intellect.

VIII

I plucked the bougainvillaea
    In Queensland in time of war;
The train stopped at the station
    And I reached it from my door.

I have never kept a flower
    And this one I never shall
I thought as I laid the blossom
    In the leaves of *Les Fleurs du Mal.*

I read my book in the desert
    In the time of death and fear,
The flower slipped from the pages
    And fell to my lap, my dear.

I sent it inside my letter,
    The purplest kiss I knew,
And thus you abused my passion
    With "A most Victorian Jew."

The Alphabet

The letters of the Jews as strict as flames
Or little terrible flowers lean
Stubbornly upwards through the perfect ages,
Singing through solid stone the sacred names.
The letters of the Jews are black and clean
And lie in chain-line over Christian pages.
The chosen letters bristle like barbed wire
That hedge the flesh of man,
Twisting and tightening the book that warns.
These words, this burning bush, this flickering pyre
Unsacrifices the bled son of man
Yet plaits his crown of thorns.

Where go the tipsy idols of the Roman
Past synagogues of patient time,
Where go the sisters of the Gothic rose,
Where go the blue eyes of the Polish women
Past the almost natural crime,
Past the still speaking embers of ghettos,
There rise the tinder flowers of the Jews.
The letters of the Jews are dancing knives
That carve the heart of darkness seven ways.
These are the letters that all men refuse
And will refuse until the king arrives
And will refuse until the death of time
And all is rolled back in the book of days.

The 151st Psalm

Are You looking for us? We are here.
Have You been gathering flowers, Elohim?
We are Your flowers, we have always been.
When will You leave us alone?
We are in America.
We have been here three hundred years.
And what new altar will You deck us with?

Whom are You following, Pillar of Fire?
What barn do You seek shelter in?
At whose gate do You whimper
In this great Palestine?
Whose wages do You take in this New World?
But Israel shall take what it shall take,
Making us ready for Your hungry Hand!

Immigrant God, You follow me;
You go with me, You are a distant tree;
You are the beast that lows in my heart's gates;
You are the dog that follows at my heel;
You are the table on which I lean;
You are the plate from which I eat.
Shepherd of the flocks of praise,
Youth of all youth, ancient of days,
Follow us.

My Father's Funeral

Lurching from gloomy limousines we slip
On the warm baby-blanket of Baltimore snow,
Wet flakes smacking our faces like distraught
Kisses on cheeks, and step upon the green
Carpet of artificial grass which crunches
Underfoot, as if it were eating, and come
To the canopy, a half-shelter which provides
A kind of room to enclose us all, and the hole,
And the camp chairs, and following after,
The scrolly walnut coffin
That has my father in it.

Minutes ago in the noncommittal chapel
I saw his face, not looking himself at all
In that compartment hinged to open and shut,
A vaudeville prop with a small waxen man,
"So cold," the widow said and shied away
In a wide arc of centrifugal motion,
To come again to stand like me beside,
In the flowerless room with electric candelabra.
If there is among our people any heaven,
We are rather ambiguous about it
And tend to ignore the subject.

The rabbi's eulogy is succinct,
Accurate and sincere, and the great prayer
That finishes the speech is simply praise
Of God, the god my father took in stride
When he made us learn Hebrew and shorthand,
Taught us to be superior, as befits
A nation of individual priests.
At my sister's house we neither pray nor cry

Nor sit, but stand and drink and joke,
So that one of the youngsters says
It's more like a cocktail party.

For Dylan's dandy villanelle,
For Sylvia's oath of damnation one reserves
A technical respect. To Miller's Willie
And Lewis's Babbitt I demur.
My father was writing a book on salesmanship
While he was dying; it was his book of poems,
Destined to be unpublished. He hadn't time
To master books but kept the house well stocked
With random volumes, like a ship's library,
Rows and rows of forgotten classics,
Books for the sake of having books.

My father in black knee-socks and high shoes
Holding a whip to whip a top upstreet;
My father the court stenographer,
My father in slouch hat in the Rockies,
My father kissing my mother,
My father kissing his secretary,
In the high-school yearbook captioned Yid,
In synagogue at six in the morning praying
Three hundred and sixty-five days for his mother's rest,
My father at my elbow on the bimah
And presiding over the Sabbath.

In the old forgotten purlieus of the city
A Jewish ghetto in its day, there lie
My father's father, mother and the rest,
Now only a ghetto lost to time,
Ungreen, unwhite, unterraced like the new
Cemetery to which my father goes.
Abaddon, the old place of destruction;
Sheol, a new-made garden of the dead
Under the snow. Shalom be to his life,
Shalom be to his death.

David Ignatow (b. 1914)

The son of immigrant parents, David Ignatow was born in Brooklyn, New York. He studied briefly at Brooklyn College and then held a variety of odd jobs, struggling to make a living while writing. His poetry began to receive critical recognition in the 1960s, and since then he has held teaching positions at numerous universities throughout the country. Ignatow's work includes ten volumes of poetry and two collections of essays. His poems, which frequently express a pessimistic view of the world, are often profoundly Jewish in both theme and subject. In the poems included here, Ignatow writes of the father-son relationship from both a personal and biblical perspective ("The Rightful One"), of his mother's death and his own isolation ("Kaddish"), and of his father's life in Russia ("1905"). He has defined himself as "an American, a Jew, . . . and a desperate believer in the One" (*The Notebooks of David Ignatow*, 1973).

The Rightful One

I heard my son burst out of his room
and shout, he is here, dad. He is here.
I understood and I managed to stand up,
melting within, and walk the hall
between our rooms to meet Him
whom I had neglected in my thoughts;
but not my son who was ill
and had searched for Him.
He had come. I saw Him standing,
his hair long, face exhausted, eyes sad
and knowing, and I bent my knee,
terrified at the reality,
but he restrained me with a hand
and said, I am a sufferer like yourself.
I have come to let you know.
And I arose, my heart swelling, and said,
I have failed and bitterness is in me.
And he replied, And forgiveness too.
Bless your son. And I blessed him
and his face brightened. And the Rightful One
was gone and left a power to feel free.

1905

While my father walked through mud
in shoes borrowed from his sister,
all Kiev attended *Prince Igor* and cheered,
and while he worked in a cellar bindery
and slept on workbenches rats leapt over
at night, Dostoevsky's *White Nights*
and *Anna Karenina* were being read avidly
amid joy, tears and protests. My father
was the silent one, walking through the streets
where the hot arguments went on about poverty
and guilt. He walked, his work bundle under arm,
from cellar to monastery, to bind holy books
and volumes of the Russian classics,
and when they had had enough of classics
and needed blood, he fled,
for his blood was real to them; only he
had worked and starved. All others were
but characters in a novel or a play—
bless Chekhov, Gogol and others for their genius,
but my father was the one who had not been
immortalized and made untouchable.
Only he was real in Russia's torment.
Only he stood for life. All else was books,
and that was the torment.

Kaddish

Mother of my birth, for how long were we together
in your love and my adoration of your self?
For the shadow of a moment, as I breathed your pain
and you breathed my suffering. As we knew
of shadows in lit rooms that would swallow the light.

Your face beneath the oxygen tent was alive
but your eyes closed, your breathing hoarse.
Your sleep was with death. I was alone
with you as when I was young
but now only alone, not with you,
to become alone forever, as I was learning
watching you become alone.

Earth now is your mother, as you were mine, my earth,
my sustenance and my strength,
and now without you I turn to your mother
and seek from her that I may meet you again
in rock and stone. Whisper to the stone,
I love you. Whisper to the rock, I found you.
Whisper to the earth, Mother, I have found her,
and I am safe and always have been.

Eve Merriam (1916–1992)

Eve Merriam was born Eva Moskovitz in Philadelphia, Pennsylvania, to Russian Jewish immigrant parents. She received a B.A. degree from the University of Pennsylvania and did graduate work at Columbia University. Thinking that anti-Semitism might be the cause of her early, failed attempts at publication, she reluctantly changed her name. In her lifetime she held a variety of positions, including radio writer for CBS, copy editor for *Glamour* magazine, and teacher. In addition to poetry, she also published many novels, stories, and plays for adults and children. Her poetry was motivated by her love of language, her hatred of social injustice, and her desire to explore Jewish identity and history. "Esther," reprinted from Merriam's early collection, *Family Circle* (1946), is a satirical portrait of "Americanized" Jews. "The Wall" and "Of Dogs and Ostriches," from *Tomorrow Morning* (1953), criticize both the purveyors of anti-Semitic hatred and those Jews who "passively despair."

Esther

Had crashed the right part of town.
Could wear a different deep-cut gown
Every night in the week.
Butlered, banqueted, butter-rich fed,
Life was a silver serving dish,
Cinderella wish.

And midnight tolled no jeering pumpkin coach;
Only personal maid unfolding the crepe-de-chine couch.
Golden slipper was merely one of many.
Munching on frilly bonbon thrills,
Mufflered in all-year mink:
Could have refused to think.

Simple to turn your back on the pinchpenny past;
The dazzling improbable dream was daylight at last,
And dark would never dawn again.
Regret, forget what went before;
Lie, deny that early station,
Your chapped hands' humiliation.

Drive limousinely up to the old neighborhood,
Lady Bountiful bestowing caviar baskets of food!
Brighten their cobweb corner.
(But stay just a little while.)
Let them stroke your shimmering coat,
Touch sapphire at your throat.

Then grandly perfect your grammar of the perfect snob:
Convince yourself all beggars like to rob,
The poor are naturally defiled,

You never were their kin—
But a royal child left at that lowly door
You need stoop to and scrub no more.

Gag their crying hands with a large and lavish bank note,
Diminishing every month till it needs a microscope . . .
Then let them shift for themselves;
You have more important demands
With your new family crest.
Besides, they always leave you depressed.

That might have been your pattern: historic renegade,
Up from the rank and file, stool pigeon bought and paid;
Except that under the heavy festooned robe, beneath the
    intricate carved pin,
You wore your common conscience like a light and
    shining skin.

The Wall

Scratch a Jew and you'll find a Wailing Wall.

Born a Jew?
Too bad for you.
Mourn, Jew.
Crawl, Jew.
Fall on your wailing wall
And cry, Jew.

For your crime, Jew
It is time Jew
That you should die.

"Jude!" tramples the storm-troop voice,
"Consider your crime!"
"Jew, you are a Jew!"

Crime like the shine of sun
Salt in the ocean
Snow on a winter day.

But Jews suffer
It is the Will   the Wall
There is no other way.

History of the Jews is a wall.
And walls are to divide,
To keep inside.

The   wall   the wall was always there.
Thousands of wailing years
And bearded tears.

The wall, barring the daylight blue.
Breathe gray the ghetto air
And passively despair.

It is the Will   the Wall
And tears cannot climb.
Black mourning shawl your cradle shroud.

                    II
Shout!
The silent wall
Become a brazen barricade!

Tears are anger frozen
An icy road to take,
Wall to leap.

(Blood is slippery on the wall
Slippery as oil . . .
But hands hold;
Wall can be scaled.)

The black mourning shawl is thrust aside,
The bride of courage goes forth,
Joins Jew the proud bridegroom,
Jew the proud fighter:
Oh, joyous wedding day
Claiming your love, your need.

Rejoice,
Shout
As
The
Wall
Thundering
Falls

Stone rises from ruin.
Stones flower with vines and fruit,
Garden for a house,
Shade for a sleeping child
Stirring in safety, smiling at being a Jew.

Of Dogs and Ostriches

Speaking as one Jew to another:
Trouble is trouble.
Need a place be set for it?

Hitler is final and flat.

Let us chat of more pastel happenings than Peekskill and
   Chicago pogroms.
Why bring the gun-butt down again upon your head
By stretching up too tall,
By standing straight?

A mere suggestion: bow low, go by the back door,
Glide down the side street quietly.
Agreed, it is narrower here, you can stumble and fall,
And if it becomes a creeping habit to walk on all fours—
Well, it's a dog's life anyway;
Roll over and play dead.
If it makes you feel any better, spit three times inside.

Your pride?
But mine fits easily into the pocket of my skin.
Understand,
There are culture patterns, tensions, balances and checks;
All can be explained
Without a sticking-out of necks.

Graceful does it.
Consider the elegant ostrich deep in the furry sand,
The most refined of burials.

PART II

NEW DAYS
FOR OLD,
OLD DAYS
FOR NEW

Howard Nemerov (1920–1991)

In addition to more than fifteen volumes of poetry, Howard Nemerov is author of a diverse range of fiction, autobiography, and criticism. In 1978, *The Collected Poems of Howard Nemerov* (1977) won both the Pulitzer Prize and the National Book Award. From 1988 to 1990, Nemerov served as Poet Laureate of the United States. Although he did not write extensively about his Jewish heritage, Nemerov did publish a number of impressive poems which explore Jewish themes. Those included here demonstrate his satiric wit ("Debate with the Rabbi"), his ability to employ biblical sources imaginatively ("Nicodemus"), and his philosophical questioning of God's harsh treatment of the Jews ("A Song of Degrees"). Nemerov was born in New York City, graduated from Harvard University, and served as a pilot during World War II. He taught at a number of institutions, including Hamilton College, Bennington College, and Washington University in St. Louis, Missouri.

A Song of Degrees

Though the road lead nowhere
I have followed the road
In its blind turnings, its descents
And the long levels where the emptiness ahead
Is inescapably seen.

I have cried for justice, I have cried
For mercy, now I desire neither.
A man may grow strong in his wandering,
His foot strong as a wheel
Turning the endless road.

Foot and hand hardened to horn,
Nose but a hook of bone, and eyes
Not liquid now but stone—I
To myself violent, fiercely exult
In Zion everywhere.

Nicodemus

I

I went under cover of night
By back streets and alleyways,
Not as one secret and ashamed
But with a natural discretion.
I passed by a boy and a girl
Embraced against the white wall
In parts of shadow, parts of light,
But though I turned my eyes away, my mind shook
Whether with dryness or their driving blood;
And a dog howled once in a stone corner.

II

Rabbi, I said,
How is a man born, being old?
From the torn sea into the world
A man may be forced only the one time
To suffer the indignation of the child,
His childish distempers and illnesses.
I would not, if I could, be born again
To suffer the miseries of the child,
The perpetual nearness to tears,
The book studied through burning eyes,
The particular malady of being always ruled
To ends he does not see or understand.

A man may be forced only the one time
To the slow perception of what is meant
That is neither final nor sufficient,
To the slow establishment of a self
Adequate to the ceremony and respect
Of other men's eyes; and to the last

Knowledge that nothing has been done,
The bitter bewilderment of his age,
A master in Israel and still a child.

III

Rabbi, all things in the springtime
Flower again, but a man may not
Flower again. I regret
The sweet smell of lilacs and the new grass
And the shoots put forth of the cedar
When we are done with the long winter.

Rabbi, sorrow has mothered me
And humiliation been my father,
But neither the ways of the flesh
Nor the pride of the spirit took me,
And I am exalted in Israel
For all that I know I do not know.

Now the end of my desire is death
For my hour is almost come.
I shall not say with Sarah
That God hath made me to laugh,
Nor the new word shall not be born
Out of the dryness of my mouth.

Rabbi, let me go up from Egypt
With Moses to the wilderness of Sinai
And to the country of the old Canaan
Where, sweeter than honey, Sarah's blood
Darkens the cold cave in the field
And the wild seed of Abraham is cold.

Debate with the Rabbi

You've lost your religion, the Rabbi said.
    It wasn't much to keep, said I.
You should affirm the spirit, said he,
and the communal solidarity.
    I don't feel so solid, I said.

We are the people of the Book, the Rabbi said.
    Not of the phone book, said I.
Ours is a great tradition, said he,
And a wonderful history.
    But history's over, I said.

We Jews are creative people, the Rabbi said.
    Make something, then, said I.
In science and in art, said he,
Violinists and physicists have we.
    Fiddle and physic indeed, I said.

Stubborn and stiff-necked man! the Rabbi cried.
    The pain you give me, said I.
Instead of bowing down, said he,
You go on in your obstinacy.
    We Jews are that way, I replied.

Grace Paley (b. 1922)

The daughter of Russian immigrants, Grace Paley was born in the Bronx, New York. She attended Hunter College, New York University, and the Merchants and Bankers Business and Secretarial School. Known primarily for her fiction, which has received ample critical praise, Paley has published three collections of poetry and three volumes of short stories. Like her fiction, her poetry, written in clear, proselike language, often concerns her present-day American Jewish milieu, the memories of her childhood, and the immigrant culture of her parents. "A Warning" expounds on the words of the psalmist: "If I forget thee, O Jerusalem." "The Sad Children's Song" laments both personal and universal loss, while "Some Days I Am Lonesome" and "People in My Family" strike similar, sad tones of disillusionment and isolation. Paley divides her time between teaching at Sarah Lawrence College and City College of the City University of New York.

A Warning

One day I forgot Jerusalem and my right arm is withered
My right arm, my moving arm, my rising and falling arm
                    my loving arm
Is withered

And my left eye, the blinker and winker is plucked out
It hangs by six threads of endless remembering.
Because I forgot Jerusalem
And wherever I go, I am known, I am recognized at once. I am
                    perceived by strangers.
Because on one day, only one day I forgot Jerusalem.

Jews everywhere, Jews, old deaths of the north and south
                    kingdoms,
Poor Jews in the ghetto walls built by the noble slav,
                    Jew princes
In Amsterdam who live in diamond houses that shine like window
                    panes
Listen to me. Wherever you go, keep the nation of that city
                    in mind
For I forgot her and now I am blind and crippled.

Even my lover, a Christian with pale eyes and the barbarian's foreskin
                    has left me.

The Sad Children's Song

This house is a wreck said the children
when they came home with their children
Your papers are all over the place
The chairs are covered with books
and look   brown leaves are piled on the floor
under the wandering Jews

Your face is a wreck said the children
when they came home with their children
There are lines all over your face
your necks are like curious turtles
Why did you let yourself go?
Where are you going without us?

This world is a wreck said the children
When they came home with their children
There are bombs all over the place
There's no water   the fields are all poisoned
Why did you leave things like this
Where can we go said the children
what can we say to our children?

Some Days I Am Lonesome

Some days I am lonesome   I want to talk to my mother
And she isn't home
Then I ask my father   Where has she been the last twenty years?
And he answers
Where do you think   you fool as usual?
        She is asleep in Abraham's bosom
        Resting from years of your incessant provocation
        Exhausted by infinite love of me
        Escaping from the boredom of days shortening to Christmas
                and the pain of days lengthening to Easter
        You know where she is   She is at ease in Zion with all
                the other dead Jews

People in My Family

In my family
people who were eighty-two were very different
from people who were ninety-two

The eighty-two year old people grew up
    it was 1914
    this is what they knew
    War   World War   War

That's why when they speak to the child
they say
    poor little one . . .

The ninety-two year old people remember
    it was the year 1905
    they went to prison
    they went into exile
    they said   ah   soon

When they speak to the grandchild
they say
    yes   there will be revolution
    then there will be revolution   then
    once more   then the earth itself
    will turn and turn and cry out   oh I
    have been made sick

        then you   my little bud
          must flower and save it

Ruth Whitman (b. 1922)

Ruth Whitman is the author of seven collections of poetry, a volume of essays, and numerous translations of Yiddish fiction and poetry. Her poetry often explores Jewish sources and themes, and is informed by her own feminist perspective as, for example, "Cutting the Jewish Bride's Hair." "Touro Synagogue," from her early collection *Blood and Milk Poems* (1963), presents a loving yet unsentimental portrait of her paternal grandfather. A more recent volume, *Laughing Gas: Poems, New and Selected 1963–1990* (1991), from which the other selections are taken, includes poems about being a Jew in contemporary America, as well as several ("Bubba Esther, 1888," "Uncle Harry at the La Brea Tar Pits," and "My Greatgreatuncle the Archbishop") that evoke tragic memories, both personal and collective. Whitman was born in New York City, attended Radcliffe College, and received an M.A. degree from Harvard University. She has taught at a number of colleges and universities, both in the United States and in Israel.

Touro Synagogue

As to an unknown lover I returned
To my father's land, a shifting land, now jeweled
And satined like a bride, a holy ark.

A stranger to his house, I heard my talk
More friendly to the twelve Ionic trees
Than to the tribes of Israel, more shy

To celebrate this birthday than to die.
White and perfect, starred with candlelight,
The sacred chamber held a secret stair.

The heart's escape leads out to everywhere,
Nowhere, but dreams still find a certain black
Connecticut hill.
                    My grandfather stands tall

And wraps me in his cemetery cloak,
Encircles me against the nightmare chill,
Till gowned in fear I follow with his ghost

Through village, town, down through the midnight past
To a second son reading by candlelight
Forbidden books that set his future free.

To an immigrant tender in his blasphemy,
Bold, repentant, joyful against death.
Rich in gesture, eloquent as earth.

Ignorant of all, I catch my breath
To hear the sharp crack of the shattered cup.
Driven to live, I grope to gather up

The windless torch of love, my tribe's rebirth.

Cutting the Jewish Bride's Hair

It's to possess more than the skin
that those old world Jews
exacted the hair of their brides.
> Good husband, lover of the Torah,
> does the calligraphy of your bride's hair
> interrupt your page?

Before the clownish friction of flesh
creating out of nothing
a mockup of its begetters,
a miraculous puppet of God,
you must first divorce her from her vanity.

She will snip off her pride,
cut back her appetite to be devoured,
she will keep herself well braided,
her love's furniture will not endanger you,
> but this little amputation
> will shift the balance of the universe.

Bubba Esther, 1888

She was still upset,
she wanted to tell me,
she kept remembering
his terrible hands:

how she came, a young girl
of seventeen, a freckled
fairskinned Jew from Kovno
to Hamburg with her uncle
and stayed in an old house
and waited while he bought
the steamship tickets
so they could sail to America

and how he came into her room
sat down on the bed, touched
her waist, took her by the
breast, said for a kiss
she could have her ticket,
her skirts were rumpled, her
petticoat torn, his teeth were
broken, his breath full of
onions, she was ashamed

still ashamed, lying
eighty years later
in the hospital bed,
trying to tell me,
trembling, weeping with anger

My Greatgreatuncle the Archbishop

The cossacks snatched him from his mother
at the age of five
to serve in the Tsar's army.

He was farmed with a family
who found him so docile, so bright
they forced him to enter the church.

One day he passed through the shtetl
where he was born, Borisov,
and he heard the sound of a melody,

mournful and familiar.
It haunted him, why was he so shaken by it?
He grew up and became an archbishop.

In the middle of a foursquare
Gregorian chant
he wept to remember

the old Hassidic notes:
di-dona-di, di-dona-di.
They drew him back, back to Borisov,

to the house of his kidnapping.
I am the brother of Yitzie Orkos, he said,
I have heard of my nephew, Yankev Leyb

(that was my grandfather),
he too wants to be enlightened, he has
secretly taught himself Russian,

let me take him, let me educate him:
I have no children of my own.
But they refused,

they denied him,
they were afraid.
It was the time of pogroms.

What was a Russian Orthodox archbishop
doing in their Jewish house?
They sent him away.

Uncle Harry at the La Brea Tar Pits

Against the iron fence surrounding pools
of black asphalt bubbling and boiling up
through geologic layers; against the fence
where this hot tar surprised and swallowed
families of mastodons forty thousand years ago
(their bones now tangled with birds, camels, antelopes,
hundreds of dire wolves and dinosaurs);
where, nine thousand years ago, a young
woman came stumbling across the treeless plain
of Los Angeles, and slipped or was hurled
by a jealous lover into the sticky black lake—
Uncle Harry poses in a jaunty fedora,
his elegant profile turned toward the camera.

  He says, life has cheated me.
  When they shipped me to America
  in 1907, I lost my friends
  and I lost the Russian theaters
  where I stayed every night
  until one or two in the morning,
  adoring the actors.

  A childish prank ruined me.

  I was the smallest of the gang,
  so they hoisted me up
  to hang a black cloth
  over the Tsar's double eagles
  in front of the prison
  while sailors from the Potemkin
  were rioting in the streets.
  Cossacks were clubbing Jews

left and right. I saw a woman
running with a baby carriage
in front of the horses' hooves.

My father said it was Siberia for me,
or America. I boarded a broken-down
ship in Leeds, bound for Boston.

Later I wandered here,
still an exile,
to Elysian Park in Los Angeles.

The feather on his hat is motheaten,
his coat torn and stained,
but he has turned his plucky collar up
like an unemployed actor from Odessa
who knows he is still handsome.
He is ninetythree.

Behind him a lifelike mastodon
made of plaster and acrylic
lifts her tusks in terror
as she struggles half-submerged in tar,
while her mammoth baby
hesitates behind her
on the edge of the black museum.

Denise Levertov (b. 1923)

Born in Essex, England, to a Welsh mother and a Russian Jewish father who converted to Christianity (and eventually became an Anglican minister), Denise Levertov emigrated to the United States in 1948. A tremendously prolific and accomplished writer, Levertov has published more than twenty volumes of poetry, essays, and translations. Although her poetry is not limited to Jewish themes, she has written a number of poems that reflect her self-proclaimed Judaism and her bond to the Jewish people. Her father's belief that he was descended from the founder of the Hasidic movement was the impetus for her poem "Illustrious Ancestors," reprinted from *Collected Earlier Poems 1940–1960* (1979). Levertov's work often reflects her lifelong opposition to war and injustice, evident in her well-known poem, "During the Eichmann Trial," reprinted from *Poems, 1960–1967* (1983). A selection from *Poems, 1968–1972* (1987), "February Evening in Boston, 1971," with its images of twilight, lovers, and those who would "reach out / toward survivors," suggests hope and continuity.

Illustrious Ancestors

The Rav
of Northern White Russia declined,
in his youth, to learn the
language of birds, because
the extraneous did not interest him; nevertheless
when he grew old it was found
he understood them anyway, having
listened well, and as it is said, 'prayed
        with the bench and the floor.' He used
what was at hand—as did
Angel Jones of Mold, whose meditations
were sewn into coats and britches.
        Well, I would like to make,
thinking some line still taut between me and them,
poems direct as what the birds said,
hard as a floor, sound as a bench,
mysterious as the silence when the tailor
would pause with his needle in the air.

During the Eichmann Trial

i   WHEN WE LOOK UP

> When we look up
> each from his being
>   —Robert Duncan

He had not looked,
pitiful man whom none

pity, whom all
must pity if they look

into their own face (given
only by glass, steel, water

barely known) all
who look up

to see—how many
faces?   How many

seen in a lifetime? (Not those
that flash by, but those

into which the gaze wanders
and is lost

and returns to tell
Here is a mystery,

a person, an
other, an I?

Count them.
Who are five million?)

'I was used from the nursery
to obedience

all my life . . .
Corpselike

obedience.' Yellow
calmed him later—

'a charming picture'
yellow of autumn leaves in

Wienerwald, a little
railroad station
nineteen-o-eight, Lemburg,

yellow sun
on the stepmother's teatable

Franz Joseph's beard
blessing his little ones.

It was the yellow
of the stars too,

stars that marked
those in whose faces

you had not
looked. "They were cast out

as if they were
some animals, some beasts.'

'And what would disobedience
have brought me? And

whom would it have served?'
'I did not let my thoughts

dwell on this—I had
seen it and that was

enough.' (The words
'slur into a harsh babble')

'A spring of blood
gushed from the earth.'
Miracle

unsung. I see
a spring of blood gush from the earth—

Earth cannot swallow
so much at once

a fountain
rushes towards the sky

unrecognized
a sign—.

Pity this man who saw it
whose obedience continued—

he, you, I, which shall I say?
He stands

isolate in a bulletproof
witness-stand of glass,

a cage, where we may view
ourselves, an apparition

telling us something he
does not know: we are members

one of another.

ii   THE PEACHTREE

The Danube orchards
are full of fruit
but in the city one tree
haunts a boy's dreams

a tree in a villa garden
the Devil's garden
a peach tree

and of its fruit one peach
calls to him

he sees it yellow and ripe
the vivid blood
bright in its round cheek

Next day he knows
he cannot withstand desire
it is no common fruit

it holds some secret
it speaks to the yellow star within him

he scales the wall
enters the garden of death
takes the peach
and death pounces

mister death who rushes out
from his villa
mister death who loves yellow

This poem is based on the earliest mention, during the trial, of this incident. In a later statement it was said that the fruit was cherries, that the boy was already in the garden, doing forced labor, when he was accused of taking the fruit, and that Eichmann killed him in a tool shed, not beneath the tree. The poem therefore is not to be taken as a report of what happened but of what I envisioned.

who wanted that yellow peach
for himself
mister death who signs papers
then eats

telegraphs simply: **Shoot them**
then eats
mister death who orders
more transports
then eats

he would have enjoyed
the sweetest of all the peaches on his tree
with sour-cream
with brandy

Son of David
's blood, vivid red
and trampled juice
yellow and sweet
flow together beneath the tree

there is more blood than
sweet juice
always more blood—mister
death goes indoors
exhausted

From blacked-out streets
    (wide avenues swept by curfew,
    alleyways, veins
    of dark within dark)

from houses whose walls
    had for a long time known
the tense stretch of skin over bone
as their brick or stone listened—

            The scream!
The awaited scream rises,
the shattering
of glass and the cracking
of bone

a polar tumult as when
black ice booms, knives
of ice and glass
splitting and splintering the silence into
innumerable screaming needles of
yes, now it is upon us, the jackboots
are running in spurts of
sudden blood-light through the
broken temples

the veils
are rent in twain
terror has a white sound
every scream
of fear is a white needle freezing the eyes
the floodlights of their trucks throw
jets of white, their shouts
cleave the wholeness of darkness into

sectors of transparent white-clouded pantomime
where all that was awaited
is happening, it is Crystal Night

it is Crystal Night
these spikes which are not
pitched in the range of common hearing
whistle through time

smashing the windows of sleep and dream
smashing the windows of history
a whiteness scattering
in hailstones
each a mirror
for man's eyes.

February Evening in Boston, 1971

The trees' black hair electric
brushed out,
          fierce haloes.

And westward
veils of geranium hold their own,
even yet. Transparent.

People are quickly, buoyantly
crossing the Common
into evening, into
a world of promises.

It was the custom of my tribe
to speak and sing;
not only to share the present, breath and sight,
but to the unborn.
Still, even now, we reach out
toward survivors. It is a covenant
of desire.

          Shall there be, by long chance,
one to hear me after the great, the gross,
                    the obscene silence,
to hear and wonder that in the last days
the seasons gave joy,
that dusk transmuted
               brilliant pink to lilac, lilac
               to smoke blue?

And lovers sat on a bench in the cold as night drew in,
laughing because the snow had melted.

Shirley Kaufman (b. 1923)

Born in Seattle, Washington, Shirley Kaufman is the daughter of Polish Jews who emigrated to the United States prior to World War I. She graduated from UCLA and then—twenty-three years later—received an M.A. degree in creative writing from San Francisco State University. A committed Zionist, Kaufman left America and settled permanently in Israel in 1973. She is the author of seven volumes of poems, as well as several translations of Hebrew poetry. Although Kaufman's poems express an awareness of her marginality as an American Israeli, they also resonate with her devotion to Israel, her knowledge of both contemporary and ancient Jewish history, and her ability to synthesize her feminist and Zionist ideologies. Kaufman writes about biblical characters, Eastern Europe before the Holocaust, and contemporary Israel. "Above Vitebsk" and "The Western Wall" are from *The Floor Keeps Turning* (1970); "Roots in the Air" and "Vows" are taken from *Roots in the Air: New and Selected Poems* (1996).

Above Vitebsk

The old man sitting on the roof
is really there. In fact,
he is an uncle.
And if the wagon gets up
off the road, it's only
one leap to roll sideways
over the town.

Such leaning and loving
high in the night sky,
who will come down?
Peddlers, sweethearts,
milkmaids with faces floating
or three-breasted dancers?

Your father in his herring shop
may have seen his fish
climb ladders, but you
conform to your own miracles,
flutter your own air.

The poet finds his head turned
upside down. The weightless
angel is in the child.
The child has wings.
The fiddle is musician,
plays itself.
What is earthbound?
Which of us must fall?

The Western Wall

What are they doing here? And why are they crying?
—Elie Wiesel

And so through the Jaffa Gate, the street
named David swaying with donkeys,
down the Street of the Chain, barrels
of spices and of fresh baked bread,
women with tin trays on their heads
and shapes of children running everywhere.

Down the old city—to the wall.
I stop and stare. The wall is thick
with its own silence. The men become
their fathers. Women cover up their arms,
their hair. And I am old with them
and they have held my children
with their dead.

I move across the whole
world to the wall and with my fingers
touch against their touch the shadows
growing out of it like vines. The stone
is cold. As if my hand lies buried
under ground, it sucks the cold,
my palm is filled with it.

And prayers.
The yellow papers in the wall, higher
than arms can reach. They fall
from every hollow, every crack,
fall in the small pores of my skin,
and I am huge with prayers I cannot hold.

Heavy with messages, I stay
until the wall goes out

beyond the wall, circles the Temple
and the Ark, the ruins below the paving
where we crowd, rocking with faces,
kings and priests, their eyes like animals
at night shining so fiercely through the dark
they pass between us and the wall,
and we become their shadows breathing
dust, breathing the place where we have been,
all that is written in the awkward flesh,
how the whole alphabet of yearning
makes no words, the unformed words
keep crying in our throats.

Roots in the Air

Over my head
the Bengal ficus
dangles its roots like seaweed
out of the sea, licking
the ashes from the air.

Sure of which way is down
but unable to get there,
one tree makes a hundred
out of the steaming soil it comes from,
replanting itself.

Not here.
The roots are shaggy
with trying in this land.
No earth, no water,
what are they doing
in the light?

Trees find their shapes again,
as the world blanches. It must be morning.

At the window I can make out the dim outlines
of the domes the towers lit by the dawn.

On the sill the dove sleeps
over her two damp birds.
She built a nest in the pot of geraniums
and yesterday they hatched,
little homemade bombs.
They are not Jews or Arabs.

Vows

Nobody wants it to rain at a wedding.
Already the trees were losing their edges
to the dark behind them. Your friends
raised the *huppa* as if they were pushing
the clouds back, lifting a portable
velvet hope.

        I wanted to lift you
again on one of the animals you chose,
swans hollowed out in the center
where we both sat, the ostrich you rode
by yourself, hanging on to its neck.
Each time you went around I'd wave.
Practicing, though I didn't know it,
for your sweet rides later, nights
I stayed up waiting like my mother
waiting to save me from the world.

Little fish on my belly. That's where
they laid you when they cut us loose.
I was afraid of your squashed face
until I saw how baffled you were,
your foggy eyes, your small mouth
begging. Sometimes I'd see in your eyes
me looking into my mother's,
sucking her angst, or grandma, tiny
and whiskered, hiding her shorn hair
under the wig like her true life
scissored in Poland.

        Someone was always
sorry. We go on being the daughters,

feeling their lonely breath on our faces
after the breasts dry or after we marry
the wrong ones. Walking backwards
into our lives.

The gray sky
was coming at us like a mudslide,
you in your clean space saying
what we all say.

Anthony Hecht (b. 1923)

Anthony Hecht is generally acknowledged to be one of the outstanding poets of his generation. There is little to distinguish Hecht's early poetry from that of his non-Jewish contemporaries. But beginning with the publication of *The Hard Hours* (1967), which won the Pulitzer Prize, Hecht began writing numerous, powerful poems linking universal themes with a more personal Jewish sensibility. " 'More Light! More Light!' " (supposedly Goethe's last words) evokes the image of the great German writer and depicts a Germany Goethe could never imagine, while "The Book of Yolek" is an even more intimate portrayal of the horrors of the Holocaust. "Adam" recalls Hecht's own son Adam, as well as his biblical namesake. Another very personal poem, "The Vow," recounts the sad details of a miscarriage, but concludes with the promise of love and hope for future offspring. "Exile" is addressed to the poet Joseph Brodsky, yet also refers to the stories of both the New and Old Testament Joseph. Hecht was born in New York City and attended Bard College and Columbia University. He has taught at Kenyon College, the University of Rochester, Smith College, and many others.

Adam

Hath the rain a father? or who hath begotten the drops of dew?

"Adam, my child, my son,
These very words you hear
Compose the fish and starlight
Of your untroubled dream.
When you awake, my child,
It shall all come true.
Know that it was for you
That all things were begun."

Adam, my child, my son,
Thus spoke Our Father in heaven
To his first, fabled child,
The father of us all.
And I, your father, tell
The words over again
As innumerable men
From ancient times have done.

Tell them again in pain,
And to the empty air.
Where you are men speak
A different mother tongue.
Will you forget our games,
Our hide-and-seek and song?
Child, it will be long
Before I see you again.

Adam, there will be
Many hard hours,
As an old poem says,
Hours of loneliness.
I cannot ease them for you;

They are our common lot.
During them, like as not,
You will dream of me.

When you are crouched away
In a strange clothes closet
Hiding from one who's "It"
And the dark crowds in,
Do not be afraid—
O, if you can, believe
In a father's love
That you shall know some day.

Think of the summer rain
Or seedpearls of the mist;
Seeing the beaded leaf,
Try to remember me.
From far away
I send my blessing out
To circle the great globe.
It shall reach you yet.

The Vow

In the third month, a sudden flow of blood.
The mirth of tabrets ceaseth, and the joy
Also of the harp. The frail image of God
Lay spilled and formless. Neither girl nor boy,
But yet blood of my blood, nearly my child.
        All that long day
Her pale face turned to the window's mild
        Featureless grey.

And for some nights she whimpered as she dreamed
The dead thing spoke, saying: "Do not recall
Pleasure at my conception. I am redeemed
From pain and sorrow. Mourn rather for all
Who breathlessly issue from the bone gates,
        The gates of horn,
For truly it is best of all the fates
        Not to be born.

"Mother, a child lay gasping for bare breath
On Christmas Eve when Santa Claus had set
Death in the stocking, and the lights of death
Flamed in the tree. O, if you can, forget
You were the child, turn to my father's lips
        Against the time
When his cold hand puts forth its fingertips
        Of jointed lime."

Doctors of Science, what is man that he
Should hope to come to a good end? *The best
Is not to have been born.* And could it be
That Jewish diligence and Irish jest
The consent of flesh and a midwinter storm

Had reconciled,
Was yet too bold a mixture to inform
        A simple child?

Even as gold is tried, Gentile and Jew.
If that ghost was a girl's, I swear to it:
Your mother shall be far more blessed than you.
And if a boy's, I swear: The flames are lit
That shall refine us; they shall not destroy
        A living hair.
Your younger brothers shall confirm in joy
        This that I swear.

"More Light! More Light!"

For Heinrich Blücher and Hannah Arendt

Composed in the Tower before his execution
These moving verses, and being brought at that time
Painfully to the stake, submitted, declaring thus:
"I implore my God to witness that I have made no crime."

Nor was he forsaken of courage, but the death was horrible,
The sack of gunpowder failing to ignite.
His legs were blistered sticks on which the black sap
Bubbled and burst as he howled for the Kindly Light.

And that was but one, and by no means one of the worst;
Permitted at least his pitiful dignity;
And such as were by made prayers in the name of Christ,
That shall judge all men, for his soul's tranquillity.

We move now to outside a German wood.
Three men are there commanded to dig a hole
In which the two Jews are ordered to lie down
And be buried alive by the third, who is a Pole.

Not light from the shrine at Weimar beyond the hill
Nor light from heaven appeared. But he did refuse.
A Lüger settled back deeply in its glove.
He was ordered to change places with the Jews.

Much casual death had drained away their souls.
The thick dirt mounted toward the quivering chin.
When only the head was exposed the order came
To dig him out again and to get back in.

No light, no light in the blue Polish eye.
When he finished a riding boot packed down the earth.
The Lüger hovered lightly in its glove.
He was shot in the belly and in three hours bled to death.

No prayers or incense rose up in those hours
Which grew to be years, and every day came mute
Ghosts from the ovens, sifting through crisp air,
And settled upon his eyes in a black soot.

Exile

For Joseph Brodsky

Vacant parade grounds swept by the winter wind,
A pile of worn-out tires crowning a knoll,
The purplish clinkers near the cinder blocks
That support the steps of an abandoned church
Still moored to a telephone pole, this sullen place
Is *terra deserta*, Joseph, this is Egypt.

You have been here before, but long ago.
The first time you were sold by your own brothers
But had a gift for dreams that somehow saved you.
The second time was familiar but still harder.
You came with wife and child, the child not yours,
The wife, whom you adored, in a way not yours,
And all that you can recall, even in dreams,
Is the birth itself, and after that the journey,
Mixed with an obscure and confusing music,
Confused with a smell of hay and steaming dung.
Nothing is clear from then on, and what became
Of the woman and child eludes you altogether.

Look, though, at the blank, expressionless faces
Here in this photograph by Walker Evans.
These are the faces that everywhere surround you;
They have all the emptiness of gravel pits.
And look, here, at this heavy growth of weeds
Where the dishwater is poured from the kitchen window
And has been ever since the house was built.
And the chimney whispers its weak diphtheria,
The hydrangeas display their gritty pollen of soot.
This is Egypt, Joseph, the old school of the soul.
You will recognize the rank smell of a stable
And the soft patience in a donkey's eyes,
Telling you you are welcome and at home.

The Book of Yolek

Wir haben ein Gesetz,
Und nach dem Gesetz soll er sterben.

The dowsed coals fume and hiss after your meal
Of grilled brook trout, and you saunter off for a walk
Down the fern trail, it doesn't matter where to,
Just so you're weeks and worlds away from home,
And among midsummer hills have set up camp
In the deep bronze glories of declining day.

You remember, peacefully, an earlier day
In childhood, remember a quite specific meal:
A corn roast and bonfire in summer camp.
That summer you got lost on a Nature Walk;
More than you dared admit, you thought of home;
No one else knows where the mind wanders to.

The fifth of August, 1942.
It was morning and very hot. It was the day
They came at dawn with rifles to The Home
For Jewish Children, cutting short the meal
Of bread and soup, lining them up to walk
In close formation off to a special camp.

How often you have thought about that camp,
As though in some strange way you were driven to.
And about the children, and how they were made to walk.
Yolek who had bad lungs, who wasn't a day
Over five years old, commanded to leave his meal
And shamble between armed guards to his long home.

We're approaching August again. It will drive home
The regulation torments of that camp
Yolek was sent to, his small, unfinished meal,

The electric fences, the numeral tattoo,
The quite extraordinary heat of the day
They all were forced to take that terrible walk.

Whether on a silent, solitary walk
Or among crowds, far off or safe at home,
You will remember, helplessly, that day,
And the smell of smoke, and the loudspeakers of the camp.
Wherever you are, Yolek will be there, too.
His unuttered name will interrupt your meal.

Prepare to receive him in your home some day.
Though they killed him in the camp they sent him to,
He will walk in as you're sitting down to a meal.

Harvey Shapiro (b. 1924)

Harvey Shapiro was born in Chicago, Illinois, and served in the U.S. Army Air Corps during the Second World War, receiving the Distinguished Flying Cross. Upon his return, he earned a B.A. from Yale and an M.A. from Columbia, and began his teaching career at Cornell University. The author of nine volumes of poetry, Shapiro has served on the faculty of a number of universities and as an editor for *Commentary, The New Yorker, The New York Times Magazine*, and *The New York Times Book Review*. His work often reflects his Orthodox religious background, as well as his war experiences, his urban existence, and a personal sense of loss and isolation. "Ditty" and "Death of a Grandmother" are from *National Cold Storage Company: New and Selected Poems* (1988); "Bible Lesson," "Loyalty," and "For Paul Celan and Primo Levi" are reprinted from *A Day's Portion* (1994). Celan and Levi were both writers who survived Nazi death camps; both later committed suicide: Celan in France in 1970, Levi in Italy in 1987.

Ditty

Where did the Jewish god go?
Up the chimney flues.
Who saw him go?
Six million souls.
How did he go?
All so still
As dew from the grass.

Death of a Grandmother

Let me borrow her corpse a little.
Over that clown in finest linen,
Over that white-dressed dummy, pretty girl
(Dressed for a party, the daughters cried),
Let me speak a line.

The dead lie in a ditch of fear,
In an earth wound, in an old mouth
That has sucked them there.
My grandmother drank tea, and wailed
As if the Wailing Wall kissed her head
Beside the kitchen window;
While the flaking, green-boxed radio
Retailed in Yiddish song
And heartache all day long.
Or laughter found her,
The sly, sexual humor of the grave.

Yet after her years of dragging leg,
Of yellowed sight,
She still found pain enough
To polish off the final hours with a shriek.
To what sweet kingdom do the old Jews go?
Now mourned by her radio and bed,
She wishes me health and children,
Who am her inheritor.

I sing her a song of praise.
She meddled with my childhood
Like a witch, and I can meet her
Curse for curse in that slum heaven where we go
When this American dream is spent—
To give her a crust of bread, a little love.

Bible Lesson

When it's time for the Sacrifice
Abraham pays for his stardom
with terror and sweat.
The risk of talking with God.
At some point he could say to you:
Listen, this is what I want you to do
for me next, take your son, your only
son whom you love . . .

For Paul Celan and Primo Levi

Because the smoke
still drifted through your lives,
because it had not settled—
what would that settling be?
A coming to terms with man's savagery?
God's savagery? The victim
digging deeper into his wound
for the ultimate face?
That would be like saying
we mourn you, when you
have taken all the mourning words
and left us a gesture
of despair. To understand despair
and be comfortable with it—
something you could not do—
is how we live. Sun
drifting through smoke
as I sit on my roof in Brooklyn
with words for the Days of Awe.

Loyalty

They have been driven insane by history,
my tribe.
They are totally crazy.
Bialik's little Talmudist
and the settler with the gun.
Don't I know firsthand
their self-dramatizations and
their absolute assurance—here in America—
about what constitutes the good life
(my dead mother still telling me from Miami).
My mother, my tribe.
Strung out on wires
in black and white.
God can forsake them, whenever.
Hasn't He?
He has the option.
I don't.

Maxine Kumin (b. 1925)

Maxine Kumin was born in Philadelphia, Pennsylvania, and studied at Radcliffe College, where she earned B.A. and M.A. degrees. After graduation, she began teaching English at Tufts University and has since held positions at a number of colleges and universities. A prolific writer, Kumin is the author of more than ten volumes of poetry, four novels, a volume of short stories, two collections of essays, and more than twenty books for children. Her poetry reflects her life and personal experiences as a daughter, a mother, a farmer, and an American Jewish woman. In the poems included here, Kumin writes of her connection to her Jewish origins ("The Chain"), her complex attachments to Israel's past and present ("The Poet Visits Egypt and Israel"), the difficult and ambiguous nature of belief ("In the Absence of Bliss"), and her vision of a Judaism that welcomes women as well as men ("Getting the Message").

The Chain

My mother's insomnia over at last,
at dawn I enter her bureau drawers.
Under the petticoats, bedjackets, corsets,
under the unfinished knitting that crossed
continents with her, an affable animal,
I come on a hatbox of type-O any-hair,
heavy braids that have lain fifty years in this oval.
Between them, my mother's mother's calling card
engraved on brittle ivory vellum:
Mrs. Abraham Simon, Star Route 3, Radford.

Radford, Virginia, three thousand souls.
Here my mother spent her girlhood, not
without complications, playing
the Methodist church organ for weddings,
funerals, and the Sunday choir.
Here her mother, holding a lily-shaped
ear trumpet, stepped down from the surrey
Grandfather drove forty miles to Roanoke
to witness the blowing of the shofar
on Rosh Hashonah and Yom Kippur.

Affirming my past, our past in
a nation losing its memory, turning
its battlegrounds into parking lots,
slicking its regional differences over
with video games, substituting outer
space for history, I mourn
the type-O any-deaths of Mecca,
Athens, Babylon, Rome,
Radford, country towns
of middle-class hopes and tall corn.

Every year a new itinerant
piano teacher. New exercises
in the key of most-flats. 1908,
the first indoor toilet. The first
running hot water. My mother
takes weekly elocution lessons.
The radio, the telephone,
the Model T arrive. One by one
her sisters are sent north to cousins
in search of kindly Jewish husbands.

Surely having lived this long confers
a kind of aristocracy on my mother,
who kept to the end these talismans,
two dry links in the chain of daughters.
In the land of burley tobacco,
of mules in the narrow furrows,
in the land of diphtheria and strangles,
of revival meetings and stillborn angels,
in the land of eleven living siblings
I make my mother a dowager queen.

I give her back the chipped ruby goblets.
I hand over the battered Sheffield tureen
and the child I was, whose once-auburn hair
she scooped up like gems from the beauty-shop floor.

The Poet Visits Egypt and Israel

Sand, sand. In the university the halls,
seats, table tops, sills, are gritty with it.
Birds fly in and out at the open windows.
During the lecture an elderly porter
splendid in turban and djellaba,
shuffles in, opens a cabinet on the apron,
plugs in a microphone, spits into it twice,
and plumps it down on the lectern.
She continues to speak, amplified,

on American women poets since World War One
to an audience familiar with Dickinson,
Poe, and at a safe remove, Walt Whitman.
Afterward, thick coffee in thimbles. Sticky cakes
with the faculty. In this polite fortress
a floating unease causes her hands to shake
although nothing is said that could trespass
on her status as guest from another, unveiled, life.
She is a goddess, rich, white, American,

and a Jew. It says so in some of her poems.
There are no visible Jews in the American
Embassy, nor at the Cultural Center, and none
turns up in Cairo or Alexandria
although an itinerant rabbi is rumored
to cross from the other side once a fortnight
and serve the remaining congregants. The one
synagogue, a beige stucco Parthenon,
sleeps in the Sabbath sun, shuttered tight
and guarded by languid soldiers with bayonets.

All that she cannot say aloud she holds
hostage in her head: the congruities
of bayonets and whips; starved donkeys
and skeletal horses pulling impossible loads;
the small, indomitable Egyptian flies
that perch on lips, settle around the eyes
and will not be waved away. Like traffic
in Cairo, they persist, closing the margin
between life and death to a line so thin

as to become imperceptible.
Transported between lectures, she is tuned
to the rich variety of auto horns, each one
shriller, more cacophonous, peremptory
than its abutter. The decibel level
means everyone drives with windows closed,
tapedeck on full, airconditioning at maximum.
Thus conveyed, fender nudging fender,
she comes to ancient Heliopolis

where the Sheraton sits apart in an oasis.
Gaudier than Las Vegas, she thinks, checking in.
Behind her in the lobby, two BMWs,
several sheiks, exotic birds in cages,
and plumbing fixtures of alabaster
ornament this nouveau riche heaven.
Backlighted to enhance their translucency,
the toilet tank and bidet bowl are radiant,
the kind of kitsch she wishes she didn't notice.

Outdoors in the sports enclave, pool attendants
in monogrammed turtlenecks, like prep-school athletes,
carry iced salvers from bar to umbrellaed table,
proffer thick towels, reposition chaises longues
for the oiled, bikini-ed, all-but-naked bodies
of salesmen's wives and hostesses on holdover.

What do they think about, the poet wonders,
as they glide among the infidels, these men
whose own wives wrap up head to toe in public,

whose cousins' cousins creep from day to day
in a state of chronic lowgrade emergency.
Anonymous again in transit,
the poet leaves for Tel Aviv at night.
She watches a pride of pregnant tabbies stalk
cockroaches in the threadbare airport lounge
for protein enough to give a litter suck.
Always the Saving Remnant learns to scrounge
to stay alive. Could she now name the ten

plagues God sent? Uneasy truce exists
between these two antagonists.
El Al's flight, a frail umbilicus
that loops three times a week to the Holy Land,
is never posted on the Departures Board.
Security's intense. Shepherded
by an Israeli packing two guns,
she's bused with a poor handful to the tarmac.
The takeoff's dodgy, as if in fear of flak,

as if God might turn aside and harden
Pharaoh's heart, again fill up the sea.
Once down, she knows the desert by its gardens,
the beachfront by its senior citizens
assembled for calisthenics on the sand.
An hour later in the Old City
she sees a dozen small white donkeys,
descendants of the one that Jesus straddled,
trot docilely beside Volkswagen Beetles,

Mercedes cabs, tour buses full of young
camera-strapped, light-metered Japanese.
She peers into archaeological digs that reach
down through limestone to the days of Babylon,

pridefully down to the first tribes of Yahweh
sacrificing scapegoats on a stone.
Down through the rubble of bones and matter
—Constantinian, Herodian, Hasmonean—
that hold up the contemporary clutter.

At the Western Wall, Sephardic Jews,
their genders separated by a grill,
clap for the bar mitzvah boy with spit curls
who struggles to lift a gold-encrusted Torah
that proclaims today he is a man.
The poet polkas, dancing to tambourine
and bongo drums with other passersby.
Behind her, dinosaurs against the sky,
two Hapag-Lloyd Ltd. cranes

raise massive stacks of facing stones,
the eighth or ninth or tenth civilization
to go up on the same fought-over bedrock.
Near the Via Dolorosa, among the schlock
for sale—amber beads, prayer rugs, camel saddles—
lamb legs are offered, always with one testicle
attached. Ubiquitous sweet figs, olive trees
botanically certified to be
sprouts from the sacred roots of Gethsemane.

She tries to haggle for a sheepskin coat
but lacks the swagger needed for cheerful insult.
A man whose concentration-camp tattoo
announces he was zero six nine eight
picks through a tangle of ripe kumquats
beside a Bedouin, her hands and face daubed blue,
who could as easily have been a Druid,
the poet thinks, and she an early Christian.
In a restored Burnt House from 70 A.D.,

the year the Romans sacked the second Temple,
she dutifully clambers down to view
scorch marks, gouged walls, some human bones, amid
a troop of new recruits in green fatigues.
Girls the shape and gawk of girls back home.
Boys whose bony wrists have overshot
their cuffs already. Not yet on alert
but destined to serve on one front or another,
eye contact in this shrine says: Jews together.

Meanwhile, clusters of Hasidic zealots
(most of them recent Brooklyn imports)
in bobbing dreadlocks and black stovepipe hats
pedal breakneck along the claustral streets
of the Arab Quarter on ten-speed bikes to await
the messianic moment any minute
now. Look for a pillar of fire and in it
the one true Blessed-be-He, whose very name
cannot be spoken in the waiting game.

The one true Blessed-be-He, who still is hidden.
The poet sees a film on television,
news clips of shock troops: Syrian women
soldiers holding live snakes, biting them
on command, chewing and spitting out
the raw flesh. *In this way we will chew
and spit out the enemy.* Guess who.
Parental discretion was advised for viewing.
As if the young in these geographies

had not yet heard of torture, frag bombs, the crying
out at night that is silenced by garrote.
Another clip, the commentator said,
closeups of Assad's crack soldiers ordered
to strangle puppies and squeeze out blood
to drink as he reviewed the troops, was censored.

Judged too depraved for any audience.
How much is propaganda, how
much real? How did we get here,

the poet wonders, in the name of God,
in the name of all gods revving up their motors
to this high-pitched hum, like tripwire
stretched taut before the spark ignites the fuse
fragmenting life for life, blood running
in the dust to mingle Shiite, Druse,
Israeli, French, American.
If I forget thee, O Jerusalem,
may my right hand forget its cunning.

In the Absence of Bliss

Museum of the Diaspora, Tel Aviv

The roasting alive of rabbis
in the ardor of the Crusades
went unremarked in *Europe from
the Holy Roman Empire to 1918,*
open without prerequisite
when I was an undergraduate.

While reciting the Sh'ma in full
expectation that their souls
would waft up to the bosom
of the Almighty the rabbis burned,
pious past the humming extremes
of pain. And their loved ones with them.
Whole communities tortured and set aflame
in Christ's name
while chanting Hear, O Israel.

Why?
Why couldn't the rabbis recant,
kiss the Cross, pretend?
Is God so simple that He can't
sort out real from sham?
Did He want
these fanatic autos-da-fé, admire
the eyeballs popping,
the corpses shrinking in the fire?

We live in an orderly
universe of discoverable laws,
writes an intelligent alumna
in *Harvard Magazine.*
Bliss is belief,

agnostics always say
a little condescendingly
as befits mandarins who function
on a higher moral plane.

Consider our contemporary
Muslim kamikazes
hurling their explosives-
packed trucks through barriers.
Isn't it all the same?
They too die cherishing the fond
certitude of a better life beyond.

We walk away from twenty-two
graphic centuries of kill-the-jew
and hail, of all things, a Mercedes
taxi. The driver is Yemeni,
loves rock music and hangs
each son's picture—three so far—
on tassels from his rearview mirror.

I do not tell him that in Yemen
Jewish men, like women, were forbidden
to ride their donkeys astride,
having just seen this humiliation
illustrated on the Museum screen.

When his parents came
to the Promised Land, they entered
the belly of an enormous
silver bird, not knowing whether
they would live or die.
No matter. As it was written,
the Messiah had drawn nigh.

I do not ask, who tied
the leaping ram inside the thicket?

Who polished, then blighted the apple?
Who loosed pigs in the Temple,
set tribe against tribe
and nailed man in His pocket?

But ask myself, what would
I die for and reciting what?
Not for Yahweh, Allah, Christ,
those patriarchal fists
in the face. But would
I die to save a child?
Rescue my lover? Would
I run into the fiery barn
to release animals,
singed and panicked, from their stalls?

Bliss is belief, but where's
the higher moral plane I roost on?
This narrow plank given to splinters.
No answers. Only questions.

Getting the Message

God, the rabbis tell us, never assigns
exalted office to a man until
He has tested his mettle in small things.
So it is written in the *Midrash*
that when a lamb escaped the flock Moses
overtook it at a brook drinking its fill
and said, I would have taken thee in my arms
and carried thee thither had I known thy thirst
whereupon a Heavenly Voice warmly
resounded, *As thou livest, thou art fit.*

Divine election's scary. The burning bush
might have been brightened by St. Elmo's fire
according to *The Interpreter's One-Volume
Commentary.* The slopes of Exodus,
scrub growth close-cropped by tough horned herds
of Jacob's sheep (now prized as an heirloom breed)
lack treetops, mountain peaks or spires
that might discharge electrical ghost-plumes.
St. Elmo's seems less science than the desire
of modern exegetes to damp the flame.

I like my Bible tales, like Scotch, straight up
incontrovertible as Dante's trip
through seven circles, Milton's map
of Paradise or Homer's wine-dark epic.
On such a stage there falls a scrim between
text and critique where burst of light may crack
and dance as if on masts of sailing ships
and heavenly voices leap from alp to plain.
In Sunday School I shivered at God's command:
Take off thy shoes, thou stand'st on holy ground

and lay awake in the hot clutch of faith
yearning yet fearful that the Lord might speak
to me in my bed or naked in my bath.
I didn't know how little risk I ran
of being asked to set my people free
from fording some metaphorical Red Sea
with a new-sprung Pharaoh raging at my back.
I didn't know the patriarchy that spared me
fame had named me chattel, handmaiden.
God's Angels looked me over but flew by.

I like to think God's talent scouts today
select for covenant without regard
for gender, reinterpreting The Word
so that holy detectives glossing the bush
(most likely wild acacia), scholars of J
E and P deciphering Exodus
will fruitfully research the several ways
divine authentication lights up truth.
Fragments of it, cryptic, fugitive
still spark the synapses that let us live.

Gerald Stern (b. 1925)

Born in 1925 in Pittsburgh, Pennsylvania, Gerald Stern attended the University of Pittsburgh, earned an M.A. degree from Columbia University, and did further graduate study at the University of Paris. He taught at Temple University and has served as Visiting Professor at Sarah Lawrence College, the University of Iowa, and Columbia University, among others. His early poetry received little critical or popular attention, but *Lucky Life* (1977) was awarded the prestigious Lamont Poetry Prize, and other honors have since followed. Much of Stern's poetry reveals his profound interest in Jewish culture and history, his use of biblical references, and his fascination with Hasidism and Jewish mysticism. The poems included here demonstrate his rich and varied use of Jewish themes, including those dealing with his own Jewish identity ("Self-Portrait"), the Holocaust ("Soap"), Jewish ritual ("Tashlikh"), the rise and fall of Yiddish culture ("Adler"), and the ethical and moral implications of what it means to be a Jew in contemporary America ("Behaving Like a Jew").

Self-Portrait

When I turn the ceiling light on
the sky turns purple and the bathroom window is filled
with a mountain of crooked limbs like a huge Van Gogh.
When I turn it off the details change,
the trunks appear, the ducks walk up the grass
and the candles begin to shine in the dark canal.
In either case I am looking at two large gum trees
sweetly shaped by years of care and now
left alone to live or die slowly and peacefully.
I will think about them all day and dream about staying here
like a secret body at the window while they change in the light
from snarled twig to violent branch to limb with shadow;
and I will dream about standing out there on the towpath
staring back at myself in this large empty house.
    Others will go to Paris, sit at the tables,
and do the River, and do the Boulevard;
I will stand at the window dressed like a prisoner
in old corduroys and Brown's Beach vest and jacket
fingering the stamped buttons and testing the pockets.
I will look at my greenish eyes in the mirror
and touch my graying hair and twist my hat.
I will think of Van Gogh in Brussels raging
against the bourgeois world, I will think of him
working all day in the sun, I'll think of him in shock;
and I will think of myself sitting in Raubsville,
the only Jew on the river, counting my poems
and—finally—counting my years; and I will think of
Van Gogh when he headed south, I will think of him giving his
life to the art of the future, I will think of his poverty,
I will think of his depressions and exaltations;
I will think of him with yellow straw hat and pipe;
I will think of him with fur cap and bandaged ear;

I will think of him against the whirling lines,
small and powerful in the hands of the blue God;
and I will think of myself walking down my road
between the rows of dogs—so familiar now
that only one still barks, the horrible Schoene,
clawing her concrete and biting her twisted fence,
and I will think of my weeds and watery places
where I can go to rest between the scourges,
and I will think of New York just two hours away
still rotting and gleaming in the golden dust.
—I will think of myself in my rabbi's suit
walking across the marshland to my car;
I will think of myself in black beard and corncob
dragging the hay or leaning against a locust;
and I will think of the mad existence of all artists
as they lean against trees, and doors, and I will look with
horror at the vile ones, the bugs eating up our leaves,
and I will dream of another artistic life for
the fiftieth time, of a small decayed city
half buried in sand, surrounded by trees and water,
with artists living together, with old newspapers lying
piled up under the porches, with that whole race
of mothers and carpenters and gardeners
living inside their houses and in their yards.
    For the sake of Van Gogh I will dream it, for the sake of his
        olive trees,
for the sake of his empty chair, for the sake of his Bible,
for the sake of his inflamed eyes, for the sake of his wild mind;
and for the sake of his black Belgians retching and gasping for air
and for the sake of his Londoners stumbling over the greasy cobbles
and for the sake of his exhausted farmers stabbing at their potatoes
and for the sake of all the lunatics of God, for the sake of the flesh-
eaters gathering after work at the Authority, for the sake of
the wagons and baby carriages lined up outside the Armory, for the
        sake of
the frozen Armenians going back into their empty towns, for the
        sake of
the Jews of Vilna waiting inside their synagogues and for the sake of

the naked boys moving between the numbered tables and for the sake
of the slowly moving bodies under Lexington Avenue and for
the sake of the horses that labored quietly for three thousand
years and for the sake of the unassimilated wolves who lay trapped
inside their own forests; and in memory of the first stones we dragged
out of the mountain and in memory of the Fire
out of which the burned doves flew looking for water
and in memory of the long life that stretches back now
almost a million years and in memory of the cold rain
that saved our lives and in memory of the leaves
that helped us breathe and in pleasant memory
of the grass that clung to our slippery arms and legs
and in memory of the nourishing sand in which we lay like dead fishes
slowly mastering the sky. In honor of Albert Einstein.
In honor of Eugene Debs. In honor of Emma Goldman.

Behaving Like a Jew

When I got there the dead opossum looked like
an enormous baby sleeping on the road.
It took me only a few seconds—just
seeing him there—with the hole in his back
and the wind blowing through his hair
to get back again into my animal sorrow.
I am sick of the country, the bloodstained
bumpers, the stiff hairs sticking out of the grilles,
the slimy highways, the heavy birds
refusing to move;
I am sick of the spirit of Lindbergh over everything,
that joy in death, that philosophical
understanding of carnage, that
concentration on the species.
—I am going to be unappeased at the opossum's death.
I am going to behave like a Jew
and touch his face, and stare into his eyes,
and pull him off the road.
I am not going to stand in a wet ditch
with the Toyotas and the Chevies passing over me
at sixty miles an hour
and praise the beauty and the balance
and lose myself in the immortal lifestream
when my hands are still a little shaky
from his stiffness and his bulk
and my eyes are still weak and misty
from his round belly and his curved fingers
and his black whiskers and his little dancing feet.

Soap

Here is a green Jew
with thin black lips.
I stole him from the men's room
of the Amelia Earhart and wrapped him in toilet paper.
Up the street in *Parfumes*
are Austrian Jews and Hungarian,
without memories really,
holding their noses in the midst of that
paradise of theirs.
There is a woman outside
who hesitates because it is almost Christmas.
"I think I'll go in and buy a Jew," she says.
"I mean some soap, some nice new lilac or lily
to soothe me over the hard parts,
some Zest, some Fleur de Loo, some Wild Gardenia."

And here is a blue Jew.
It is his color, you know,
and he feels better buried in it, imprisoned
in all that sky, the land of death and plenty.
If he is an old one he dances,
or he sits stiffly,
listening to the meek words and admiring the vile actions
of first the Goths and then the Ostrogoths.
Inside is a lovely young girl,
a Dane, who gave good comfort
and sad support to soap of all kinds and sorts
during the war and during the occupation.
She touches my hand with unguents and salves.
She puts one under my nose all wrapped in tissue,
and squeezes his cheeks.

I buy a black Rumanian for my shelf.
I use him for hair and beard,
and even for teeth when things get bitter and sad.
He had one dream, this piece of soap,
if I'm getting it right,
he wanted to live in Wien
and sit behind a hedge on Sunday afternoon
listening to music and eating a tender schnitzel.
That was delirium. Other than that he'd dream
of America sometimes, but he was a kind of cynic,
and kind of lazy—conservative—even in his dream,
and for this he would pay, he paid for his lack of dream.
The Germans killed him because he didn't dream
enough, because he had no vision.

I buy a brush for my back, a simple plastic
handle with gentle bristles. I buy some dust
to sweeten my body. I buy a yellow cream
for my hairy face. From time to time I meet
a piece of soap on Broadway, a sliver really,
without much on him, sometimes I meet two friends
stuck together the way those slivers get
and bow a little, I bow to hide my horror,
my grief, sometimes the soap is so thin
the light goes through it, these are the thin old men
and thin old women the light goes through, these are
the Jews who were born in 1865
or 1870, for them I cringe, for them
I whimper a little, they are the ones who remember
the eighteenth century, they are the ones who listened
to heavenly voices, they were lied to and cheated.

My counterpart was born in 1925
in a city in Poland—I don't like to see him born
in a little village fifty miles from Kiev
and have to fight so wildly just for access
to books, I don't want to see him struggle

half his life to see a painting or just to
sit in one of the plush chairs listening to music.
He was dragged away in 1940
and turned to some use in 1941,
although he may have fought a little, piled
some bricks up or poured some dirty gasoline
over a German truck. His color was rose
and he floated for me for days and days; I love
the way he smelled the air, I love how he looked,
how his eyes lighted up, how his cheeks were almost pink
when he was happy. I loved how he dreamed, how he almost
disappeared when he was in thought. For him
I write this poem, for my little brother, if I
should call him that—maybe he is the ghost
that lives in the place I have forgotten, that dear one
that died instead of me—oh ghost, forgive me!—
Maybe he stayed so I could leave, the *older* one
who stayed so I could leave—oh live forever!
forever!—Maybe he is a Being from the other
world, his left arm agate, his left eye crystal,
and he has come back again for the twentieth time,
this time to Poland, to Warsaw or Bialystok,
to see what hell is like. I think it's that,
he has come back to live in our hell, if he could
even prick his agate arm or even weep
with those crystal eyes—oh weep with your crystal eyes,
dear helpless Being, dear helpless Being. I'm writing this
in Iowa and Pennsylvania and New York City,
in time for Christmas, 1982,
the odor of Irish Spring, the stench of Ivory.

Adler

The Jewish King Lear is getting ready
for some kind of horror—he is whispering
in the ears of Regan and Goneril: I know
the past, I know the future, my little hovel

will be in Pennsylvania, I will be
an old man eating from a newspaper,
I will stop to read the news, my fish
will soak the petty world up, it will stretch

from Sears on the left to Gimbels on the right,
my table will be a crate and I will cover
the little spaces with tape, it is enough
for my thin elbows. They will look at him

with hatred reminiscent of the Plains
of Auschwitz—Buchenwald—and drive him mad
an inch at a time. Nothing either in England
or Germany could equal his ferocity,

could equal his rage, even if the Yiddish
could make you laugh. There is a famous picture
of a German soldier plucking a beard; I think
of gentle Gloucester every time I see

that picture. There is a point where even Yiddish
becomes a tragic tongue and even Adler
can make you weep. They sit in their chairs for hours
to hear him curse his God; he looks at the dust

and asks, What have I done, what have I done,
for Him to turn on me; that audience murmurs,
Daughters, daughters, it cries for the sadness that came
to all of them in America. King Lear,

may the Lord keep him, hums in agony,
he is a monster of suffering, so many holes
that he is more like a whistle than like a king,
and yet when sometimes he comes across the stage

crowned with burdocks and nettles and cuckoo flowers
we forget it is Adler, we are so terrified,
we are so touched by pity. It is said
that Isadora Duncan came to worship him,

that John Barrymore came to study his acting,
that when he died they carried his coffin around
from theater to theater, that people mourned in the streets,
that he lay in a Windsor tie and a black silk coat.

One time he carried Cordelia around in his arms
he almost forgot his words, he was so moved
by his own grief, there were tears and groans
for him when they remembered his misfortune.

I thank God they were able to weep
and wring their hands for Lear, and sweet Cordelia,
that it happened almost forty years
before our hell, that there was still time then

to walk out of the theater in the sunlight
and discuss tragedy on the bright sidewalk
and live a while by mercy and innocence
with a king like Adler keeping the tremors alive

in their voices and the tears brimming in their eyes.
Thank God they died so early, that they were buried

one at a time, each with his own service,
that they were not lined up beside the trucks

or the cattle cars. I think when they saw him put
a feather over her lips they were relieved
to see her dead. I think they knew her life
was the last claim against him—the last delusion,

one or two would say. Now he was free,
now he was fully changed, he was *created*,
which is something they could have to talk about
going back to their stairways and their crowded tables

with real streaks of remorse on their faces—
more than forty years, almost fifty,
before the dead were dragged from their places
and dumped on the ground or put in orderly piles—

I think they used a broom on the charred faces
to see if there was breath—and a match or two
was dropped on the naked bodies. For the sake of art
there always was a German or Ukrainian

walking around like a dignified Albany,
or one made sad repentant noises like Kent
and one was philosophical like Edgar,
giving lectures to the burning corpses,

those with gold in their mouths, and those with skin
the color of yellow roses, and those with an arm
or a hand that dropped affectionately on another,
and those whose heads were buried, and those whose black tongues—

as if there were mountains, as if there were cold water
flowing through the ravines, as if there were wine cups
sitting on top of the barrels, as if there were flowers—
still sang in bitterness, still wept and warbled in sorrow.

Tashlikh

This one shows me standing by the Delaware
for the last time. There is a book in one hand
and I am making cunning motions with the other,
chopping and weaving motions to illustrate
what I am reading, or I am just enlarging
the text with my hand the way a good Jew did
before the 1930s. I am wearing
a Russian cap and a black overcoat
I bought in Pittsburgh in 1978,
a *Cavalier*, from Kaufmann's, a gabardine
with bluish buttons. Behind me in the locusts
and up and down the banks are ten or twelve others
in coats and hats, with books in their hands. We sing
a song for the year and throw our sticks in the water.
We empty our pockets of paper and lint. I know
that there are fish there in the Delaware
so we are linked to the silver chain, and I know
that the fire is wet and sputtering, a fire
to rest your boots on, perfect for the smoke
to rise just a little and move an inch at a time
across the water. I throw another stick—
this one a maple—onto the greasy rocks
and climb the hill, the rubber steps and the saplings.
I make a kissing sound with my hand—I guess
we all do. This was a painful year, a painful
two years. It is a joy to be here, sailing
back and forth across the highway, smelling
one thing or another, not just living
in terror, sleeping again, and breathing.

Tashlikh—An ancient Jewish ceremony in which sins, in the form of bread, are cast into a body of
running water. It is observed late in the afternoon during the first day of Rosh Ha-Shanah. The
core of the ceremony is a recitation from Micah.

Allen Ginsberg (1926–1997)

Allen Ginsberg was born in Newark, New Jersey; his mother was a Russian Jewish immigrant and his father was an American Jewish high school teacher and published poet. While attending Columbia University in the 1940s, Ginsberg met Jack Kerouac, William Burroughs, and Gregory Corso—writers with whom he was to inaugurate the Beat movement. Known more for his association with the Beats and for his angry and irreverent condemnations of American society, Ginsberg was also influenced by his Jewish upbringing—as evidenced in "To Aunt Rose," reprinted here from *Kaddish and Other Poems, 1958–1960* (1961). Since the publication of *Kaddish*, much of Ginsberg's work has reflected his interest in Buddhism and Eastern philosophy. Yet several of the poems in his 1994 collection, *Cosmopolitan Greetings: Poems 1986–1992* (from which "Visiting Father & Friends" and "Yiddishe Kopf" are taken) indicate a return to a more narrative, less fiery poetry, and renewed attention to his early Jewish memories.

To Aunt Rose

Aunt Rose—now—might I see you
with your thin face and buck tooth smile and pain
                of rheumatism—and a long black heavy shoe
                        for your bony left leg
limping down the long hall in Newark on the running carpet
                past the black grand piano
                in the day room
                        where the parties were
        and I sang Spanish loyalist songs
        in a high squeaky voice
                (hysterical) the committee listening
        while you limped around the room
                collected the money—
Aunt Honey, Uncle Sam, a stranger with a cloth arm
                in his pocket
                and huge young bald head
                        of Abraham Lincoln Brigade

—your long sad face
        your tears of sexual frustration
                (what smothered sobs and bony hips
                        under the pillows of Osborne Terrace)
        —the time I stood on the toilet seat naked
                and you powdered my thighs with Calomine
                against the poison ivy—my tender
                        and shamed first black curled hairs
        what were you thinking in secret heart then
                knowing me a man already—
and I an ignorant girl of family silence on the thin pedestal
                of my legs in the bathroom—Museum of Newark.

                    Aunt Rose
      Hitler is dead, Hitler is in Eternity; Hitler is with
                Tamburlane and Emily Brontë

Though I see you walking still, a ghost on Osborne Terrace
                down the long dark hall to the front door
                limping a little with a pinched smile
                in what must have been a silken
                      flower dress
      welcoming my father, the Poet, on his visit to Newark
                —see you arriving in the living room
                dancing on your crippled leg
                and clapping hands his book
                had been accepted by Liveright

Hitler is dead and Liveright's gone out of business
The Attic of the Past and *Everlasting Minute* are out of print
                Uncle Harry sold his last silk stocking
                Claire quit interpretive dancing school
                Buba sits a wrinkled monument in Old
                      Ladies Home blinking at new babies

last time I saw you was the hospital
                pale skull protruding under ashen skin
                blue veined unconscious girl
                in an oxygen tent
                the war in Spain has ended long ago
                Aunt Rose

Visiting Father & Friends

I climbed the hillside to the lady's house.
There was Gregory, dressed as a velvet ape,
japing and laughing, elegant-handed, tumbling
somersaults and consulting with the hostess,
girls and wives familiar, feeding him like a baby.
He looked healthy, remarkable energy, up all night
talking jewelry, winding his watches, hair over his eyes,
jumping from one apartment to another.

Neal Cassady rosy-faced indifferent and affectionate
entertaining himself in company far from China
back in the USA old 1950s–1980s still kicking
his way thru the city, up Riverside Drive without a car.
He hugged me & turned attention to the night ladies
appearing disappearing in the bar, in apartments
and the street, his continued jackanapes wasting his time
& everyone else's but mysterious, maybe up to something.
Good—keep us all from committing more crimes,
political wars, or peace protests angrier than wars'
cannonball noises. He needed a place to sleep.

Then my father appeared, lone forlorn & healthy
still living by himself in an apartment a block up
the hill from Peter's ancient habitual pad, I hadn't
noticed where Louis lived these days, somehow obliterated
his home condition from my mind, took it for granted
tho never'd been curious enough to visit—but as I'd no place
to go tonight, & wonder'd why I'd not visited him recently,
I asked could I spend the night & bed down
there with him, his place had bedroom and bath
a giant Jewish residence apartment on Riverside Drive
refugees inhabited, driven away from Europe by Hitler,

where now my father lived—I entered, he showed me his couch
& told me get comfortable, I slept the night, but woke
when he shifted his sleeping pad closer to mine I got up
—he'd slept badly on a green inch-thick dusty
foam rubber plastic mattress I'd thrown out years ago,
poor cold mat upon the concrete cellar warehouse floor—
so that was it! He'd given his bed for my comfort!

No no I said, take back your bed, sleep comfortable
weary you deserve it, amazing you still get around,
I'm sorry I hadn't visited before, just didn't know
where you lived, here you are a block upstreet
from Peter, hospitable to me Neal & Gregory &
girlfriends of the night, old sweet Bohemian heart
don't sleep on the floor like that I'll take your place
on the mat & pass the night ok.
                                                I went upstairs, happy to see
he had a place to lay his head for good, and woke in China.
Peter alive, though drinking a problem, Neal was dead
more years than my father Louis no longer
smiling alive, no wonder I'd not visited this place
he'd retired to a decade ago, How good to see him home, and take
his fatherly hospitality for granted among the living
and dead. Now wash my face, dress in my suit
on time for teaching classroom poetry at 8am Beijing,
far round the world away from Louis' grave in Jersey.

Yiddishe Kopf

I'm Jewish because love my family matzoh ball soup.

I'm Jewish because my fathers mothers uncles grandmothers said "Jewish," all the way back to Vitebsk & Kaminetz-Podolska via Lvov.

Jewish because reading Dostoyevsky at 13 I write poems at restaurant tables Lower East Side, perfect delicatessen intellectual.

Jewish because violent Zionists make my blood boil, Progressive indignation.

Jewish because Buddhist, my anger's transparent hot air, I shrug my shoulders.

Jewish because monotheist Jews Catholics Moslems're intolerable intolerant—

Blake sd. "6000 years of sleep" since antique Nobodaddy Adonai's mind trap—Oy! such Meshuggeneh absolutes—

Senior Citizen Jewish paid my dues got half-fare card buses subways, discount movies—

Can't imagine how these young people make a life, make a living.

How can they stand it, going out in the world with only $10 and a hydrogen bomb?

Philip Levine (b. 1928)

Philip Levine, the son of Russian immigrants, was born in Detroit, Michigan, and educated at Wayne State University, the University of Iowa, and Stanford University. He worked for several years in a factory before beginning a teaching career at California State University in Fresno. Levine is the author of more than a dozen volumes of poetry, including *The Simple Truth* (1994), which received the Pulitzer Prize. Much of his poetry relies on his early, urban Jewish experiences, although Levine's most successful poems speak to both Jewish and universal concerns. His most frequent subjects are those associated with father and son relationships (his own father died when Levine was five), exile and suffering, and his sense of loss and alienation. The four poems reprinted here all include portraits of family members (his grandfather, uncle, father, brother), but transcend the personal in order to treat wider issues of love, belief, despair, and hope.

Zaydee

Why does the sea burn? Why do the hills cry?
My grandfather opens a fresh box
of English Ovals, lights up, and lets the smoke
drift like clouds from his lips.

Where did my father go in my fifth autumn?
In the blind night of Detroit
on the front porch, Grandfather points up
at a constellation shaped like a cock and balls.

A tiny man, at 13 I outgrew his shirts.
I then beheld a closet of stolen suits,
a hive of elevator shoes, crisp hankies,
new bills in the cupboard, old in the wash.

I held the spotted hands that passed over
the breasts of airlines stewardesses,
that moved in the fields like a wind
stirring the long hairs of grain.

Where is the ocean? the flying fish?
the God who speaks from a cloud?
He carries a card table out under the moon
and plays gin rummy and cheats.

He took me up in his arms
when I couldn't walk and carried me
into the grove where the bees sang
and the stream paused forever.

He laughs in the movies, cries in the streets,
the judges in their gowns are monkeys,

the lawyers mice, a cop is a fat hand.
He holds up a strawberry and bites it.

He sings a song of freestone peaches
all in a box,
in the street he sings out Idaho potatoes
California, California oranges.

He sings the months in prison,
sings salt pouring down the sunlight,
shovelling all night in the stove factory
he sings the oven breathing fire.

Where did he go when his autumn came?
He sat before the steering wheel
of the black Packard, he turned the key,
pressed the starter, and he went.

The maples blazed golden and red
a moment and then were still,
the long streets were still and the snow
swirled where I lay down to rest.

New Days for Old, Old Days for New

The old moon fades, the flies tune their voices
for the dawn song. Morning glories
trumpet from the fence, the shadows hide.

My brother Priscolnik wanders lost between
Nîmes and Dombrovitz. A dust cloud carries
the gospel of his final words, his curses,

his sighs, all the volumes of his loss—
my tiny brother, the peddler, the magician
whose hands transformed old shirts to new.

Don't tell me nothing about discipline.
I come from a people of the road, a line
of prophets who slept on sticks and stones,

who called the day down in the language
of Abraham and Isaac. At the well my father
had only sand to drink, his father drank

his own life down, breath by last breath.
So when I waken on a pillow of moonlight
I take it all, nightmares, daydreams,

the stories my children scatter down
the arteries of my care. The mind runs on,
even under a stone, the mind runs on and on.
A new day's here, with or without the moon.

The Old Testament

My twin brother swears that at age thirteen
I'd take on anyone who called me kike
no matter how old or how big he was.
I only wish I'd been that tiny kid
who fought back through his tears, swearing
he would not go quietly. I go quietly
packing bark chips and loam into the rose beds,
while in his memory I remain the constant child
daring him to wrest Detroit from lean gentiles
in LaSalle convertibles and golf clothes
who step slowly into the world we have tainted,
and have their revenge. I remember none of this.
He insists, he names the drug store where I poured
a milkshake over the head of an Episcopalian
with quick fists as tight as croquet balls.
He remembers his license plate, his thin lips,
the exact angle at which this seventeen year old dropped
his shoulder to throw the last punch. He's making
it up. Wasn't I always terrified?
"Of course," he tells me, "that's the miracle,
you were even more scared than me, so scared
you went insane, you became a whirlwind,
an avenging angel."
                    I remember planting
my first Victory Garden behind the house, hauling
dark loam in a borrowed wagon, and putting in
carrots, corn that never grew, radishes that did.
I remember saving for weeks to buy a tea rose,
a little stick packed in dirt and burlap,
my mother's favorite. I remember the white bud
of my first peony that one morning burst
beside the mock orange that cost me 69¢.

(Fifty years later the orange is still there,
the only thing left beside a cage for watch dogs,
empty now, in what had become a tiny yard.)
I remember putting myself to sleep dreaming
of the tomatoes coming into fullness, the pansies
laughing in the spring winds, the magical wisteria
climbing along the garage, and dreaming of Hitler,
of firing a single shot from a foot away, one
that would tear his face into a caricature of mine,
tear stained, bloodied, begging for a moment's peace.

My Father with Cigarette
Twelve Years Before the Nazis
Could Break His Heart

I remember the room in which he held
a kitchen match and with his thumbnail
commanded it to flame: a brown sofa,
two easy chairs, one covered with flowers,
a black piano no one ever played half
covered by a long-fringed ornamental scarf
Ray Estrada brought back from Mexico
in 1931. How new the world is, you say.
In that room someone is speaking about money,
asking why it matters, and my father exhales
the blue smoke, and says a million dollars
even in large bills would be impossible.
He's telling me because, I see now, I'm
the one who asked, for I dream of money,
always coins and bills that run through my hands,
money I find in the corners of unknown rooms
or in metal boxes I dig up in the backyard
flower beds of houses I've never seen.
My father rises now and goes to the closet.
It's as though someone were directing a play
and my father's part called for him to stand
so that the audience, which must be you,
could see him in white shirt, dark trousers,
held up by suspenders, a sign of the times,
and conclude he is taller than his son
will ever be, and as he dips into his jacket,
you'll know his role calls for him to exit
by the front door, leaving something
unfinished, the closet light still on,
the cigarette still burning dangerously,
a Yiddish paper folded to the right place

so that a photograph of Hindenburg
in full military regalia swims up
to you out of all the details we lived.
I remember the way the match flared
blue and yellow in the deepening light
of a cool afternoon in early September,
and the sound, part iron, part animal,
part music, as the air rushed toward it
out of my mouth, and his intake of breath
through the Lucky Strike, and the smoke
hanging on after the door closed and the play
ran out of acts and actors, and the audience—
which must be you—grew tired of these lives
that finally come to nothing or no more
than the furniture and the cotton drapes
left open so the darkening sky can seem
to have the last word, with half a moon
and a showering of fake stars to say what
the stars always say about the ordinary.
Oh, you're still here, 60 years later,
you wonder what became of us, why
someone put it in a book, and left
the book open to a page no one reads.
Everything tells you he never came back,
though he did before he didn't, everything
suggests it was the year Hitler came
to power, the year my grandmother learned
to read English novels and fell in love
with *David Copperfield* and *Oliver Twist*
which she read to me seated on a stool
beside my bed until I fell asleep.
Everything tells you this is a preface
to something important, the Second World War,
the news that leaked back from Poland
that the villages were gone. The truth is—
if there is a truth—I remember the room,
I remember the flame, the blue smoke,

how bright and slippery were the secret coins,
how David Copperfield doubted his own name,
how sweet the stars seemed, peeping and blinking,
how close the moon, how utterly silent the piano.

Irving Feldman (b. 1928)

Born in Brooklyn, New York, Irving Feldman attended the City College of New York and earned an M.A. degree from Columbia University. He has taught English and creative writing at a number of colleges and universities, most recently the State University of New York at Buffalo. The author of nine collections of poetry, Feldman frequently writes of his experiences as a second-generation American Jew. "The Pripet Marshes" and "To the Six Million," from *New and Selected Poems* (1979), are powerful meditations on the Holocaust and its psychological aftermath, while "The Handball Players at Brighton Beach," lighter in tone, captures the flavor and spirit of the first generation of American-born Jews. "The Dream," from Feldman's 1994 collection, *The Life and Letters*, is based on the poet's memories of his mother.

The Pripet Marshes

Often I think of my Jewish friends and seize them as they are
    and transport them in my mind to the *shtetlach* and ghettos,

And set them walking the streets, visiting, praying in *shul*,
    feasting and dancing. The men I set to arguing, because I
    love dialectic and song—my ears tingle when I hear their
    voices—and the girls and women I set to promenading or to
    cooking in the kitchens, for the sake of their tiny feet and
    clever hands.

And put kerchiefs and long dresses on them, and some of the
    men I dress in black and reward with beards. And all of them
    I set among the mists of the Pripet Marshes, which I have
    never seen, among wooden buildings that loom up suddenly
    one at a time, because I have only heard of them in stories,
    and that long ago.

It is the moment before the Germans will arrive.

Maury is there, uncomfortable, and pigeon-toed, his voice is
    rapid and slurred, and he is brilliant;
And Frank who is good-hearted and has the hair and yellow skin
    of a Tartar and is like a flame turned low;
And blond Lottie who is coarse and miserable, her full mouth is
    turning down with a self-contempt she can never hide, while
    the steamroller of her voice flattens every delicacy;
And Marian, her long body, her face pale under her bewildered
    black hair and of the purest oval of those Greek signets she
    loves; her head tilts now like the heads of the birds she draws;
And Adele who is sullen and an orphan and so like a beaten
    creature she trusts no one, and who doesn't know what to do

with herself, lurching with her magnificent body like a
   despoiled tigress;
And Munji, moping melancholy clown, arms too short for his
   barrel chest, his penny-whistle nose, and mocking
   nearsighted eyes that want to be straightforward and good;
And Abbie who, when I listen closely, is speaking to me,
   beautiful with her large nose and witty mouth, her coloring
   that always wants lavender, her vitality that body and mind
   can't quite master;
And my mother whose gray eyes are touched with yellow, and
   who is as merry as a young girl;
And my brown-eyed son who is glowing like a messenger
   impatient to be gone and who may stand for me.
I cannot breathe when I think of him there.
And my red-haired sisters, and all my family, our embarrassed
   love bantering our tenderness away.

Others, others, in crowds filling the town on a day I have made
   sunny for them; the streets are warm and they are at their
   ease.

How clearly I see them all now, how miraculously we are
   linked! And sometimes I make them speak Yiddish in
   timbres whose unfamiliarity thrills me.

But in a moment the Germans will come.

What, will Maury die? Will Marian die?

Not a one of them who is not transfigured then!

The brilliant in mind have bodies that glimmer with a total
   dialectic;
The stupid suffer an inward illumination; their stupidity is a
   subtle tenderness that glows in and around them;
The sullen are surrounded with great tortured shadows raging
   with pain, against whom they struggle like titans;

In Frank's low flame I discover an enormous perspectiveless
    depth;
The gray of my mother's eyes dazzles me with our love;
No one is more beautiful than my red-haired sisters.
And always I imagine the least among them last, one I did not
    love, who was almost a stranger to me.
I can barely see her blond hair under the kerchief; her cheeks are
    large and faintly pitted, her raucous laugh is tinged with
    shame as it subsides; her bravado forces her into still another
    lie;
But her vulgarity is touched with a humanity I cannot exhaust,
    her wretched self-hatred is as radiant as the faith of Abraham,
    or indistinguishable from that faith.
I can never believe my eyes when this happens, and I want to
    kiss her hand, to exchange a blessing

In the moment when the Germans are beginning to enter the
    town.

But there isn't a second to lose, I snatch them all back,
For, when I want to, I can be a God.
No, the Germans won't have one of them!
This is my people, they are mine!

And I flee with them, crowd out with them: I hide myself in a
    pillowcase stuffed with clothing, in a woman's knotted
    handkerchief, in a shoebox.

And one by one I cover them in mist, I take them out.
The German motorcycles zoom through the town,
They break their fists on the hollow doors.
But I can't hold out any longer. My mind clouds over.
I sink down as though drugged or beaten.

To the Six Million

But put forth thine hand now, and touch his bones and his flesh . . .

I

If there is a god,
he descends from the power.
But who is the god rising from death?
(So, thunder invades the room, and brings with it
a treble, chilly and intimate, of panes rattling
on a cloudy day in winter.
But when I look through the window,
a sudden blaze of sun is in the streets,
which are, however, empty and still. The thunder
repeats.) Thunder here. The emptiness resounds
here on the gods' struggle-ground
where the infinite negative retreats,
annihilating where it runs,
and the god who must possess pursues, pressing
on window panes, passing through.
Nothing's in the room but light
wavering beneath the lamp
like a frosty rose the winter bled.
No one is in the room (I possess nothing),
only power pursuing, trying
corpses where the other god went,
running quickly under the door. In
the chill, the empty room
reverberates. I look from the window.

* * *

There is someone missing.
Is it I who am missing?
And many are missing.
And outside, the frozen street extends
from me like a string, divides, circles,
with an emptiness the sun

is burnishing.
                    In the street
there is nothing, for many are missing,
or there is the death of many
missing, annulled, dispossessed,
filling the street, pressing their vacancy
against the walls, the sunlight, the thunder.
Is a god
in the street? where nothing is left
to possess, nothing to kill;
and I am standing
dead at the window looking out.

                    *   *   *

What did you kill? Whom did you save? I ask
myself aloud, clinging to the window
of a winter day.
                    Survivor, who are you?
ask the voices that disappeared,
the faces broken and expunged.
I am the one who was not there.
Of such accidents I have made my death.

Should I have been with them
on other winter days in the snow
of the camps and ghettos?
And on the days of their death that was
the acrid Polish air?—
I who lay between the mountain of myrrh
and the hill of frankincense,
dead and surviving, and dared not breathe,
and asked, By what right am I myself?

Who I am I do not know,
but I believe myself to be one
who should have died, and the dead one
who did die.
Here on the struggle-ground, impostor

of a death, I survive reviving,
perpetuating the accident.
And who is at the window pane,
clinging, lifting himself like a child
to the scene of a snowless day?

* * *

"Whatsoever is under the whole heaven
Is mine." Charred, abandoned, all this,
who will call these things his own?

Who died not
to be dying, to survive
my death dead as I am
at the window (possessing nothing),
and died not to know
agony of the absence,
revive on a day
when thunder rattles the panes,
possessed by no one;
bone and flesh of me, because
you died on other days
of actual snow and sun,
under mists and chronic rain,
my death is cut to the bone,
my survival is torn from me.
I would cover my nakedness
in dust and ashes. They burn,
they are hot to the touch. Can my
death live? The chill treble
squeaks for a bone. I was
as a point in a space,
by what right can I be myself?
At the window and in the streets,
among the roots of barbed wire,
and by springs of the sea,
to be dying my death again

and with you,
in the womb of ice, and where
the necessity of our lives is hid.
Bone and flesh of me,
I have not survived,
I would praise the skies,
leap to the treasures of snow.

II

By night on my bed I sought him whom my soul loveth: I sought him, but I found him not.

I will rise now, and go about the city in the streets, and in the broad ways I will seek him whom my soul loveth. . . .

What can I say?
            Dear ones, what can I say?
You died, and emptied the streets
and my breath, and went from my seeing.
And I awoke, dying at the window
of my wedding day, because
I was nowhere; the morning that revived
was pain, and my life that began again was pain,
I could not see you.
            What can I say?
My helpless love overwhelmed me,
sometimes I thought I touched your faces,
my blindness sought your brows again,
and your necks that are towers,
your temples that are as pieces
of pomegranate within your locks.
Dead and alive,
your shadows escaped me. I went
into the streets, you were not there,
for you were murdered and befouled.
And I sought you in the city,
which was empty, and I found you not,

for you were bleeding at the dayspring
and in the air. That emptiness
mingled with my heart's emptiness,
and was at home there, my heart
that wished to bear you again, and bore
the agony of its labor, the pain
of no birth. And I sought for you
about the city in the streets, armed
with the love hundreds had borne me.
And before the melancholy in the mazes,
and the emptiness in the streets,
in the instant before our deaths,
I heard the air (that was
to be ashen) and the flesh
(that was to be broken), I heard
cry out, Possess me!
And I found you whom my soul loves;
I held you, and would not let you go
until I had brought you
into my mother's house, and into the chamber
of her that conceived me.

Dear ones, what can I say?
I must possess you no matter how,
father you, befriend you,
and bring you to the lighthearted dance
beside the treasures and the springs,
and be your brother and your son.
Sweetness, my soul's bride,
come to the feast I have made,
my bone and my flesh of me,
broken and touched,
come in your widow's raiment of dust and ashes,
bereaved, newborn, gasping for
the breath that was torn from you,
that is returned to you.
There will I take your hand
and lead you under the awning,

and speak the words it behooves to speak.
My heart is full, only the speech
of the ritual can express it.
And after a little while,
I will rouse you from your dawn sleep
and accompany you in the streets.

The Handball Players at Brighton Beach

To David Ritz

And then the blue world daring onward
discovers them, the indigenes, aging,
oiled, and bronzing sons of immigrants,
the handball players of the new world
on Brooklyn's bright eroding shore
who yawp, who quarrel, who shove,
who shout themselves hoarse, don't
get out of the way, grab for odds,
hustle a handicap, all crust,
all bluster, all con and gusto all
on show, tumultuous, blaring,
grunting as they lunge. True,
their manners lack grandeur, and
yes, elsewhere under the sun legs
are less bowed, bellies are less
potted, pates less bald or blanched,
backs less burned, less hairy.
                              So?
So what! the sun does not snub,
does not overlook them, shines,

and the fair day flares,
the blue universe booms and blooms,

the sea-space, the summer high, focuses
its great unclouded scope in ecstatic
perspection—and you see it too
at the edge of the crowd, edge of the sea,
between multitudes and immensity:
from gray cement ball courts under
the borough's sycamores' golden boughs,
against the odds in pure speculation

Brighton's handball heroes leap up half
a step toward heaven in burgundy, blue,
or buttercup bathing trunks, in black
sneakers still stylish after forty years,
in pigskin gloves buckled at the wrist,
to keep the ball alive, the sun up,
the eye open, the air ardent,
festive, clear, crowded with delight.

The Dream

Once, years after your death, I dreamt
you were alive and that I'd found you
living once more in the old apartment.
But I had taken a woman up there
to make love to in the empty rooms.
I was angry at you who'd borne and loved me
and because of whom I believe in heaven.
I regretted your return from the dead
and said to myself almost bitterly,
"For godsakes, what was the big rush,
couldn't she wait one more day?"

And just so daily somewhere Messiah
is shunned like a beggar at the door because
someone has something he wants to finish
or just something better to do, something
he prefers not to put off forever
—some little pleasure so deeply wished
that Heaven's coming has to seem bad luck
or worse, God's intruding selfishness!

But you always turned Messiah away
with a penny and a cake for his trouble
—because wash had to be done, because
who could let dinner boil over and burn,
because everything had to be festive for
your husband, your daughters, your son.

Cynthia Ozick (b. 1928)

One of the most renowned American Jewish fiction writers, Cynthia Ozick was born in New York City to Russian immigrant parents. She attended New York University and earned an M.A. degree from Ohio State University. Although Ozick grew up in a Jewish milieu, the strong sense of Jewish history and folklore that characterizes her work is a result of her own learning and research. The idea of a literature that is, as she states, "centrally Jewish in its concerns" is essential to Ozick's poetry and prose. While her stories, novellas, and novels have received wide critical acclaim, her poems (which remain uncollected) have gone virtually unnoticed. They are nevertheless interesting investigations of such themes as Hasidic lore ("The Wonder-Teacher"), Jewish ritual and history ("Yom Kippur, 5726" and "Origins, Divergences"), biblical story ("When That with Tragic Rapture Moses Stood"), and the loss of faith ("In the Synagogue").

The Wonder-Teacher

The rabbi of Kobryn said: "We paid no attention to the miracles our teacher worked, and when sometimes a miracle did not come to pass, he gained in our eyes." —*Martin Buber*, TALES OF THE HASIDIM

When the morning hymn
unbound its alphabet to fall
like flies into his hand, when he would call
Ayin to stand upon its limb
and utter (who was mute)
voices of the living flute,
and bid lame *Lamèd* caper to his whim,
we thrust our watching to the wall.

Another time he made
the letters into curds,
fed beggars on the foam, and feasted birds.
That day we swallowed blessings unafraid,
prayer was silken-white like cheese;
what our mouths sang, our teeth would seize.
Repast mounted on our brains and weighed
so burdensome we beat away his words.

And once we saw him levitate.
He tramped on nothing, stuttered like a wire;
hanged, he gnawed for the leash to shock him higher
in holy space, and longed to wait
in air for the unknotting of the Name.
He was a maimed man when he came
back down to us and toed our common slate.
But we hugged the floor and fled the cord of his desire.

Last night he said: "I am worn
of working wonders. Custom's stung
my magickings, my craft limps witless on your tongue.

What are my labors?—Like the ram's horn:
swift to enter, the dwindling door a trap."

So saying, he laid his head within a pupil's lap
and slept like any one of us, as if to scorn
all prodigy. We huddled near the marvel of his lung.

Origins, Divergences

(My grandmother steals out of Russia)

Mark Twain said he wouldn't want to be a boy again
unless magnolia swelled in an always-summer,
but we don't know magnolia
and suppose it's winter where we once were?

A veil of moths revolves beyond the bloom of breath:
snow, and the knife-footed droshky leaves two clean crusts
             behind
for the beggar wind to muffle in his coat.
A girl named Natasha rides in frozen white slippers and
             a white peaked hood.

Or there's a border wood: two bristling countries, and
             wolves between,
agreed and incorruptible, unlike the guards.
Smother if not the wail the baby, it's all the same.
But Grandma Rachel saw a vigilant pine-point nudging God.

Yom Kippur, 5726

i

Abstaining from the congregation
Torah is a meal I do not take
Synagogue a stomach of allegation
God the fast I will not break.

ii

From feeding on too much Jew
History reels with cramp:
The century a pew
For those who sigh and stamp.

iii

Beat on the door of the rib!
(As much go cup the dead.)
Kiss the Law's spangled bib!
(On Yom Kippur peddle bread.)

iv

The world will not down,
Digestion is shallow.
What God will not disown,
Who can swallow?

v

Sooner will the proton halt
Than he revoke:
Wherefore this feast of salt
And smoke.

vi

The hour is singled out:
Let God renounce what's done
And for his absence and my doubt
Atone.

vii

Let each man sup
On seasoned blows,
On armament and whip.
Then let the banquet close.

viii

(Jerusalem the city
Lasts deeper than our days
But a famine of pity
Gluts always.)

When That with Tragic Rapture Moses Stood

When that with tragic rapture Moses stood on the edge and ledge,
   the edge of the Land overlooked from the mountain's ledge,
      the ledge of life which death, like all the others law
   and being of the Law, might not overlook,

bound on that double threshold to cross the ledge but not the edge,
   to see the plain of the valley and the palm and the wave-scaly
      boundary of the sea fretting near, Judah's shining lip,
   but not to go over,
to see the commanded boundary of Sheol and death its commander
   and captain, likewise a leader of men according to the law and a
      lawgiver, that promised country's single-minded king,
   and sworn to go over,
loving limits because loving law, but liking not these to Land
   and life;

when that he, the plucker of the Law from the thorny desert who
   pricked the brows of idolators obeisant,
      who cracked Sinai's pillar for the holy stones its marrow-ore,
   those grains and pebbles chipped from Rock more than rock of
      mountain, being mountain-maker,
and early wept for the oppressors whom the silt sucked in, and for
   the mares whose eye-whites reddened with the splattered yolk
      of the broken wave, and for the chariot's axle hewn of
   straight young trees, all being God's and though oppressors
      all divine, men and steeds and wondrous wheels,
when that he ascended: ascended Nebo, he whose head history had
   hammered holy, hoary, heavy, bending down from Pisgah toward
      the rabble's luring ground rich with seed,
himself allured, him whom history brought to the edge and ledge of
   denial
lest history fever with more history that history-howling heart;

when that he ascended, and with proud lieutenant's measure the
    given territory scanned, given not for him but for the fickle mob,
in that moment it was enough: history dropped him from her beak,
    too fastidious for carrion,
        and led in the gilded mob. Not that he was less than they,
he who unbewildered the mazy riddle of the way through forty years
    of nomadry,
and laid his head upon the rock to be a chamber for the thunder's
    voice,
not that he was less!—but was, being man, not more,
    going squired, though the mob's ex-squire, to the territory
        given him.

            Its situation no man knows.

And since the border-crossing was jubilant, flag-wild and roaring
    triumph, the pageant already winking sidewise at some
        Canaanitish lady-baal with breasts of sanded wood and
        smelling piney,
and he from Pisgah saw how we, the mob, noses barely over the
    border and feet still prickled with the wilderness, raced
        crying after abominations, again and after all,
no wonder he praised history for halting him at humanity, and
    bringing him unhallowed to an unknown grave.

We would raise a sepulchre if we guessed the place, and over that
    a palace,
and on every edge and ledge would lift his sacred likeness,
        commissioned and called art,
in tapestry and marble, in majesty and crimson, hiding God in
    Moses' pleats,
we adoring till God departed in disgust, and left us to the idol
        we deserved;
or failing this, forgetting Sinai we'd suppose it all a symbol
    and a dream, deafening ourselves with that technique
until once more we stood, a babbling rabble in the desert,
    waiting for another Moses to give us back our ears,
        more driven than desirous.

In the Synagogue

I do not understand
the book in my hand.

Who will teach me to return?
Loss of custom, ruin of will,
a memory of a memory
thinner than a vein.
Who will teach us to return?

To whom nothing speaks.
Not shofar, not song, not homily.

On whom nothing was wrought.
Not slaughter, not horror, not holocaust.

History is not my concern.

Suppose even God
turned out to be a god?

We do not want to come back.
We do not know where we are.
Not knowing where we are, how can we know
      where we should go?

John Hollander (b. 1929)

The author of more than twenty volumes of poetry, John Hollander is one of America's most prolific and respected poets. Considered "academic," his poetry is most often formal, allusive, and intellectual. His early work did not generally make use of Jewish motifs. With the publication of *Spectral Emanations: New and Selected Poems* (1978), however, Hollander began in many of his poems to explore Jewish mystical sources (such as the *Zohar*, one of the central texts of Kabbalism), Yiddish literature, and Jewish folklore and tradition. Of the poems included here, "Song at the End of a Meal" is based on a traditional Passover song, while "At the New Year" embodies a lyrical prayer for the coming year. In "Letter to Jorge Luis Borges: Apropos of the Golem," the poet recounts the myth of the Golem, a legendary Jewish monster. Born in New York City, Hollander received B.A. and M.A. degrees from Columbia University, and a Ph.D. from Indiana University. He has taught at universities and colleges both in the United States and abroad, and is currently a member of the English faculty at Yale University.

At the New Year

Every single instant begins another new year;
    Sunlight flashing on water, or plunging into a clearing
In quiet woods announces; the hovering gull proclaims
    Even in wide midsummer a point of turning: and fading
Late winter daylight close behind the huddled backs
    Of houses close to the edge of town flares up and shatters
As well as any screeching ram's horn can, wheel
    Unbroken, uncomprehended continuity,
Making a starting point of a moment along the way,
    Spinning the year about one day's pivot of change.
But if there is to be a high moment of turning
    When a great, autumnal page, say, takes up its curved
Flight in memory's spaces, and with a final sigh,
    As of every door in the world shutting at once, subsides
Into the bed of its fellows; if there is to be
    A time of tallying, recounting and rereading
Illuminated annals, crowded with black and white
    And here and there a capital flaring with silver and bright
Blue, then let it come at a time like this, not at winter's
    Night, when a few dead leaves crusted with frost lie shivering
On our doorsteps to be counted, or when our moments of coldness
    Rise up to chill us again. But let us say at a golden
Moment just on the edge of harvesting, "Yes. Now."
    Times of counting are times of remembering; here amidst
        showers
Of shiny fruits, both the sweet and the bitter-tasting results,
    The honey of promises gleams on apples that turn to mud
In our innermost of mouths, we can sit facing westward
    Toward imminent rich tents, telling and remembering.

Not like merchants with pursed hearts, counting in dearth and
    darkness,

But as when from a shining eminence, someone walking starts
At the sudden view of imperturbable blue on one hand
    And wide green fields on the other. Not at the reddening sands
Behind, nor yet at the blind gleam, ahead, of something
    Golden, looking at such a distance and in such sunlight,
Like something given—so, at this time, our counting begins,
    Whirling all its syllables into the circling wind
That plays about our faces with a force between a blow's
    And a caress', like the strength of a blessing, as we go
Quietly on with what we shall be doing, and sing
    Thanks for being enabled, again, to begin this instant.

Letter to Jorge Luis Borges: Apropos of the Golem

I've never been to Prague, and the last time
That I was there its stones sang in the rain;
The river dreamed them and that dream lay plain
Upon its surface, shallow and sublime.

The residues of years of dream remained
Solidified in structures on each bank;
Other dreams than of Prague and Raining sank
Under dark water as their memory waned.

And far beneath the surface of reflection
Lay a deep dream that was not Prague, but of it,
Of silent light from the gray sky above it,
The river running in some dreamed direction.

O Borges, I remember this too clearly—
Staring at paper now, having translated
Your poem of Prague, my flood of ink abated—
To have recalled it from my last trip, merely.

Three mythical cronies my great-grandfather
Was known to speak of nurture dark designs
Against my childhood: from between the lines
Of what was told me of them, I infer

How Haschele Bizensis, Chaim Pip,
The Bab Menucha and his friends, conspire
Over old pipes; sparks in a beard catch fire,
The smoke grows heavier with each slow sip . . .

I scream and wake from sleep into a room
I only remember now in dreams; my mother

Calms me with tales of Prague back in another
Time. All I remember is a tomb

Near what was called the Old-New Synagogue;
Under a baroque stone whose urn and column
Emerge in the first dawn lies, dead and solemn,
My ancestor, the Rabbi Loew of Prague.

He made The Golem (which means "embryo,"
"Potential person," much more than "machine")
And quickened him with a Name that has been
Hidden behind all names that one could know.

We have our family secrets: How the creature
Tried for the Rabbi's daughter, upped her dress
Till nacreous and bushy nakedness
Shone in the moonlight; groped; but failed to reach her—

How once, when heat throbbed in the August skies
And children were playing hide-and-seek, the Golem
Trailed the one who was It, and nearly stole him
Before the shadows rang with all their cries.

But was he circumcised? What glimmerings rose
In his thick face at evening? Were they sham?
Did he and nine men make a quorum? I am
Not, alas, at liberty to disclose.

(But how he saved the Jews of Prague is told
In a late story—from a Polish source?—
Not to be taken seriously, of course,
No more than one about the Emperor's gold.)

These tales jostle each other in their corner
At the eye's edge, skirting the light of day
(The Bab Menucha lurks not far away,
As if around a grave, like a paid mourner).

Too dumb to live, he could not touch, but muddy:
Lest the virgin Sabbath be desecrated,
The rabbi spoke. It was deanimated;
Half-baked ceramic moldered in his study . . .

Save for the Fire of process, elements
Mix sadly: Mud is born of Water and Earth;
Air knows Water—a bubble comes to birth;
Earth and Air—nothing that makes any sense.

But bubble, mud and that incoherent third,
When animated by the Meta-Name
That is no mere breath of air itself, became
The myth whose footsteps we just overheard

Together, shuffling down a hallway, Borges,
Toward its own decreation, dull and lonely,
Lost in the meager world of one and only
One Golem, but so many Johns and Jorges.

Song at the End of a Meal

The kid was already noxious carrion
That poisoned our kitty when she lunched on it;
The cat clawed at the neighbor's dog who bit
At her tail—infection left the dog undone,
But not before he snapped a stick in two
That fell across his flanks as if to beat
The beast as with a will of its own; the heat
Of a fire that burned the stick was made to rue
The day on which it was born, as half the stick
Flew through the air and knocked its flames apart.
(The fire meanwhile vaporized the wet heart
Of the water that sought to quench it, that made sick
The ox that sought to drink it, who in turn
Brought down with nasty anthrax the butcher who would
Have slaughtered him; that butcher pierced the hood
Of the Angel of Death, from whom we all must learn.)
But how did that dark Angel turn his wrath upon
His would-be punisher, Blessed be He, the Holy One?

Adrienne Rich (b. 1929)

One of America's most accomplished poets and critics, Rich has pub-
lished more than fifteen volumes of poetry and several collections of es-
says. Her many honors include the National Book Award in 1974 for
Diving Into the Wreck and a MacArthur Fellowship in 1994. Born in
Baltimore, Maryland, to a Jewish father and a Protestant-born mother,
Rich described herself in an early poem as "split at the root, neither
Gentile nor Jew" ("Readings of History," 1960). Yet throughout her ca-
reer, Jewish themes, especially those associated with anti-Semitism
and persecution, have been prevalent in her work. In "At the Jewish
New Year," Rich meditates on the meaning of Jewish history; "Jerusa-
lem," originally published in *Leaflets* (1969), delineates the tragic cir-
cumstances of a violent, war-torn city. In "Yom Kippur 1984" the poet
explores the themes of solitude and isolation in terms of her marginal-
ity as a Jew, a woman, and a lesbian. Part 10 from "Eastern War Time"
expresses her lifelong concern with injustice, prejudice, and war.
"Food Packages: 1947," from Rich's 1995 collection, *Dark Fields of the
Republic*, juxtaposes the themes of personal devotion and historical
destruction.

At the Jewish New Year

For more than five thousand years
This calm September day
With yellow in the leaf
Has lain in the kernel of Time
While the world outside the walls
Has had its turbulent say
And history like a long
Snake has crawled on its way
And is crawling onward still.
And we have little to tell
On this or any feast
Except of the terrible past.
Five thousand years are cast
Down before the wondering child
Who must expiate them all.

Some of us have replied
In the bitterness of youth
Or the qualms of middle-age:
"If Time is unsatisfied,
And all our fathers have suffered
Can never be enough,
Why, then, we choose to forget.
Let our forgetting begin
With those age-old arguments
In which their minds were wound
Like musty phylacteries;
And we choose to forget as well
Those cherished histories
That made our old men fond,
And already are strange to us.

"Or let us, being today
Too rational to cry out,
Or trample underfoot
What after all preserves
a certain savor yet—
Though torn up by the roots—
Let us make our compromise
With the terror and the guilt
And view as curious relics
Once found in daily use
The mythology, the names
That, however Time has corrupted
Their ancient purity
Still burn like yellow flames,
But their fire is not for us."

And yet, however we choose
To deny or to remember,
Though on the calendars
We wake and suffer by,
This day is merely one
Of thirty in September—
In the kernel of the mind
The new year must renew
This day, as for our kind
Over five thousand years,
The task of being ourselves.
Whatever we strain to forget,
Our memory must be long.

May the taste of honey linger
Under the bitterest tongue.

Jerusalem

In my dream, children
are stoning other children
with blackened carob-pods
I dream my son is riding
on an old grey mare
to a half-dead war
on a dead-grey road
through the cactus and thistles
and dried brook-beds.

In my dream, children
are swaddled in smoke
and their uncut hair smolders
even here, here
where trees have no shade
and rocks have no shadow
trees have no memories
only the stones and
the hairs of the head.

I dream his hair is growing
and has never been shorn
from slender temples hanging
like curls of barbed wire
and his first beard is growing
smoldering like fire

his beard is smoke and fire
and I dream him riding
patiently to the war.

What I dream of the city
is how hard it is to leave
and how useless to walk
outside the blasted walls
picking up the shells
from a half-dead war
and I wake up in tears
and hear the sirens screaming
and the carob-tree is bare.

Yom Kippur 1984

I drew solitude over me, on the long shore.
                    —*Robinson Jeffers*, "PRELUDE"

For whoever does not afflict his soul throughout
this day, shall be cut off from his people.
                    —LEVITICUS 23:29

What is a Jew in solitude?
What would it mean not to feel lonely or afraid
far from your own or those you have called your own?
What is a woman in solitude: a queer woman or man?
In the empty street, on the empty beach, in the desert
what in this world as it is can solitude mean?

The glassy, concrete octagon suspended from the cliffs
with its electric gate, its perfected privacy
is not what I mean
the pick-up with a gun parked at a turn-out in Utah or the Golan
          Heights
is not what I mean
the poet's tower facing the western ocean, acres of forest planted to
          the east, the woman reading in the cabin, her
          attack dog suddenly risen
is not what I mean

Three thousand miles from what I once called home
I open a book searching for some lines I remember
about flowers, something to bind me to this coast as lilacs in the
          dooryard once
bound me back there—yes, lupines on a burnt mountainside,
something that bloomed and faded and was written down
in the poet's book, forever:
Opening the poet's book
I find the hatred in the poet's heart: . . . *the hateful-eyed*
and human-bodied are all about me: you that love multitude may
     have them

Robinson Jeffers, multitude
is the blur flung by distinct forms against these landward valleys
and the farms that run down to the sea; the lupines
are multitude, and the torched poppies, the grey Pacific unrolling
        its scrolls of surf,
and the separate persons, stooped
over sewing machines in denim dust, bent under the shattering
        skies of harvest
who sleep by shifts in never-empty beds have their various dreams
Hands that pick, pack, steam, stitch, strip, stuff, shell, scrape,
        scour, belong to a brain like no other
Must I argue the love of multitude in the blur or defend
a solitude of barbed-wire and searchlights, the survivalist's final
        solution, have I a choice?

To wander far from your own or those you have called your own
to hear strangeness calling you from far away
and walk in that direction, long and far, not calculating risk
to go to meet the Stranger without fear or weapon, protection
        nowhere on your mind
(the Jew on the icy, rutted road on Christmas Eve prays for another
        Jew
the woman in the ungainly twisting shadows of the street: *Make
        those be a woman's footsteps*; as if she could believe
        in a woman's god)

Find someone like yourself.   Find others.
Agree you will never desert each other.
Understand that any rift among you
means power to those who want to do you in.
Close to the center, safety; toward the edges, danger.
But I have a nightmare to tell: I am trying to say
that to be with my people is my dearest wish
but that I also love strangers
that I crave separateness
I hear myself stuttering these words
to my worst friends and my best enemies
who watch for my mistakes in grammar

my mistakes in love.
This is the day of atonement; but do my people forgive me?
If a cloud knew loneliness and fear, I would be that cloud.

To love the Stranger, to love solitude—am I writing merely about
        privilege
about drifting from the center, drawn to edges,
a privilege we can't afford in the world that is,
who are hated as being of our kind: faggot kicked into the icy
        river, woman dragged from her stalled car
into the mist-struck mountains, used and hacked to death
young scholar shot at the university gates on a summer evening
        walk, his prizes and studies nothing, nothing
        availing his Blackness
Jew deluded that she's escaped the tribe, the laws of her exclusion,
        the men too holy to touch her hand;   Jew who has
        turned her back
on *midrash* and *mitzvah* (yet wears the *chai* on a thong between
        her breasts) hiking alone
found with a swastika carved in her back at the foot of the cliffs
        (did she die as queer or as Jew?)

Solitude, O taboo, endangered species
on the mist-struck spur of the mountain, I want a gun to defend
        you
In the desert, on the deserted street, I want what I can't have:
your elder sister, Justice, her great peasant's hand outspread
her eye, half-hooded, sharp and true
And I ask myself, have I thrown courage away?
have I traded off something I don't name?
To what extreme will I go to meet the extremist?
What will I do to defend my want or anyone's want to search for
        her spirit-vision
far from the protection of those she has called her own?
Will I find O solitude
your plumes, your breasts, your hair

against my face, as in childhood, your voice like the mockingbird's
singing *Yes, you are loved, why else this song?*
in the old places, anywhere?

What is a Jew in solitude?
What is a woman in solitude, a queer woman or man?
When the winter flood-tides wrench the tower from the rock,
      crumble the prophet's headland, and the farms slide
      into the sea
when leviathan is endangered and Jonah becomes revenger
when center and edges are crushed together, the extremities
      crushed together on which the world was founded
when our souls crash together, Arab and Jew, howling our
      loneliness within the tribes
when the refugee child and the exile's child re-open the blasted and
      forbidden city
when we who refuse to be women and men as women and men
      are chartered, tell our stories of solitude spent in
      multitude
in that world as it may be, newborn and haunted, what will
      solitude mean?

Eastern War Time

10

Memory says: Want to do right? Don't count on me.
I'm a canal in Europe where bodies are floating
I'm a mass grave   I'm the life that returns
I'm a table set with room for the Stranger
I'm a field with corners left for the landless
I'm accused of child-death   of drinking blood
I'm a man-child praising God he's a man
I'm a woman bargaining for a chicken
I'm a woman who sells for a boat ticket
I'm a family dispersed between night and fog
I'm an immigrant tailor who says *A coat*
is not a piece of cloth only   I sway
in the learnings of the master-mystics
I have dreamed of Zion   I've dreamed of world revolution
I have dreamed my children could live at last like others
I have walked the children of others through ranks of hatred
I'm a corpse dredged from a canal in Berlin
a river in Mississippi   I'm a woman standing
with other women dressed in black
on the streets of Haifa, Tel Aviv, Jerusalem
there is spit on my sleeve there are phonecalls in the night
I am a woman standing in line for gasmasks
I stand on a road in Ramallah   with naked face   listening
I am standing here in your poem   unsatisfied
lifting my smoky mirror

Food Packages: 1947

Powdered milk, chocolate bars, canned fruit, tea,
salamis, aspirin:
Four packages a month to her old professor in Heidelberg
and his Jewish wife:
Europe is trying to revive an intellectual life
and the widow of the great sociologist needs flour.

Europe is trying/to revive/
with the Jews somewhere else.

The young ex-philosopher tries to feed her teachers
all the way from New York, with orders for butter from Denmark,
sending dispatches into the fog
of the European spirit:
I am no longer German. I am a Jew and the German language
was once my home.

PART III

STRUGGLING

TO SING

WITH ANGELS

Jerome Rothenberg (b. 1931)

Jerome Rothenberg was born in New York City to Polish immigrant parents, and educated at City College of New York and the University of Michigan. A prolific poet and translator, he has published more than twenty-five collections of poetry and translations. As a prominent avant-garde critic, he has also worked to develop the practice of "ethnopoetics," the study of ancient and neglected poetic traditions and the translation of those works into modern idiom. Rothenberg's own poetry is acutely attuned to historic Jewish sources: the thirteenth-century Kabbalist, Abulafia; Kabbalistic interpretation of the Hebrew alphabet as ontology; Eastern European shtetl life before the Holocaust; and the Holocaust itself. "The Connoisseur of Jews" and "Portrait of a Jew Old Country Style" are reprinted from *Vienna Blood and Other Poems* (1980). "In the Dark Word, Khurbn" and "Nokh Aushvits (After Auschwitz)" are from *Khurbn and Other Poems* (1989). *Khurbn* ("total destruction") is the Yiddish word for the Holocaust.

The Connoisseur of Jews

if there were locomotives to ride home on
& no jews
there would still be jews & locomotives
just as there are jews & oranges
& jews & jars
there would still be someone to write the jewish poem
others to write their mothers' names in light—
just as others, born angry
have the moon's face burnt onto their arms
& don't complain
my love, my lady, be a connoisseur of jews
the fur across your lap
was shedding
on the sheet were hairs
the first jew to come to you is mad
the train pulls into lodz
he calls you
by your polish name
then he tells the other passengers a story
there are jews & there are alphabets
he tells them
but there are also jewish alphabets
just as there are jewish locomotives
& jewish hair
& just as there are some with jewish fingers
such men are jews
just as other men are not jews
not mad
don't call you by your polish name
or ride the train to lodz
if there are men who ride the train to lodz
there are still jews

just as there are still oranges
& jars
there is still someone to write the jewish poem
others to write their mothers' names in light
shoes were the craft all our friends
got into first
like his brother-in-law we called
THE UNCLE
I remember in a basement shop
somewhere "downtown"
bent over shoes he stitched
how many years would pass
till nineteen-fifty maybe
when I saw him last
his lungs gone in east bronx tenement
he slept behind a curtain
seeing me he thought
I was my brother   old & crazy
he was the oldest jew I knew
my grandfather had died
in nineteen-twenty
on the night my parents
ran to warsaw
to get married   my father
left for U.S.A. the next day
no one told him of his father's death
he would never be a talmudist
would go from shoes
to insurance
from insurance back to shoes
later an entrepreneur & bust
he was always clean
shaven   my grandmother
the religious one I mean
saw the first beard
I'd ever grown   got angry
"jews dont wear beards"
(she said) no

not in golden U.S.A.
the old man had fled from
to his Polish death
for which reason I deny autobiography
or that the life of a man
matters more or less
      "We are all one man"
      Cezanne said
I count the failures of these jews
as proof of their election
they are divine because they all die
                  screaming
      like the first
   universal jew
     the gentiles
       will tell you had some special deal

Portrait of a Jew Old Country Style

visitor to warsaw
          old man with open fly
      flesh girls could suck
              mothers would die to catch sight of
sometimes would pass your door
              his song was
      a generation is a day, time floweth
coldly he blew his nose
reached a hand around his high round waist
          money was pinned to caftan
              aches & pains
a jew's a jew he says
love brings him to the words he needs
              but sadly
      no
              I cannot stay
              for breakfast loving
              the taste of duck eggs loving
              little rolls & butter
              loving cereals in metal pans
he tells them
          all we touch is love
          & feeds us
this is a portrait of a jew old country style
the gentile will fail to understand
the jew come on better days will run from it
how real
the grandfathers become

              my grandfather the baker son of bakers
              YOSEL DOVID ben SHMIEL

who was a hasid at the court in Rizhyn
came to U. S. A. circa 1913
but found the country godless
tho he worked in leather

In the Dark Word, Khurbn

all their lights went out

their words were silences,
memories
drifting along the horse roads
onto malkiner street

a disaster in the mother's tongue
her words emptied
by speaking

returning to a single word
the child word
spoken, redeyed on
the frozen pond

was how they spoke it,
how I would take it from your voice
& cradle it

that ancient & dark word

those who spoke it in the old days
now held their tongues

Nokh Aushvits (After Auschwitz)

the poem is ugly & they make it uglier
wherein the power resides
that duncan did—or didn't—understand
when listening that evening to the other poet read
he said   "that was pure ugliness"   & oh it was
it was   & it made my heart skip a beat
because the poem wouldn't allow it   no
not a moment's grace nor beauty to obstruct
whatever the age demanded   or the poem
shit poured on wall & floor
sex shredded   genitals torn loose by dog claws
& the ugliness that you were to suffer
later   that they had suffered
not as dante dreamed it but in the funnel
they ran through & that the others called
the road to heaven   little hills & holes now
& beneath   upon   among them
broken mirrors kettles pans enameled teapots
the braided candlesticks of sabbath
prayershawl scraps & scraps of bodies   bones
his child's   he said   leaping
into the mud the pool of bones
& slime   the frail limbs separating
each time he pulls at one   the mystery of body
not a mystery   bodies naked   then bodies
boned & rotten   how he must fight
his rage for beauty must make a poem
so ugly it can drive out the other voices
like artaud's squawk the poem addressed
to ugliness   must resist
even the artistry of death   a stage set
at treblinka   ticket windows   a large clock

the signs that read: change for bialystok
but the man cries who has seen
the piles of clothing   jews
it is not good it is your own sad meat
that hangs here   poor & bagged   like animals
the blood coagulated into a jell
an armpit through which a ventricle has burst
& left him dangling screaming
a raw prong stuck through his tongue
another through his scrotal sac   he sees
a mouth   a hole   a red hole
the scarlet remnants of the children's flesh
their eyes like frozen baby scallops
so succulent that the blond ukrainian guard
sulking beneath his parasol leaps up
& sucks them inward past his iron teeth
& down his gullet, shitting
globules of fat & shit
that trickle down the pit in which the victim—
the girl without a tongue—stares up
& reads her final heartbreak

Linda Pastan (b. 1932)

Born in the Bronx, New York, Linda Pastan attended Radcliffe College and did graduate work at Simmons College and Brandeis University. Although she won *Mademoiselle*'s Dylan Thomas Poetry Award her senior year in college (Sylvia Plath was the runner-up), Pastan delayed a writing career to raise three children. Her first collection of poetry, *A Perfect Circle of Sun*, was published in 1971. Other volumes followed, as did critical recognition. In 1991 she was named the Poet Laureate of Maryland. Pastan's subjects often concern Jewish history, family life, and contemporary American Jewish culture. In "Passover," the poet sees correspondences between ancient Egypt and her present suburban existence. "A Name" and "Old Photograph Album" represent a more somber aspect of Pastan's work, one in which the poet explores the themes of loss and separation, as well as her own tenuous connections with past generations. Both "At the Jewish Museum" and "Rachel (rā'chal), a ewe" express Pastan's link to the Jewish past, to the victims of the Holocaust, and to her immigrant forebears.

A Name

For Susan who became Shoshana

David means beloved.
Peter is a rock. They named me
Linda which means beautiful
in Spanish—a language
I never learned.
Even naked
we wear our names.
In the end we leave them behind
carved into desktops
and gravestones, inscribed
on the flyleaf of Bibles
where on another page
God names the generations
of Shem, Ham, and Japheth.

Homer cast a spell with names
giving us the list
of warriors and their ships
I read my children to sleep by.
There are as many names underfoot
as leaves in October;
they burn as briefly on the tongue,
and their smoke could darken
the morning sky to dusk.
Remember the boy of seven
who wandered the Holocaust alone
and lost not his life
but his name? Or the prince whose name
was stolen with his kingdom?

When I took my husband's name
and fastened it to mine

I was as changed
as a child
when the priest sprinkles it
with water and the name
that saves it a place in heaven.
My grandfather gave me a name
in Hebrew I never heard,
but it died with him.
If I had taken that name
who would I be,
and if he calls me now
how will I know to answer?

At the Jewish Museum

The Lower East Side: Portal To American Life, 1887–1924

We can endure the eyes
of these children lightly,
because they stare
from the faces of our fathers
who have grown old before us.
Their hungers have always been
our surfeit. We turn again
from the rank streets, from
marred expectancies and laundry
that hangs like a portent
over everything.
Here in a new museum
we walk past all the faces
the cameras have stolen from time.
We carry them like piecework
to finish at home,
knowing how our childrens' sins
still fall upon the old Jew
in a coal cellar, on Ludlow street,
in nineteen hundred.

Passover

1

I set my table with metaphor:
the curling parsley—green sign nailed to the doors
of God's underground; salt of desert and eyes;
the roasted shank bone of a Pascal lamb,
relic of sacrifice and bleating spring.
Down the long table, past fresh shoots of a root
they have been hacking at for centuries,
you hold up the unleavened bread—a baked scroll
whose wavy lines are indecipherable.

2

The wise son and the wicked, the simple son
and the son who doesn't ask, are all my son
leaning tonight as it is written,
slouching his father calls it. His hair is long:
hippie hair, hassid hair, how strangely alike
they seem tonight.
                    First Born, a live child cried
among the bulrushes, but the only root
you know stirs between your legs, ready
to spill its seed in gentile gardens.
And if the flowers be delicate and fair
I only mind this one night of the year
when far beyond the lights of Jersey
Jerusalem still beckons us, in tongues.

3

What black-throated bird
in a warm country
sings spirituals,
sings spirituals
to Moses now?

4

One exodus prefigures the next.
The glaciers fled before hot whips of air.
Waves bowed at God's gesture
for fugitive Israel to pass;
while fish, caught then behind windows
of water, remembered how their brothers once
pulled themselves painfully from the sea,
willing legs to grow
from slanted fins.
Now the blossoms pass from April's tree,
refugee raindrops mar the glass,
borders are transitory.
And the changling gene, still seeking
stone sanctuary, moves on.

5

Far from Egypt, I have sighted blood,
have heard the throaty mating of frogs.
My city knows vermin, animals loose in hallways,
boils, sickness, hail.
In the suburban gardens
seventeen-year locusts rise
from their heavy beds
in small explosions of sod.
Darkness of newsprint.
My son, my son.

Rachel (rā'chal), a ewe

We named you
for the sake
of the syllables
and for the small boat
that followed the Pequod,
gathering lost children
of the sea.

We named you
for the dark-eyed girl
who waited at the well
while her lover
worked seven years
and again
seven.

We named you
for the small daughters
of the Holocaust
who followed their six-pointed stars
to death
and were all of them
known as
Rachel.

Old Photograph Album

These pages, crumbling under my fingers
as I turn them, chronicle the lives
of the people I loved, years before
I was there to love them. Mother.
Great aunts and cousins. Here are their naked
infancies on sheepskin rugs; their exodus
across decades of childhood and youth;
the shy solemnity of their weddings.
In the old country my father in knickers
clowns and spends his foreign dollars
on his last visit before that country
closes down. The Adirondacks.
The Catskills. New York—its pushcarts,
its ancient children—more foreign
to me than the streets of Troy or Rome.
The glue loosens under the small black
triangles that hold the pictures in place,
reminding me of those torn
pieces of mourning ribbon pinned
to our blouses or coats at funerals.
Here are the people I have lost
because I can't believe in the green
pastureland of hymns or in the haloed
faces of angels, outlined
in golden threads on altar cloths:
Grandma and Grandpa,
Ada and Ruth. If only I thought
we would meet just one more time
even in purgatory, that anteroom
to someone else's heaven, with its horsehair sofas
and shabby twenties furniture, peopled
with ghosts in high starched collars and velvet hats.

Stephen Berg (b. 1934)

The poetry of Stephen Berg, a gifted poet and translator, resonates with sadness and the sense of loss. In *Grief* (1975), Berg explores the implications of the then-recent death of his father and his own understanding of the father-son relationship. He also writes movingly of the Holocaust and the suffering of the Jews at the hands of the Nazis. In "Desnos Reading the Palms of Men on Their Way to the Gas Chambers," reprinted here from *Grief*, Robert Desnos—the French poet who supposedly read palms and predicted good fortunes of those about to enter the gas chambers at Buchenwald—serves as Berg's alter ego, visualizing and interpreting the ineffable and rendering it in dream imagery. "Prayer," from *New and Selected Poems* (1992), reveals the anguished uncertainty of a poet who continually questions religious belief and the existence of God. Berg, the author of five volumes of poetry, was born in Philadelphia, Pennsylvania, where he lives and teaches.

Desnos Reading the Palms of Men
on Their Way to the Gas Chambers

Our suffering would be unbearable if we couldn't
think of it as a passing and sentimental disorder.
—Robert Desnos
March 28, 1944, Buchenwald

Maybe I should go back to the white leather
sofa and bull terrier
of my childhood, when my grandfather died,
but I can't.
It rained and there were beaks of light.
Who was it
picking my hand up where it hung
against my naked thigh?
What matters is how we act before we die,
whether we have a joke ready
and can make all the terrified sad faces
around us laugh and weep,
whether we can make everyone kiss.
Who was it? Who holds us here?
Whom should we touch?

You squeeze my hand.
The orchestra's notes from across the road
weave upward in the smoke,
the frozen eyes, the brown angular light
off center, rows, stacks, glasses
without anyone's eyes behind them
and nothing except
the smile of a boot,
the eyes of gloves,
the mouth of a belt

It is reported that the French poet Robert Desnos broke out of a line of naked prisoners on their
way to the gas chambers at Buchenwald and went from prisoner to prisoner reading palms, pre-
dicting good fortune and happiness.

and the holes.
Holes.
I squeeze your hand.

You don't love anyone.
I'm sorry. You never loved anyone.
Probably it's because your planets
are mixed, or Jewish.
But there's a cross down by the wrist
on the edge of the mound of Venus
and lines tangling violently
along the third finger.
You're a sexual person.
Still, those lines webbed
under the thumb are bright.
The agony is false.
The earth has been here beneath us
less than an hour
and we are shuffling forward.
Nobody looks at us.
Say anything,
say we are somewhere else,
each violin has
long curved eyes
tilted seaward and up
like your hand in mine.

And yours, little boy with dark brown eyes,
is wetter than the fake soup
of urine and grass the Nazis give us.
You hide your penis fearfully
behind it, making a pathetic cup
while the other hand dangles
like a noose
that will open on no one,
close on no one.
But I predict one last moment of
incredible joy

when you see yourself melt
into the hundreds gasping around you,
and the doors are pulled
and the gas sighs once, reminding
the Father of you.

Nothing is lost. One guard sprouts wings
in his sleep. He is presented a robe of
spun blond hair and a throne
of tiny nuggets.
In the morning on the parade ground
he opens his fly and prays for us
and is shot
and chopped up for the dogs.
But the next night he returns,
an amputated wing
branding its shadow in miniature
on twelve foreheads.

Like a blind clown I dance between
rifles and the laughter of kings,
and it must be my withered cock and balls,
the color of stone walls,
that cause so much happiness
in the ranks,
as I stumble through the prisoners to hold them,
needing to touch as many as I can
before I go.

There's a shallow hole over the bed
on the wall behind my head
where my dreams live on
after I have waked and knelt
and bled
thousands of times.
I look into it and if I concentrate
I see bodies decorated with
God's toil and ashes.

They drift
into the mouths and eyes
of the living
until there is nothing
but children
like us
here.

Shaggy grains of frost
cling to the ground.
The barracks glitter, the sky hugs
itself like a girl whose arms
have been hacked off, and the wire
hums invisibly in the night air except when a
strand goes white for a second
from no source.
O I want to be that thread, tiny
barrier, bodiless vein, line
that the wind reads.
When I chew on what looks like a finger
and tastes like sour wine
I remember you running, stretching your arms out
to be caught or to fling yourself
through space
until your laughter choked in the sand.
I remember nothing.

You ask me why.
I stand facing you
and speak your name,
whatever it is.
Your name over and over
like a lullaby
until we kiss.
I put my hand on your breast.
It is beautiful, and ugly,
and as empty
as we will be soon.

Lights begin passing
in your eyes
like cities going to sleep
or like those thick lamps on the masts
of fishing boats.
I love you more than I
have loved anyone.
You touch my hair and cry.

Are you different from the one
I just touched? Who are you?
Everyone looks so young suddenly
as if this were the beginning
of the world.
Everything is as silent as this hand
laid up in my palm,
except for a slight hissing somewhere.
What would you say if I spoke?
I will marry a beautiful woman
named Youki,
have children, a cottage
in the forest near Compiègne
and live many years?
I will marry and have children.

Sometimes a message flutters down,
and someone picks it up
and reads:

then goes back home.
The wheels clack.

Unbearable, the wrong parents, the sun
funneling down like the wings
of judgment. Love suffers.
                              I
dance in any direction now,
kissing the guards, soothing their faces

with my torn hands, singing like a child
after a long illness
who is here, here and here,
knowing you by the lost warmth
of your hands
in Philadelphia, Cape May,
New York, wherever I could not be.
Who is it?
I slide under the uniforms
and fill them,
and as I swim the sorrow and depth
of a stranger's blood, of
a belly held in by a bulletproof vest,
I know it was not a mistake
to be here.

I am my sister, but I have none.
My brother, but I have none.

Living men, what have you done?
In a strand
of invisible scorched nerve
scenes we won't remember
never stop flashing toward us,
unreceived,
like us.
The last wisps of gas
rise from our sleeves

and what I danced is danced again where
you smile about love
and eat with friends
the last smile is smiled first
and I am both of them
on the last mouth

and I am the light you see by
fingers tracing the breast

a cloud chilling the street suddenly
what you need, say, lie down
next to in hours
of common terror
I am the face
touch touch

and who it is is who it is

a boot's O empties itself eternally
as radiant in the holiness
of presence as
any

I go back
and can't
but I hear myself
call the flesh
call what I love
what I love is not listening

Don't you hear it?
It says "The pain will soon be over"
It says "The lovely season is near"

Don't you hear it?

Prayer

Nobody understands so let the Rabbi
mutter his texts advise tell us how life should be
let the cantor wail open us
his jagged voice inconsolable praise

I took my mother's face into my hands and kissed her face
    and put my face
against her face and pressed my face against her face her tears
    my tears
and kept my face against her face listened in the dark hospital room
"My mother never held me I never told anyone . . . this . . ."

"How we manage to live so much in the trivial emotion of the daily
when we know what's really important lurks there waiting for us,
and, always, one way or another, finds us," wrote my friend Charlie
and Chekhov's "The soul of another lies in darkness . . ."

I quote these here to console

Myra Sklarew (b. 1934)

Myra Sklarew was born in Baltimore, Maryland, and educated at Tufts University and Johns Hopkins University. Although less well-known than some others in this collection, Sklarew has published several well-received volumes of poetry, including *From the Backyard of the Diaspora* (1976), *The Science of Goodbyes* (1982), and *Lithuania: New and Selected Poems* (1995). Her poems, which almost always express Jewish concerns, are clear, simple, and direct. They are also capable of evoking strong emotions, especially those, such as "After Theresienstadt," "On Muranowska Street," and part 1 of "Lithuania," that deal with the Holocaust and the pogroms of Eastern Europe. "A Three-Course Meal for the New Year," is her somewhat wry depiction of organized American Judaism. Sklarew is a member of the English faculty at The American University in Washington, D.C.

A Three-Course Meal for the New Year

This stalk of day-old bread
cannot move my soul
into the new year.
I am left behind again
in the synagogue
where the rabbi quotes
divorce statistics and heals
loneliness with transcendental
Jewish meditation.

I am left behind
holding the yellow ticket
which provides me
one unreserved seat
on the hard bench
of the sanctuary. I wave it
like a bee on a string,
afraid it will sting me,
afraid to let go.

Come to the synagogue,
the rabbi says,
but leave, he cautions,
with deliberate speed.
Four services going on
at the same time—
a little god spread thin
on next year's sandwich.

His fingers parted
in the cabalistic blessing,
I slip through the spaces

and come home, the new year
already at table before me.
The small husks of the days
of the old year hover in my room.
Later on I will take them out
to the river. And later
I will visit the grave
of my mother and offer praise
without knocking on wood
and take my first taste
of the sweet year.

After Theresienstadt

For Vera

It does not matter;
it is only a word:

Maria Theresia's fortress,
a collection of stones.

If you move the letters around
like furniture—thick

and upholstered as great-aunts—
they will not complain.

Here is the word
which you entered in childhood

and here is the word
which took away

your breathing
and here is the word

grown wrinkled and dangerous
which labors to spit you

back into the world again.

Theresienstadt—Collection point for the gas chambers.

On Muranowska Street

I have always loved particulars: the angels
bearing a martyr's palm, the way the hair
of the worshippers forms waves or
filaments, the flowers embroidered
on your sleeve. Even my sleep
contains them: the pointed teeth
of mice, a black camera aimed
at my grief. Yet when you ask for the truth
I summon words empty
as air as if I were guarding a sorrow,
encapsulating it that nothing
might come into its vicinity, letting it
ripen. Like the foot of this woman swollen
with callouses, bearing
bits of earth and tar, thorns, remnants
salvaged in it like the map
of the world, pebbles filled with carbon
when the earth was young, fern still
coiled in sandstone. Never mind that he draws
this foot to his lips and kisses the world
that lies embedded in it, or that beneath
the bellies rolling down to her knees
he sees only the loveliest bones hidden
there, caverns and wetlands he traverses
easily, moving from opening
to opening like a bird metabolizing at a rate
too high to measure. He does not hear
the rifle fire behind her nor the fleeting
sound of hooves. He does not see
twenty men standing on Muranowska
Street, their hands raised in the air.

Lithuania

1

At three-thirty in the morning in America
I have filled an enamel soup pot with cold water
from the sink and I am watering
the apple tree I planted a summer ago,
I am watering the false camellia tree I planted
in March, the crown-of-thorns cactus,
the plant with tiny blue flowers. I am trying
to remember something.

I am trying to remember something I couldn't
possibly know. I am trying,
as I was two days ago in Lithuania,
to move by feel, to know when I was close
to where they had been. At first
I just walked in the Jew's town
without anyone helping me, without anyone
telling me. I walked until I remembered.

But how could I? I had not been here
before. Who could show me
the way? Neither stones
nor saints nor royalty. Perhaps a man
who bit the throat of a Lithuanian
before they cut him into pieces. Perhaps
a tiny red poppy I picked from the trench
of the massacre of Keidan—they say the weeds grew

here twice as tall as anywhere else. How
beautiful it is in Lithuania. See how at Ponar they come
to fetch mushrooms. It was their land long ago. This
was not the only killing they have known. They pick

apples and plums in this season. They pick
cherries. At Ponar they dig for
mushrooms and carry them home
and cook them and eat them—the mycelium

four hundred years in the making nourished
by countless wars, by betrayals, by blood and
bone, by the tears of the dead, by hair and skin. Every
hill is suspect, every ravine, every tree. If you put
your foot down on the earth in Keidan or Datnuva or
Ponar, if you stop walking and read the shape
of the earth under your foot, you can feel the skull
or a bone of someone you knew, someone

you almost remembered. In Kovno a man keeps
the bones of his family from Ponar in a glass
jar on his bookshelf, bones and a bit of earth.
A man keeps a list of the killers. Sometimes
he sends them anonymous letters,
warning them their time has come. Sometimes
he goes further, confronting them directly. He has
nothing more to lose. At his age he endangers

only himself. At Ponar there is a ladder on wheels,
its two parts fold down to the ground. What
is this for? It was used to climb up to the top
of the mound of dead bodies in order to throw
more of the dead onto the pile,
to burn them, to hide the evidence of what
was done here. In Kovno a man keeps a list
of the righteous among the nations. Case by case he documents

acts of kindness and rescue, the names
of those who risked their own lives to save others. Ponar
is a forest, a beautiful forest. The Jews walked
here at night in the dark. Some say they lit candles
to help them see where they were going. Others

say it was fear that showed them the way.
Dante was comforting: in his catalogue
of descents, cause and effect still reigned.

Even he took pity upon Paolo
and Francesca—lovers he treated so tenderly.
But here there was no reason
apart from designation. I name you, tree,
for death. I name you, star, for death, you
grass, you earth, you sister, father. I
name you Christ, I name you Jew name you.
In the territory of the forbidden

like the green ailanthus which dares to grow
in the interstices of stone, they found
what home they could. They occupied air.

Robert Mezey (b. 1935)

Born in Philadelphia, Pennsylvania, Robert Mezey attended Kenyon College and the University of Iowa, and did graduate work at Stanford University. He has taught and served as writer-in-residence at a number of colleges and universities, including Franklin and Marshall, the University of Utah, and Pomona College. He is the author and translator (from Hebrew) of more than ten volumes of poetry, as well as the editor of several other collections. Mezey's Jewish poems include several that delineate his own sense of dislocation as an American Jew, most notably "The Wandering Jew," and the humorous, ironic portrait of his typically "Jewish" mother, "My Mother." "To Levine on the Day of Atonement," is addressed to the poet Philip Levine, and strikes a more somber, reflective tone, as does "The Silence." The first three poems reprinted here are from *The Door Standing Open: New and Selected Poems 1954–1969* (1970); "The Silence" is from *Evening Wind* (1987).

To Levine on the Day of Atonement

Impenitent, we meet again,
As Gentile as your wife or mine,
And pour into a jelly glass
The cheapest California wine.

Jewless in Gaza, we have come
Where worldly likenesses commence
Gathering fury, and still we keep
Some dark, essential difference.

Is it the large half-chiseled nose,
That monument to daily breath?
Is it some fiber in the heart
That makes the heart believe in death?

God only knows. And who is he?
That cold comedian of our harm.
I wear its red stains on my sleeve,
You like a scar on either arm,

But neither knows what good it does.
The voiceless darkness falls again
On this elaborate wilderness
And fills the empty minds of men

Where they sit drinking with their wives,
Children asleep but not in bed,
Nothing to atone for but the long,
Blurred perspectives of the dead.

The Wandering Jew

When I was a child and thought as a child, I put
The golden prayershawl tassel to my lips
As if I kissed God's hem in my child thought.
I touched the scroll with burning fingertips.

On my left temple there is a shallow dent;
Rabbi called it "the forceps of His will."
I was a boy then, and obedient;
I read the blessings and I read them well.

I strapped my arm and forehead in the faith
With the four thongs of the phylacteries,
Imagining how when we were nearest death,
God brought the proud Egyptians to their knees.

The savage poems, the legends of his mercy
Fell on these years like rain and made them green—
What simple years they were. I loved him fiercely
For loving the Jews and hating the Philistines.

Leaving for evening prayers, I felt the breath
Of the hot street on my face, I saw a door
Alive with shadow, hips and breasts and mouth,
And thought, Is she one? with a thrill of fear.

Filthy scarlet neon. A black drunk
Holding his head together with a rag.
The squad car parked across the street. A bank.
And FUCK YOU chalked on the wall of the synagogue.

One great door took me in, as in a dream.
Rich darkness falling on the congregation,

A voice in the darkness crying Elohim!
And I cried with it, drunk on sweet emotion.

I cannot now remember when I left
That house and its habitual old men
Swaying before the Ark. I was adrift,
And much in need of something I had seen.

At morning and at evening in my head,
A girl in clear silk over nothing on
Smiled with her eyes and all the while her hands
Played with the closing and opening of her gown.

I made the rounds then, married and unmarried,
And either way I seldom slept alone,
But always a familiar presence tarried
Behind the headboard and would not be gone.

Or so I thought. Leaving a girl one night,
I saw how my whole life had been arranged
To meet his anger in a traffic light,
And suddenly I laughed, and the light changed.

And the next night, obedient to my nature,
My head was filled with dew as I leaned to kiss.
Why should I leave this Egypt, while most creatures
Were killing each other in the wilderness?

Sucking for milk and honey at her breasts,
I strained against her till I ground on bone,
And still I heard a whispering of the past
When I awoke beside her in the dawn.

I lay unmoving in the small blue light—
What were the years then but the merest ash
Sprayed by a breath? And what half-buried thought
Fastened its pincers in my naked flesh?

Rabbis, I came, pounding with red knuckles
On the closed Ark, demanding whether a lord
Lived in the vacuum of the Tabernacle
Or had departed, leaving only his word—

For years I ate the radish of affliction
Till I was sick of it, and all along
The sparks flew upward, upward. Crucifixion
Screamed at my delicacies of right and wrong.

Blacks swarmed on the stone hills of the city—
Women fucked and abandoned gathered around me—
A sea of voices crying Pity! Pity!
My life's misery rose as if to drown me.

Taste your own bondage in the lives of others—
Isn't it bitter, indigestible food?
If all the wretched of the earth were brothers,
How could I find their father in my god?

I could find rest until a dream of death
Flooded the idling mechanism of my heart:
Nightly now, nomads with broken teeth
Come mumbling brokenly of a black report.

Reeking of gas, they tell what ancient fame,
What mad privation made them what they are,
The dead, the dying—I am one of them—
Dark-blooded aliens pierced with a white star,

A flock of people prey to every horror,
Shattered by thirty centuries of war,
The sport of Christian duke and Hauptsturmfuehrer—
Is this the covenant we were chosen for?

Sometimes, at noon, the dull sun seems to me
A jahrzeit candle for the millions gone

—As if that far, indifferent fire could be
Anything to the black exploded bone!

Tempted and fallen, your Lord God is brooding
Over the ashes where Job sits in pain,
And yet his tribe is ashes, ashes bleeding
And crying out to the sun and to the rain.

I speak of those that lived by rope and spade,
Of those that dug a pit for friend and brother
And later lay down naked in its shade—
There, at last, the prisoners rest together.

I speak it in an anguish of the spirit—
What is man, I ask—what am I?
Am I but one of many to inherit
The barren mountain and the empty sky?

It is a brutal habit of the mind
To look at flesh and tear its clothes away,
It makes consoling speech a figment of wind
And rescue seems like something in a play.

The nights are darker than they used to be.
A squalid ghost has come to share my room
And every night I bring him home with me,
If one can call dissatisfaction home.

All week long I have read in the Pentateuch
Of how I have not lived, and my poor body
Wrestled with every sentence in the book.
If there is Judgment, I will not be ready.

The book I read last night will be my last;
I have come too far lacking a metaphysic.
Live, says the Law—I sit here doing my best,
Relishing meat, listening to music.

My Mother

My mother writes from Trenton,
a comedian to the bone
but underneath serious
and all heart. 'Honey,' she says,
'be a mensch and Mary too,
its no good, to worry, you
are doing the best you can
your Dad and everyone
thinks you turned out very well
as long as you pay your bills
nobody can say a word
you can tell them, to drop dead
so save a dollar it can't
hurt—remember Frank you went
to highschool with? he still lives
with his wife's mother, his wife
works while he writes his books and
did he ever sell a one
the four kids run around naked
36, and he's never had,
you'll forgive my expression
even a pot to piss in
or a window to throw it,
such a smart boy he couldnt
read the footprints on the wall
honey you think you know all
the answers you dont, please, try
to put some money away
believe me it wouldn't hurt
artist shmartist life's too short
for that kind of, forgive me,
horseshit, I know what you want

better than you, all that counts
is to make a good living
and the best of everything,
as Sholem Aleichem said,
he was a great writer did
you ever read his books dear,
you should make what he makes a year
anyway he says some place
Poverty is no disgrace
but its no honor either
that's what I say,
                    love,
                         Mother'

The Silence

How many times God will remember
the silence of the beginning,
that silence which even God himself couldn't endure,
which was finally to blame for our being here now—
he lost his head, and clawing at the earth, picked up some
      mud and made us.

And thus ended the silence,
and then began the howling,
interrupted now and then by a faint chattering
when we make love in our sleep.

Marge Piercy (b. 1936)

Born in Detroit, Michigan, Marge Piercy received a B.A. degree from
the University of Michigan and an M.A. from Northwestern Univer-
sity. Equally productive as a novelist and a poet, she has published
more than twenty volumes of poetry and fiction. Piercy's writing is in-
spired by her commitment to feminism, the environment, radical poli-
tics, and Reconstructionist Judaism. In her recent collections of poetry
(*Available Light*, 1988; *Mars and Her Children*, 1992; and *What Are
Big Girls Made Of?*, 1997) Piercy frequently investigates religious
meaning within the context of nature, family, and women's experience.
In the poems included here, she explores Jewish identity through a
sense of history ("Maggid"—the title comes from the biblical term for
an itinerant preacher or teacher), childhood memory ("A candle in a
glass"), a reinterpretation of women's rituals ("At the new moon: Rosh
Hodesh"), and her own, post-Holocaust consciousness ("Growing up
haunted").

A candle in a glass

When you died, it was time to light the first
candle of the eight. The dark tidal shifts
of the Jewish calendar of waters and the moon
that grows like a belly and starves like a rabbit
in winter have carried that holiday forward
and back since then. I light only your candle
at sunset, as the red wax of the sun melts
into the rumpled waters of the bay.

The ancient words pass like cold water
out of stone over my tongue as I say kaddish.
When I am silent and the twilight drifts
in on skeins of unraveling woolly snow
blowing over the hill dark with pitch pines,
I have a moment of missing that pierces
my brain like sugar stabbing a cavity
till the nerve lights its burning wire.

Grandmother Hannah comes to me at Pesach
and when I am lighting the sabbath candles.
The sweet wine in the cup has her breath.
The challah is braided like her long, long hair.
She smiles vaguely, nods, is gone like a savor
passing. You come oftener when I am putting
up pears or tomatoes, baking apple cake.
You are in my throat laughing or in my eyes.

When someone dies, it is the unspoken words
that spoil in the mind and ferment to wine
and to vinegar. I obey you still, going
out in the saw toothed wind to feed the birds
you protected. When I lie in the arms of my love,

I know how you climbed like a peavine twining,
lush, grasping for the sun, toward love
and always you were pinched back, denied.

It's a little low light the yahrzeit candle
makes, you couldn't read by it or even warm
your hands. So the dead are with us only
as the scent of fresh coffee, of cinnamon,
of pansies excites the nose and then fades,
with us as the small candle burns in its glass.
We lose and we go on losing as long as we live,
a little winter no spring can melt.

Maggid

The courage to let go of the door, the handle.
The courage to shed the familiar walls whose very
stains and leaks are comfortable as the little moles
of the upper arm; stains that recall a feast,
a child's naughtiness, a loud blattering storm
that slapped the roof hard, pouring through.

The courage to abandon the graves dug into the hill,
the small bones of children and the brittle bones
of the old whose marrow hunger had stolen;
the courage to desert the tree planted and only
begun to bear; the riverside where promises were
shaped; the street where their empty pots were broken.

The courage to leave the place whose language you learned
as early as your own, whose customs however dan-
gerous or demeaning, bind you like a halter
you have learned to pull inside, to move your load;
the land fertile with the blood spilled on it;
the roads mapped and annotated for survival.

The courage to walk out of the pain that is known
into the pain that cannot be imagined,
mapless, walking into the wilderness, going
barefoot with a canteen into the desert;
stuffed in the stinking hold of a rotting ship
sailing off the map into dragons' mouths,

Cathay, India, Siberia, goldeneh medina,
leaving bodies by the way like abandoned treasure.
So they walked out of Egypt. So they bribed their way

out of Russia under loads of straw; so they steamed
out of the bloody smoking charnelhouse of Europe
on overloaded freighters forbidden all ports—

out of pain into death or freedom or a different
painful dignity, into squalor and politics.
We Jews are all born of wanderers, with shoes
under our pillows and a memory of blood that is ours
raining down. We honor only those Jews who changed
tonight, those who chose the desert over bondage,

who walked into the strange and became strangers
and gave birth to children who could look down
on them standing on their shoulders for having
been slaves. We honor those who let go of every-
thing but freedom, who ran, who revolted, who fought,
who became other by saving themselves.

At the new moon: Rosh Hodesh

Once a two day holiday, the most sacred stretches
in the slow swing of the epicycling year;
then a remnant, a half holiday for women,
a little something to keep us less unsatisfied;
then abandoned at enlightenment along with herbals
and amulets, bobbe-mysehs, grandmothers' stories.

Now we fetch it up from the bottom of the harbor,
a bone on which the water has etched itself,
and from this bone we fashion a bird, extinct
and never yet born, evolving feathers
from our hair, blood from our salt, strength
from our backs, vision from our brains.

Fly out over the city, dove of the light,
owl of the moon, for we are weaving your wings
from our longings, diaphanous and bony.
Pilots and rabbis soared. The only females
to fly were witches and demons, the power
to endure and the power to destroy alone

granted us. But we too can invent,
can make, can do, undo. Here we stand
in a circle, the oldest meeting, the shape
women assume when we come together
that echoes ours, the flower, the mouth,
breast, opening, pool, the source.

We greet the moon that is not gone
but only hidden, unreflecting, inturned
and introspective, gathering strength to grow

as we greet the first slim nail paring
of her returning light. Don't we understand
the strength that wells out of retreat?

Can we not learn to turn in to our circle,
to sink into the caves of our silence,
to drink lingering by those deep cold wells,
to dive into the darkness of the heart's storm
until under the crashing surge of waves
it is still except for our slow roaring breath?

We need a large pattern of how things change
that shows us not a straight eight-lane tearing
through hills blasted into bedrock; not stairs
mounting to the sacrificial pyramid where hearts
are torn out to feed the gods of power, but the coil
of the moon, that epicycling wheel

that grows fat and skinny, advances and withers,
four steps forward and three back, and yet nothing
remains the same, for the mountains are piled up
and worn down, for the rivers eat into the stone
and the fields blow away and the sea makes sand
spits and islands and carries off the dune.

Let the half day festival of the new moon
remind us how to retreat and grow strong, how to
reflect and learn, how to push our bellies forward,
how to roll and turn and pull the tides up, up
when we need them, how to come back each time
we look dead, making a new season shine.

Growing up haunted

When I enter through the hatch of memory
those claustrophobic chambers,
my adolescence in the booming fifties
of General Eisenhower, General Foods
and General Motors, I see our dreams
obsolescent mannequins in Dior frocks,
armored, prefabricated bodies;
and I see our nightmares, powerful
as a wine red sky and wall of fire.

Fear was the underside of every leaf
we turned, the knowledge that our
cousins, our other selves, had been
starved and butchered to ghosts.
The question every smoggy morning
presented like a covered dish:
why are you living and all those
mirror selves, sisters, gone
into smoke like stolen cigarettes.

I remember my grandmother's cry
when she learned the death of all she
remembered, girls she bathed with,
young men with whom she shyly
flirted, wooden shul where
her father rocked and prayed,
red haired aunt plucking the
balalaika, world of sun and snow
turned to shadows on a yellow page.

Assume no future you may not have
to fight for, to die for, muttered

ghosts gathered on the foot
of my bed each night. What you
carry in your blood is us,
the books we did not write,
music we could not make, a world
gone from gristle to smoke, only
as real now as words can make it.

C. K. Williams (b. 1936)

C. K. (Charles Kenneth) Williams's early poetry is characterized by vit-
riolic anger and filled with images of despair and anguish. His poems
of this period on Jewish subjects are especially bleak, focusing as they
often do on the Holocaust as ultimate proof of humankind's cal-
lousness and brutality. In the powerful "A Day for Anne Frank," re-
printed from *Lies* (1969), Williams vividly imagines the Nazi persecu-
tion of Jews through the persona of Anne Frank. The poem's terrible
epigraph, "God hates you!" reflects Williams's pessimism and nihilis-
tic vision. "Spit," from *With Ignorance* (1977), a haunting dreamlike
narrative of the Holocaust, is equally disturbing. Williams's more re-
cent poetry is softer in tone and evinces a less hostile, although sim-
ilarly introspective, view of the world—as for example, "The Vessel,"
reprinted from *A Dream of Mind* (1992). Williams was born in New-
ark, New Jersey, and educated at Bucknell and the University of
Pennsylvania.

A Day for Anne Frank

God hates you!
—*St. John Chrysostom*

1

I look onto an alley here
where, though tough weeds and flowers thrust up
through cracks and strain
toward the dulled sunlight,
there is the usual filth spilling from cans,
the heavy soot shifting in the gutters.
People come by mostly
to walk their dogs or take the shortcut
between the roaring main streets,
or just to walk
and stare up at the smoky windows,
but this morning when I looked out
children were there running back and forth
between the houses toward me.
They were playing with turtles—
skimming them down the street
like pennies or flat stones,
and bolting, shouting, after the broken corpses.
One had a harmonica, and as he ran,
his cheeks bloating and collapsing like a heart,
I could hear its bleat, and then the girls' screams
suspended behind them with their hair,
and all of them: their hard, young breath,
their feet pounding wildly on the pavement to the corner.

2

I thought of you at that age.
Little Sister, I thought of you,
thin as a door,
and of how your thighs would have swelled
and softened like cake,

your breasts have bleached
and the new hair growing on you like song
would have stiffened and gone dark.
There was rain for a while, and then not.
Because no one came, I slept again,
and dreamed that you were here with me,
snarled on me like wire,
tangled so closely to me that we were vines
or underbrush together,
or hands clenched.

3

They are cutting babies in half on bets.
The beautiful sergeant has enough money to drink
for a week.
The beautiful lieutenant can't stop betting.
The little boy whimpers
he'll be good.
The beautiful cook is gathering up meat
for the dogs.
The beautiful dogs
love it all.
Their flanks glisten.
They curl up in their warm kennels
and breathe.
They breathe.

4

Little Sister,
you are a clot
in the snow,
blackened,
a chunk of phlegm
or puke

and there are men with faces
leaning over you with watercans

watering you!
in the snow, as though flowers would sprout
from your armpits
and genitals.

Little Sister,
I am afraid of the flowers sprouting from you

I am afraid of the silver petals
that crackle
of the stems darting
in the wind
of the roots

5

The twilight rots.
Over the greasy bridges and factories,
it dissolves
and the clouds swamp in its rose
to nothing.
I think sometimes the slag heaps by the river
should be bodies
and that the pods of moral terror
men make of their flesh should split
and foam their cold, sterile seeds into the tides
like snow
or ash.

6

Stacks of hair were there
little mountains
the gestapo children must have played in
and made love in and loved
the way children love haystacks or mountains

O God the stink
of hair oil and dandruff

their mothers must have thrown them into their tubs
like puppies and sent them to bed

coming home so filthy stinking

of jew's hair

of gold fillings, of eyelids

7

Under me on a roof
a sparrow little by little
is being blown away.
A cage of bone is left,
part of its wings,
a stain.

8

And in Germany the streetcar conductors go to work
in their stiff hats,
depositing workers and housewives
where they belong,
pulling the bell chains,
moving drive levers forward or back.

9

I am saying goodbye to you before our death. Dear Father: I am say-
ing goodbye to you before my death. We are so anxious to live, but all
is lost—we are not allowed! I am so afraid of this death, because little
children are thrown into graves alive. Goodbye forever.
                                        I kiss you.

10

Come with me Anne.
Come,
it is awful not to be anywhere at all,

to have no one
like an old whore,
a general.

Come sit with me here
kiss me; my heart too is wounded
with forgiveness.

There is an end now.
Stay.
Your foot hooked through mine
your hand against my hand
your hip touching me lightly

it will end now
it will not begin again

Stay
they will pass
and not know us

the cold brute earth
is asleep

there is no danger

there is nothing

Anne

there is nothing

Spit

. . . then the son of the "superior race" began to spit into the Rabbi's mouth
so that the Rabbi could continue to spit on the Torah . . .

—THE BLACK BOOK

After this much time, it's still impossible. The SS man with his stiff
     hair and his uniform;
the Rabbi, probably in a torn overcoat, probably with a stained beard
     the other would be clutching;
the Torah, God's word, on the altar, the letters blurring under the
     blended phlegm;
the Rabbi's parched mouth, the SS man perfectly absorbed, obsessed
     with perfect humiliation.
So many years and what is there to say still about the soldiers waiting
     impatiently in the snow,
about the one stamping his feet, thinking, Kill him! Get it over with!
while back there the lips of the Rabbi and the other would have brushed
and if time had stopped you would have thought they were lovers,
so lightly kissing, the sharp, luger hand under the dear chin,
the eyes furled slightly and then when it started again the eyelashes of
     both of them
shyly fluttering as wonderfully as the pulse of a baby.
Maybe we don't have to speak of it at all, it's still the same.
War, that happens and stops happening but is always somehow right
     there, twisting and hardening us;
then what we make of God—words, spit, degradation, murder,
     shame; every conceivable torment.
All these ways to live that have something to do with how we live
and that we're almost ashamed to use as metaphors for what goes on
     in us
but that we do anyway, so that love is battle and we watch ourselves
     in love
become maddened with pride and incompletion, and God is what it is
     when we're alone

wrestling with solitude and everything speaking in our souls turns
        against us like His fury
and just facing another person, there is so much terror and hatred that
        yes,
spitting in someone's mouth, trying to make him defile his own
        meaning,
would signify the struggle to survive each other and what we'll enact to
        accomplish it.

There's another legend.
It's about Moses, that when they first brought him as a child before
        Pharaoh,
the king tested him by putting a diamond and a live coal in front of him
and Moses picked up the red ember and popped it into his mouth
so for the rest of his life he was tongue-tied and Aaron had to speak for
        him.
What must his scarred tongue have felt like in his mouth?
It must have been like always carrying something there that weighed
        too much,
something leathery and dead whose greatest gravity was to loll out
        like an ox's,
and when it moved, it must have been like a thick embryo slowly
        coming alive,
butting itself against the inner sides of his teeth and cheeks.
And when God burned in the bush, how could he not cleave to him?
How could he not know that all of us were on fire and that every word
        we said would burn forever,
in pain, unquenchably, and that God knew it, too, and would say
        nothing Himself ever again beyond this,
ever, but would only live in the flesh that we use like firewood,
in all the caves of the body, the gut cave, the speech cave:
He would slobber and howl like something just barely a man that
        beats itself again and again onto the dark,
moist walls away from the light, away from whatever would be light
        for this last eternity.
"Now therefore go," He said, "and I will be with thy mouth."

The Vessel

I'm trying to pray; one of the voices of my mind says, "God, please
    help me do this,"
but another voice intervenes: "How conceive God's interest would be
    to help you believe?"

Is this prayer? Might this exercise be a sign, however impure, that
    such an act's under way,
that I'd allowed myself, or that God had allowed me, to surrender to
    this need in myself?

What makes me think, though, that the region of my soul in which all
    this activity's occurring
is a site which God might consider an engaging or even an acceptable
    spiritual location?

I thought I'd kept the lack of a sacred place in myself from myself,
    therefore from God.
Is *this* prayer, recognizing that my isolation from myself is a secret I no
    longer can keep?

Might prayer be an awareness that even our most belittling secrets are
    absurd before God?
Might God's mercy be letting us think we haven't betrayed those
    secrets to Him until now?

If I believe that there exists a thing I can call God's mercy, might I be
    praying at last?
If I were, what would it mean: that my sad loneliness for God might
    be nearing its end?

I imagine that were I in a real relation with God instead of just being
    lonely for Him,

the way I'd apprehend Him would have nothing to do with secrets I'd
  kept, from Him or myself.

I'd empty like a cup: that would be prayer, to empty, then fill with a
  substance other than myself.
Empty myself of what, though? And what would God deign fill me
  with except my own prayer?

Is this prayer now, believing that my offering to God would be what
  He'd offered me?
I'm trying to pray, but I know that whatever I'm doing I'm not: why
  aren't I, when will I?

Marvin Bell (b. 1937)

Marvin Bell, the son of a Russian Jewish father and an American Jewish mother, was born in New York City. He attended Alfred University in upstate New York and did graduate work at the University of Chicago and the University of Iowa. Since 1965 he has taught in the writing program at the University of Iowa. The author of over a dozen collections of poetry, Bell writes frequently of family relationships, love, marriage, children, the Holocaust, and Jewish history. His poetry can be clever ("The Israeli Navy"), realistic ("The Extermination of the Jews"), or sadly personal ("Getting Lost in Nazi Germany"). Bell's more recent poems, however, explore the theme of the Holocaust and its relevance to contemporary history in a more unconventional, surrealistic fashion—as for example his 1997 poem "The Book of the Dead Man (#58)," included here.

The Israeli Navy

The Israeli Navy,
sailing to the end of the world,
stocked with grain
and books black with God's verse,
turned back,
rather than sail on the Sabbath.
Six days, was the consensus,
was enough for anyone.

So the world, it was concluded,
was three days wide
in each direction,
allowing three days back.
And Saturdays were given over
to keeping close,
while Sundays the Navy,
all decked out in white
and many-colored skull caps,
would sail furiously,
trying to go off the deep end.

Yo-ho-ho, would say the sailors,
for six days.
While on the shore their women moaned.

For years, their boats were slow,
and all show.
And they turned into families
on the only land they knew.

The Extermination of the Jews

A thousand years from now
they will be remembered as heroes.
A thousand years from now
they will still be promised their past.

Objects of beauty notwithstanding,
once more they will appear
for their ruin, seeking a purse,
hard bread or a heavy weapon

for those who must survive,
but no one shall survive.
We who have not forgotten,
our children shall outremember:

their victims' pious chanting—
last wishes, last Yiddish, last dreaming—
were defeats with which the Gestapo
continues ceasing and ceasing.

Getting Lost in Nazi Germany

You do not move about, but try
to maintain your position. Would you eat
the fruit of the corpses?—You would.
Your friends are the points of a star
now a golden, unattainable "elsewhere"
because there is no elsewhere for a Jew.

Men have closed their daughters to you,
and now the borders like neat hairlines
limiting your ideas to hatred and escape.
This way, they have already begun
the experiments with your brain—
later to be quartered and posted.

Cremation of what remains?
In a dream like this one, a weathered face
will drive you off under a load of hay
at the very moment the Commandant calls.
You could swear the voice you hear is kind,
calling you home, little Jewboy in alarm.

The Book of the Dead Man (#58)

1. ABOUT THE DEAD MAN OUTSIDE

They came to the door because he was small or went to some church
    or other or was seen in the company of girls or boys.
Well, he was small and went to synagogue and didn't know what to
    make of it.
They said he was from some tribe, but he didn't understand it.
They acted as if they knew what they were doing.
They were the executioners of brown eyes and brown hair, and he
    happened to have both.
Well, he said, and they went away before he awoke.
They were a dream he was having before he became the dead man.
Today the dead man lives where others died.
He passes the crematoriums without breathing.
He enters the pit graves and emerges ashen or lime-laced.
He shreds the beautiful tapestries of history and hangs in their place
    the rough shirts and dank pants forsaken at the showers, and the
    tiny work caps.
He mounts the hewn chips of shoe soles, the twisted spectacles, the
    tortured belts and suspenders, the stained handkerchiefs.
Here, he says, is history, maternity, inheritance.

2. MORE ABOUT THE DEAD MAN OUTSIDE

Let none pardon the Devil lest he have to begin again.
Let no one weep easily, let no one build portfolios of disaster
    snapshots or record the lingo of the know-betters, let no one
    speak who has not considered the fatalities of geography.
The dead man does not suffer skinheads lightly, their evil is legion.
With an olive branch, he whips the villains into a frenzy of
    repentance.

The dead man tattoos the war criminals with the numbers.
The dead man wonders what America would be like if every war were
    a wall engraved with the names of the lost.
Well, they said, he was from some tribe or other, and he didn't
    understand it.
When the dead man was a dead child, he thought as a child.
Now the dead man lives that others may die, and dies that others may live.
Let the victims gather, the dead man stays on the outside looking in.
Let the saved celebrate, the dead man stands distant, remote.
The dead man listens for the sound of fascist boots.
They will be going again to his grave to try to cut down his family tree.
This time the dead man will see them in Hell.

David Meltzer (b. 1937)

David Meltzer, like his California colleague and sometime coeditor, Jerome Rothenberg, often writes about nonrational aspects of human behavior using appropriately alternative or experimental forms of literary expression. Like Rothenberg, Meltzer has been influenced by Kabbalistic texts and the writing of Abraham ben Samuel Abulafia, the thirteenth-century Kabbalist and author. Meltzer, who began his literary career as part of the California Beat movement, has published more than twenty-five volumes of poetry, fiction, and translations of esoteric medieval texts. He was born in Rochester, New York, moved with his family as a teenager to Los Angeles, and attended Los Angeles City College and the University of California, Los Angeles. He teaches in the Poetics Department at the New College of California in San Francisco. The poems that follow illustrate Meltzer's wide range of Jewish interests, as well as his unorthodox poetic language and form.

Tell Them I'm Struggling to Sing with Angels

Tell them I'm struggling to sing with angels
who hint at it in black words printed on old paper gold-edged by
    time
Tell them I wrestle the mirror every morning
Tell them I sit here invisible in space
nose running, coffee cold & bitter
Tell them I tell them everything
& everything is never enough
Tell them I'm another cross-wired babbling being
songs coming out all ends to meet & flash above the disc above my
    brain
Tell them I'm a dreamer, new-born shaman
sitting cross-legged in trance-stupor
turning into the magic feather contemplated
Tell them there are moments when clay peels off my bones
& feeds a river passing faces downstream
Tell them I'm davening & voices rise up from within to startle
    children
Tell them I walk off into the woods to sing
Tell them I sing loudest next to waterfalls
Tell them the books get fewer, words go deeper
some take months to get thru
Tell them there are moments when it's all perfect
above & below, it's perfect
even moments in between where sparks in space
(terrible, beautiful sparks in space)
are merely metaphors for the void between
one pore & another

Who's the Jew

who's the jew where is he she it that looms up in your face
unavoidable hiding behind the scenery manipulating agitating
convulsively difficult and wordy

who's the jew on the tree bleached into Aryan calendar art

who's the jew in tubs of intestines and folds of eroticism
overwhelming orifices with Wilhold sperm percolating
metastasizing permutations of monstrosity

who's the jew in blood of shrugs and connivance pulling back
the silken shroud sequentially breaking wings without regard
for sound or pain

who's the jew on the freeway wheeling dealing and anxious
to please to acquire taboo eliminating all competition

who's the jew inventing America

who's the jew with perfect anonymous plastic generic mask
nose thinned lips blue contacts

who's the jew taking inventory of Taiwanese schlock

who's the jew on the tube with his dick in his mouth on
overdrive plugging product

who's the jew who knew the waiter at the place everyone pre-
tends not to be jews pretending not to be

who's the jew crossing the line of pubic hairs in mountain-
range formation elephantine tongue roots and scavenges for
more

who's the jew on stage in putty nose kvetching about who's
the jew

who's the jew in church behind a pew smelling of putrid knees

who's the jew kids throw ka ka swastikas at tearing away the
awning of a gauze temple

who's the jew he she it of corpses and grossness mulching
gardens molting meanings constantly overturned

who's the jew wormed inside brains expanding to devour words
holding the world together in a perfect circle

who's the jew shrewd ferret weasel alien darkness fouling
paper with copyright and power

who's the jew who knew you once when there were no jews

who's the jew you told secrets to

who's the jew we feed to history

who's the jew night gives ink to

who's the jew in chalk-white pies skidding into laughing death

who's the jew who can't say no but won't say yes

who's the jew talking to

who's the jew's friend

who's the jew to you

who are you are you the jew

Tishah B'Ov / 1952

Tishah B'Ov (the 9th day of the Jewish month Ov) is a day of mourning, during which Jews fast and bewail the destruction of the Temple and Jerusalem.

—*Schauss*, GUIDE TO JEWISH HOLY DAYS

Marty was the first holy man I knew. He was a pale seventeen-year-old rabbinical student at the Yeshivah University. I spent Tishah B'Ov with Marty in 1952. We fasted, went to shul, then walked on the Rockaway Boardwalk, looking at the sea, watching sea gulls strut & scavenge in the sand.

Months later, we strolled thru a State Park. Marty was profoundly silent. I was silent too, hoping a Revelation would come into his sacred skull & I'd be there to hear it & humbly transcribe it for all mankind.

We came to an empty playground & sat upon swings, swaying back & forth, our toes gliding through the dirt.

Beyond the trees I could hear sounds of trucks and cars passing over the highway. Our silence was so huge, I could hear twigs move, I heard my blood moving through my veins. Finally Marty spoke.

—Do you see those cars going down the highway?

I nodded.

—Do you see those trees?

—Yes.

—Do you know what?

—No, Marty, what? I asked him, keeper of the Great Secret Key to numbers, letters, & God.

—Bullshit, said Marty softly. —They're all bullshit. The trees, the cars, the leaves, your sneakers. Bullshit. Everything is bullshit.

* * *

Grey Rockaway sky, is this it? Twilight
low tide, wicker chairs rolled home by the wind
vanishing into shadows into rooms
through kitchens into a bedroom, a bed & there
Immediate death

* * *

O Lord O Elohim my heart
will go to You when I grow old
heavy with sorrow having spent Summer
in a parked car's dark feeling
beneath her silk garments, smoking
cigarettes, fearing nothing

tribal grief soothed by great unblinking seas
which part before the atoning eye
why mourn?
why blacken my horned head with *kippah*
stipple my brain with *Mishna*
burden my face with pious beard?

Tradition is energy
and will in time reshape my face
as I in time release its shadows
sending them into Your Light.
O Shaddai, your endless sea doth start & end in me
& I spill it into new life
it wets my work, flows into all points.
I seek and serve You as I can, as I will, as I'm able.

* * *

To shut my eyes & awaken years later
in a yellow stucco room. Green
leaf shadows, currents of air,
move across thin curtains.
Feel a cool breeze & look down
dazzled by new white sheets.

Eleanor Wilner (b. 1937)

Born in Cleveland, Ohio, Eleanor Wilner received a B.A. degree from Goucher College and M.A. and Ph.D. degrees in English from Johns Hopkins University. She has served on the faculty and as poet-in-residence at Goucher College, the University of Iowa, the University of Chicago, and Warren Wilson College. Wilner's first volume of poetry, *Maya*, appeared in 1979. This was followed by three highly praised collections: *Shekhinah* (1984), *Sarah's Choice* (1989), and *Otherwise* (1993). Her poems are often philosophical and meditative, drawing upon Jewish historical and biblical sources and making use of those sources to explore the situation—both historically and presently—of the Jewish woman. "Miriam's Song" and "Sarah's Choice" are imaginative recreations of the respective stories of Miriam (the mother of Moses) and Sarah (the mother of Isaac). Similarly, "When Asked to Lie Down on the Altar" reinterprets the motif of biblical motherhood from a contemporary, female point of view.

Miriam's Song

Death to the first-born sons, always—
the first fruits to the gods of men.
She had not meant it so, standing in the reeds
back then, the current tugging at her skirt
like hands, she had only meant to save
her little brother, Moses,
red-faced with rage when he was given
to the river. The long curve of the Nile
would keep their line, the promised land
around the bend. Years later
when the gray angel, like the smoke trail
of a dying comet, passed by the houses
with blood smeared over doorways,
Miriam, her head hot in her hands, wept
as the city swelled
with the wail of Egypt's women.
Then she straightened up, slowly plaited
her hair and wound it tight around her head,
drew her long white cloak with its deep blue threads
around her, went out to watch the river
where Osiris, in his golden funeral barge,
floated by forever . . .

as if in offering, she placed a basket on the river,
this time an empty one, without the precious cargo
of tomorrow. She watched it drift a little
from the shore. She threw one small stone in it,
then another, and another, till its weight
was too much for the water and it slowly turned
and sank. She watched the Nile gape and shudder,
then heal its own green skin. She went
to join the others, to leave one ruler

for another, one Egypt for the next.
Some nights you still can see her, by some river
where the willows hang, listening to the heavy tread
of armies, those sons once hidden dark
in baskets, and in her mind she sees her sister,
the black-eyed Pharaoh's daughter, lift the baby
like a gift from the brown flood waters
and take him home to save him, such a pretty
boy and so disarming, as his dimpled hands
reach up, his mouth already open
for the breast.

Sarah's Choice

A little late rain   The testing
the desert in the beauty of its winter   *of Sarah*
bloom, the cactus ablaze
with yellow flowers that glow
even at night in the reflected light
of moon and the shattered crystal of sand
when time was so new
that God still walked
among the tents, leaving no prints
in the sand, but a brand burned into
the heart—on such a night
it must have been, although
it is not written in the Book
how God spoke to Sarah
what he demanded of her
how many questions came of it
how a certain faith was
fractured, as a stone is split
by its own fault, a climate of extremes
and one last drastic change
in the temperature.

"Go!" said the Voice. "Take your son,
your only son, whom you love,
take him to the mountain, bind him
and make of him a burnt offering."
Now Isaac was the son of Sarah's age,
a gift, so she thought, from God. And how
could he ask her even to imagine such a thing—
to take the knife
of the butcher and thrust it
into such a trusting heart, then

331

light the pyre on which tomorrow burns.
What fear could be more holy
than the fear of *that*?

"Go!" said the Voice, Authority's own.
And Sarah rose to her feet, stepped out
of the tent of Abraham to stand between
the desert and the distant sky, holding its stars
like tears it was too cold to shed.
Perhaps she was afraid the firmament
would shudder and give way, crushing her
like a line of ants who, watching
the ants ahead marching safe under the arch,
are suddenly smashed by the heel
they never suspected. For Sarah,
with her desert-dwelling mind, could
see the grander scale in which the heel
might simply be the underside of some Divine
intention. On such a scale, what is
a human son? So there she stood, absurd
in the cosmic scene, an old woman bent
as a question mark, a mote in the eye
of God. And then it was that Sarah spoke
in a soft voice, a speech
the canon does not record.

"No," said Sarah to the Voice.   *The*
"I will not be chosen. Nor shall my son—   *teachings*
if I can help it. You have promised Abraham,   *of Sarah*
through this boy, a great nation. So either
this sacrifice is sham, or else it is a sin.
Shame," she said, for such is the presumption
of mothers, "for thinking me a fool,
for asking such a thing. You must have known
I would choose Isaac. What use have I
for History—an arrow already bent
when it is fired from the bow?"

Saying that, Sarah went into the tent
and found her restless son awake, as if
he'd grown aware of the narrow bed in which he lay.
And Sarah spoke out of the silence
she had herself created, or that had been there
all along. "Tomorrow you will be
a man. Tonight, then, I must tell you
the little that I know. You can be chosen
or you can choose. Not both.

The voice of the prophet grows shrill.
He will read even defeat as a sign
of distinction, until pain itself
becomes holy. In that day, how shall we tell
the victims from the saints,
the torturers from the agents of God?"

"But mother," said Isaac, "if we were not God's
chosen people, what then should we be? I am afraid
of being nothing." And Sarah laughed.

Then she reached out her hand. "Isaac,   *The*
I am going now, before Abraham awakes, before   *unbinding*
the sun, to find Hagar the Egyptian and her son   *of Isaac*
whom I cast out, drunk on pride,
God's promises, the seed of Abraham
in my own late-blooming loins."

"But Ishmael," said Isaac, "how should I greet him?"
"As you greet yourself," she said, "when you bend
over the well to draw water and see your image,
not knowing it reversed. You must know your brother
now, or you will see your own face looking back
the day you're at each other's throats."

She wrapped herself in a thick dark cloak
against the desert's enmity, and tying up

her stylus, bowl, some dates, a gourd
for water—she swung her bundle on her back,
reached out once more toward Isaac.
"It's time," she said. "Choose now."

"But what will happen if we go?" the boy
Isaac asked. "I don't know," Sarah said
"But it is written   what will happen   if you stay."

When Asked to Lie Down on the Altar

For Marie Howe, and her "Isaac"

A guiding hand raised
above us, haloed in sun, the glint
of silver on the blade like the sheen
of sperm . . .
               there was the boy,
tadpole swimming upriver, a miracle
about to unravel again, the birth
a matter (each time) of amazement,
and there, on the hill, as always,
sharpening his knife, the sad man
with the headache, the servants,
the high opinion of himself, the sand
it was built on, the mountain
his stand-in—raising its stones
toward the heavens, straining against the rain,
the wind, the merciless years that were wearing it
down, inexorably, the undulant way
that stone is worn
by the tongue of the rivers . . .
                   so, lowering himself
on the woman—the pride of his flocks, the power
of his tents in his member—he launches
this Isaac, tail still thrashing, who
grows in that inland sea where
the children of deserts lie down in still
waters, and there, in the placid place
of beginning, rock in the haven of dark.

Back on that mountain, the cold
dry air of an unforgiving
climate, the father
forces the animal onto the stone,
and now, the sun draws nearer,

the sweat pours into our eyes
and blurs our sight, so we can no longer
tell which is the boy Isaac, which is
the ram, for when the man
looks down he sees, in the face
of the boy looking up at him, the wet
eyes of the uncomprehending sheep, and
as he buries his fingers in the ram's
deep wool, he feels the bony shoulders
of his son, and everywhere (is it
the heat?) the world swims in red, and
his hands, the stones, the altar, the split
side of the mountain, the curve of the earth
run with it, the rivers are stained
with it, the tides are a strange burnt
umber, the waves wash into the shores
the color of rusted iron, the red
of a knife that has lost its edge,
that has spent years exposed
to the rain, so when you reach
to pick it up, it crumbles in your hand
like a cake of dried mud, and the air
picks up the grains of it, moving
them in slow spirals of dust
and smoke, sending them
like signals toward
a lost tribe
in a buried village
of tents folded like the wings
of dead moths
under the burned out lamp
of heaven.

And it wasn't a lamb, but the strong ram
of manhood we dreamed, women
dipping our urns again and again
into the darkening well;
                          it was not a son

but the man himself we lost, the man
who sacrificed what might have been
to his fear, and who came home
a stranger to the tent
smelling of blood
and the death
of what we had stayed for,
late, after the others
had given up hope,
after the others
had changed
to receive him.

Alicia Suskin Ostriker (b. 1937)

Alicia Suskin Ostriker was born in Brooklyn, New York, and raised in Manhattan. Recognized for her literary scholarship as well as for her poetry, she holds a Ph.D. degree from the University of Wisconsin and is a professor of English at Rutgers University. In addition to several respected critical studies, Ostriker is the author of eight volumes of poetry, including *Green Age* (1989) and *The Crack in Everything* (1996), which was nominated for a National Book Award. Both her poetry and her scholarship have focused on women's experience and writing. In recent years, her poems have often dealt with specific Jewish concerns within the context of gender-related issues. In both "The Bride" and "A Meditation in Seven Days," Ostriker seeks to redefine the historical and religious role of the Jewish woman. Similarly, "The Opinion of Hagar" reinterprets the biblical stories of Hagar and Sarah. "The Eighth and Thirteenth" (the title refers to Shostakovich symphonies) is a lyrical and complex investigation into the nature and function of artistic creation within the context of Nazi extermination.

The Bride

i

Jerusalem sits on her mountains, a woman
Who knits and frowns, going over and over her story,
Sifting it, every detail memorized, magnified,
Interpreted. How many lovers, what caresses, what golden
Fornications, what children of brilliant intellect
Sucking hard at her nipples,
What warriors, what artists.

There was a time for riches, a time for poverty.
She has gone begging in the streets, yes,
And she has danced in her rags.

And today they are killing for her
Among the stones. What woman would not
Be thoroughly proud. They love her, they love her
Above the queens
Of the earth, above the other beauties.

ii

The cats in Jerusalem form the secret
Government. They are sisters. They have hearts
As black as eels, or hearts as red
And wise as pomegranates.

They insinuate everywhere, everywhere.
Under the shady orange trees
Sit three or four,
By the ruined wall a score,
Nine surround the Dome of the Rock.
Six yawn, their mouths open as orchids,
Revealing needle teeth.

So forget the rabbis and their frozen Law,
A rod that likes
Hitting a child's fingers, and making
That satisfying sting of punishment.
Forget about the members
Of Parliament, shouting yet reasonable
Like jewelry merchants counting on your goodwill.
Forget the competitive brands of Christians
Selling postcards of sexy crucifixions
Who peer from shadowy galleries of the Church
Of the Holy Sepulchre, its livid saints
And martyrs dissolving into grimy mosaic darkness.
Forget the revolutionary students.
Cheap thrills, cheap thrills.
Forget even the fleshy mothers
Sarah and Hagar,
Praying, shopping, cooking,
Complaining. Forget their apartments, their leaky
Sinks, and the shortened screams when the bad news comes
On the evening radio about their sons
Who were tall and handsome, who were slightly careless
In Hebron, or the Golan, or Beirut.

Forget the mayor, his rosy stitching and patching.
Forget making the world a better place.

Blood and sand.
What is reality and what is fiction?
The cats crouch, the cats
Have a saying: You've seen one corpse,
You've seen them all. The black, the white, the gray,
Stealthy, overt, and sleek,
The runners, the striped ones,
The ones that look like apricots and milk,
Are receiving orders from a small, blackened
Bronze Egyptian cat
In the Rockefeller Museum

Near the Damascus gate,
The cat of dire memory, whose heart,
The size of an olive, is heavier
Than an iron cannonball.

Heavy because so angry,
So angry.

A Meditation in Seven Days

i

Hear O Israel
the Lord our God
the Lord is One
—DEUTERONOMY 6:4

If your mother is a Jew, you are a Jew
—Here is the unpredictable

Residue, but of what archaic power
Why the chain of this nation matrilineal

When the Holy One, the One
Who creates heaven and earth from formless void

Is utterly, violently masculine, with his chosen
Fathers and judges, his kings

And priests in their ritual linen, their gold and blue,
And purple and scarlet, his prophets clothed only

In a ragged vision of righteousness, angry
Voices promising a destructive fire

And even in exile, his rabbis with their flaming eyes
The small boys sent to the house of study

To sit on the benches
To recite, with their soft lips, a sacred language

To become the vessels of memory,
Of learning, of prayer,

Across the vast lands of the earth, kissing
His Book, though martyred, though twisted

Into starving rags, in
The village mud, or in wealth and grandeur

Kissing his Book, and the words of the Lord
Became fire on their lips

—What were they all but men in the image
Of God, where is their mother

   *   *   *

The lines of another story, inscribed
And reinscribed like an endless chain

A proud old woman, her face desert-bitten
Has named her son: laughter

Laughter for bodily pleasure, laughter for old age triumph
Hagar the rival stumbles away

In the hot sand, along with her son Ishmael
They nearly die of thirst, God pities them

But among us each son and daughter
Is the child of Sarah, whom God made to laugh

   *   *   *

Sarah, legitimate wife
Woman of power

My mother is a Jew, I am a Jew
Does it teach me enough

In the taste of every truth a sweeter truth
In the bowels of every injustice an older injustice

In memory
A tangle of sandy footprints

ii

Whoever teaches his daughter Torah,
teaches her obscenity.
                    —Rabbi Eleazer

If a woman is a Jew
Of what is she the vessel

If she is unclean in her sex, if she is
Created to be a defilement and a temptation

A snake with breasts like a female
A succubus, a flying vagina

So that the singing of God
The secret of God

The name winged in the hues of the rainbow
Is withheld from her, so that she is the unschooled

Property of her father, then of her husband
And if no man beside her husband

May lawfully touch her hand
Or gaze at her almond eyes, if when the dancers

Ecstatically dance, it is not with her,
Of what is she the vessel

If a curtain divides her prayer
From a man's prayer—

iii

Solomon's foreign wives, and the Canaanite daughters
Who with Ishtar mourned the death of Tammuz

Who *on the high places, under every green tree, and alongside*
The altars set fig boughs, images of Ashtoreth

Who *offered incense to the queen of heaven*
And sang in a corner of the temple, passing from hand to hand

In token of joy the fruited branch, body
Of the goddess their mothers loved

Who made cakes bearing her features
And their husbands knew

The Lady of Snakes
The Lady of Lilies

She who makes prosper the house
Who promulgates goodness, without whom is famine

Cursed by the furious prophet, scattered screaming
Burned alive according to law, for witchcraft

Stoned to death by her brothers, perhaps by men
She has nakedly loved, for the free act of love

In her city square
Her eyes finally downcast

Her head shaved
Is she too the vessel of memory

iv

For out of Zion shall go forth the law, and the word of the Lord from Jerusalem.
And he shall judge among the nations, and shall rebuke many people: and they
shall beat their swords into plowshares, and their spears into pruninghooks: na-
tion shall not lift up sword against nation, neither shall they learn war any more.

—ISAIAH 2:3-4

Here is another story: the ark burned,
The marble pillars buried, the remnant scattered

A thousand years, two thousand years
In every patch of the globe, the gentle remnant

Of whom our rabbis boast: *Compassionate sons*
Of compassionate fathers

In love not with the Law, but with the kindness
They claim to be the whole of the Torah

Torn from a whole cloth
From the hills of Judea

That ran with sweetness, and from the streams
That were jewels, yearning for wholeness, next

Year in Jerusalem, surely, there would be
Milk and honey, they could see

The thing plainly, an ideal society
Of workers, the wise, the holy hill flowing

Finally with righteousness—
Here they are, in the photographs of the 1880s,

The young women, with their serious eyes
Their lace collars and cameo brooches

Are the partners of these serious young men
Who stand shaven, who have combed their hair smoothly

They are writing pamphlets together, which describe
In many little stitches the word *shalom*

They have climbed out of the gloomy villages
They have kissed the rigid parents good-bye

Soon they will be a light to the nations
They will make the desert bloom, they are going to form

The plough and pruninghook Isaiah promised
After tears of fire, of blood, of mud

Of the sword and shame
Eighty generations

Here in their eyes the light of justice from Sinai
And the light of pure reason from Europe

The Opinion of Hagar

And Sarah saw the son of Hagar the Egyptian, which she had borne unto Abra-
ham, mocking. Wherefore she said unto Abraham, Cast out this bondwoman and
her son: for the son of this bondwoman shall not be heir with my son, even Isaac.

—GENESIS 21:9–10

And the living nations wait,
Each sequestered in its hate.
—W. H. Auden

I have no opinion
I am an Egyptian woman
They sold me and made me her slave
Like everyone else I was in love
With her beauty
She pretended to care for me
Forget about our nationalities, forget
About social rank, she would say
We are women together
That is what matters, Hagar
She used me
When she couldn't have a child herself
She made me sleep with her husband
—That old, creepy man—
When my son was born
She was yellow with jealousy
Of my round breasts, of my strong healthy boy
Finally she too had a son
What a laugh, a thin stick of a baby
Who whined and spit up his food all day
Just what you would expect
From those threadbare sacks of parents
But that was the end of me
She threw me away
Like garbage
You see how humble I am
My son is another story

Not like me, he is free and courageous
A wild ass of a man
He can read and write
He can run a printing press
He can shoot an AK-47
I call him Ishmael, I whisper to him:
Fight to your dying breath

But I still wonder
Why could she not love me
We were women together

The Eighth and Thirteenth

The Eighth of Shostakovich,
Music about the worst
Horror history offers,
They played on public radio
Again last night. In solitude
I sipped my wine, I drank
That somber symphony
To the vile lees. The composer
Draws out the minor thirds, the brass
Tumbles overhead like virgin logs
Felled from their forest, washing downriver,
And the rivermen at song. Like ravens
Who know when meat is in the offing.
Oboes form a ring. An avalanche
Of iron violins. At Leningrad
During the years of siege
Between bombardment, hunger,
And three subfreezing winters,
Three million dead were born
Out of Christ's bloody side. Like icy
Fetuses. For months
One could not bury them, the earth
And they alike were adamant.
You stacked the dead like sticks until May's mud,
When, of course, there was pestilence.
But the music continues. It has no other choice.
Stalin hated the music and forbade it.
Not patriotic, not Russian, not Soviet.
But the music continues. It has no other choice.
Peer in as far as you like, it stays
Exactly as bleak as now. The composer
Opens his notebook. *Tyrants like to present themselves as*

patrons of the arts. That's a well-known fact. But tyrants
understand nothing about art. Why? Because tyranny is a
perversion and a tyrant is a pervert. He is attracted by the
chance to crush people, to mock them, stepping over
corpses. . . . And so, having satisfied his perverted desires,
the man becomes a leader, and now the perversions continue
because power has to be defended against madmen like
yourself. For even if there are no such enemies, you have
to invent them, because otherwise you can't flex your
muscles completely, you can't oppress the people completely,
making the blood spurt. And without that, what pleasure is
there in power? Very little. The composer
Looks out the door of his dacha, it's April,
He watches farm children at play,
He forgets nothing. For the thirteenth—
I slip its cassette into my car
Radio—they made Kiev's Jews undress
After a march to the suburb,
Shot the hesitant quickly,
Battered some of the lame,
And screamed at everyone.
Valises were taken, would
Not be needed, packed
So abruptly, tied with such
Frayed rope. Soldiers next
Killed a few more. The living ones,
Penises of the men like string,
Breasts of the women bobbling
As at athletics, were told to run
Through a copse, to where
Wet with saliva
The ravine opened her mouth.
Marksmen shot the remainder
Then, there, by the tens of thousands,
Cleverly, so that bodies toppled
In without lugging. An officer
Strode upon the dead,
Shot what stirred.

How it would feel, such uneasy
Footing, even wearing boots
That caressed one's calves, leather
And lambswool, the soles thick rubber,
Such the music's patient inquiry.
What then is the essence of reality?
Of the good? The mind's fuse sputters,
The heart aborts, it smells like wet ashes,
The hands lift to cover their eyes,
Only the music continues. We'll try,
for the first movement,
A full chorus.
The immediate reverse of Beethoven.
An axe between the shoulder blades
Of Herr Wagner. *People knew about Babi Yar*
before Yevtushenko's poem, but they were silent. And when
they read the poem, the silence was broken, Art destroys
silence. I know that many will not agree with me and will
point out other, more noble aims of art. They'll talk about
beauty, grace, and other high qualities. But you won't catch
me with that bait. I'm like Sobakevich in Dead Souls: *you can*
sugarcoat a toad, and I still won't put it in my mouth.

Most of my symphonies are tombstones, said Shostakovich.

All poets are Jews, said Tsvetaeva.

The words *never again*
Clashing against the words
Again and again
—That music.

Robert Pinsky (b. 1940)

Born and raised in Long Branch, New Jersey, Pinsky received an undergraduate degree from Rutgers University and a Ph.D. from Stanford. A poet, essayist, and translator, Pinsky has published several important critical works, translations of Dante's *Inferno* and the poetry of Czeslaw Milosz, and five widely admired volumes of poetry. Pinsky's poetry is often autobiographical; he writes of the suburban, lower- and middle-class Jewish world of his youth with both nostalgia and irony, but also with an intellectual's frame of reference. "Poem with Refrains," for instance, has the poet's mother as its main figure, but incorporates various quotations from several British poets (Campion, Greville, Peele, and Swinburne). "Avenue" describes Pinsky's dreamlike recollections of the High Holy Days; "The Night Game" recalls the image of Sandy Koufax, the legendary Jewish baseball star of the 1950s and 1960s. Pinsky, who teaches English and creative writing at Wellesley College, was named the Poet Laureate of the United States in 1997.

Poem with Refrains

The opening scene. The yellow, coal-fed fog
Uncurling over the tainted city river,
A young girl rowing and her anxious father
Scavenging for corpses. Funeral meats. The clever
Abandoned orphan. The great athletic killer
Sulking in his tent. As though all stories began
With someone dying.

         When her mother died,
My mother refused to attend the funeral—
In fact, she sulked in her tent all through the year
Of the old lady's dying. I don't know why:
She said, because she loved her mother so much
She couldn't bear to see the way the doctors,
Or her father, or—someone—was letting her mother die.
"Follow your saint, follow the accents sweet;
Haste you, sad notes, fall at her flying feet."

She fogs things up, she scavenges the taint.
Possibly that's the reason I write these poems.

But they did speak: on the phone. Wept and argued,
So fiercely one or the other often cut off
A sentence by hanging up in rage—like lovers,
But all that year she never saw her face.

They lived on the same block, four doors apart.
"Absence my presence is; strangeness my grace;
With them that walk against me is my sun."

"Synagogue" is a word I never heard,
We called it *shul*, the Yiddish word for school.

354

Elms, terra-cotta, the ocean a few blocks east.
"Lay institution": she taught me we didn't think
God lived in it. The rabbi just a teacher.
But what about the hereditary priests,
Descendants of the Cohanes of the Temple,
Like Walter Holtz—I called him Uncle Walter,
When I was small. A big man with a face
Just like a boxer dog or a cartoon sergeant.
She told me whenever he helped a pretty woman
Try on a shoe in his store, he'd touch her calf
And ask her, "How does that feel?" I was too little
To get the point but pretended to understand.
"Desire, be steady; hope is your delight,
An orb wherein no creature can be sorry."

She didn't go to my bar mitzvah, either.
I can't say why: she was there, and then she wasn't.
I looked around before I mounted the steps
To chant that babble and the speech the rabbi wrote
And there she wasn't, and there was Uncle Walter
The Cohane frowning with his doggy face:
"She's missing her own son's *musaf.*" Maybe she just
Doesn't like rituals. Afterwards, she had a reason
I don't remember. I wasn't upset: the truth
Is, I had decided to be the clever orphan
Some time before. By now, it's all a myth.
What is a myth but something that seems to happen
Always for the first time over and over again?
And ten years later, she missed my brother's, too.
I'm sorry: I think it was something about a hat.
"Hot sun, cool fire, tempered with sweet air,
Black shade, fair nurse, shadow my white hair;
Shine, sun; burn, fire; breathe, air, and ease me."

She sees the minister of the Nation of Islam
On television, though she's half-blind in one eye.
His bow tie is lime, his jacket crocodile green.
Vigorously he denounces the Jews who traded in slaves,

The Jews who run the newspapers and the banks.
"I see what this guy is mad about now," she says,
"It must have been some Jew that sold him the suit."
"And the same wind sang and the same wave whitened,
And or ever the garden's last petals were shed,
In the lips that had whispered, the eyes that had lightened."

But when they unveiled her mother's memorial stone,
Gathered at the graveside one year after the death,
According to custom, while we were standing around
About to begin the prayers, her car appeared.
It was a black car; the ground was deep in snow.
My mother got out and walked toward us, across
The field of gravestones capped with snow, her coat
Black as the car, and they waited to start the prayers
Until she arrived. I think she enjoyed the drama.
I can't remember if she prayed or not,
But that may be the way I'll remember her best:
Dark figure, awaited, attended, aware, apart.
"The present time upon time passèd striketh;
With Phoebus's wandering course the earth is graced.

The air still moves, and by its moving, cleareth;
The fire up ascends, and planets feedeth;
The water passeth on, and all lets weareth;
The earth stands still, yet change of changes breedeth."

The italicized lines are quoted from, in order: Thomas Campion, Fulke Greville, Greville again,
George Peele, Algernon Swinburne, and Greville again.

Avenue

They stack bright pyramids of goods and gather
Mop-helves in sidewalk barrels. They keen, they boogie.
Paints, fruits, clean bolts of cottons and synthetics,
Clarity and plumage of October skies.

Way of the costermonger's wooden barrow
And also the secular marble cinquefoil and lancet
Of the great store. They persist. The jobber tells
The teller in the bank and she retells

Whatever it is to the shopper and the shopper
Mentions it to the retailer by the way.
They mutter and stumble, derelict. They write
These theys I write. Scant storefront pushbroom Jesus

Of Haitian hardware—they travel in shadows, they flog
Sephardic softgoods. They strain. Mid-hustle they faint
And shrivel. Or snoring on grates they rise to thrive.
Bonemen and pumpkins of All Saints. Kol Nidre,

Blunt shovel of atonement, a blade of song
From the terra-cotta temple: Lord, forgive us
Our promises, we chant. Or we churn our wino
Syllables and stares on the Avenue. We, they—

Jack. Mrs. Whisenant from the bakery. Sam Lee.
This is the way, its pavement crackwork burnished
With plantain. In strollers they bawl and claw. They flourish.
Furniture, Florist, Pets. My mongrel tongue

Of *nudnik* and *criminentlies*, the tarnished flute
And brogue of quidnuncs in the bars, in Casey's

Black amber air of spent Hiram Walker, attuned.
Sweet ash of White Owl. Ten High. They touch. Eyes blurred

Stricken with passion as in a Persian lyric
They flower and stroke. They couple. From the Korean,
Staples and greens. From the Christian Lebanese,
Home electronics. Why is that Friday "Good"?

Why "Day of Atonement" for release from vows?
Because we tried us, to be at one, because
We say as one we traffic, we dice, we stare.
Some they remember that won't remember them—

Their headlights found me stoned, like a bundled sack
Lying in the Avenue, late. They didn't speak
My language. For them, a small adventure. They hefted
Me over the curb and bore me to an entry

Out of the way. Illuminated footwear
On both sides. How I stank. Dead drunk. They left me
Breathing in my bower between the Halloween
Brogans and pumps on crystal pedestals.

But I was dead to the world. The midnight city
In autumn. Day of attainment, tall saints
Who saved me. My taints, day of anointment. Oil
Of rose and almond in the haircutting parlor,

Motor oil swirling rainbows in gutter water.
Ritually unattainted, the congregation
File from the place of worship and resume
The rumbling drum and hautbois of conversation,

Speech of the granary, of the cloven lanes
Of traffic, of salvaged silver. Not shriven and yet
Not rent, they stride the Avenue, banter, barter.
Capering, on fire, they cleave to the riven hub.

The Night Game

Some of us believe
We would have conceived romantic
Love out of our own passions
With no precedents,
Without songs and poetry—
Or have invented poetry and music
As a comb of cells for the honey.

Shaped by ignorance,
A succession of new worlds,
Congruities improvised by
Immigrants or children.

I once thought most people were Italian,
Jewish or Colored.
To be white and called
Something like *Ed Ford*
Seemed aristocratic,
A rare distinction.

Possibly I believed only gentiles
And blonds could be left-handed.

Already famous
After one year in the majors,
Whitey Ford was drafted by the Army
To play ball in the flannels
Of the Signal Corps, stationed
In Long Branch, New Jersey.

A night game, the silver potion
Of the lights, his pink skin
Shining like a burn.

Never a player
I liked or hated: a Yankee,
A mere success.

But white the chalked-off lines
In the grass, white and green
The immaculate uniform,
And white the unpigmented
Halo of his hair
When he shifted his cap:

So ordinary and distinct,
So close up, that I felt
As if I could have made him up,
Imagined him as I imagined

The ball, a scintilla
High in the black backdrop
Of the sky. Tight red stitches.
Rawlings. The bleached

Horsehide white: the color
Of nothing. Color of the past
And of the future, of the movie screen
At rest and of blank paper.

"I could have." The mind. The black
Backdrop, the white
Fly picked out by the towering
Lights. A few years later

On a blanket in the grass
By the same river
A girl and I came into

Being together
To the faint muttering
Of unthinkable
Troubadours and radios.

The emerald
Theater, the night.
Another time,
I devised a left-hander
Even more gifted
Than Whitey Ford: a Dodger.
People were amazed by him.
Once, when he was young,
He refused to pitch on Yom Kippur.

Susan Fromberg Schaeffer (b. 1941)

Better known as a novelist and short story writer than as a poet, Susan Fromberg Schaeffer has published a dozen volumes of fiction and several collections of poetry. Although her range of themes is wide, her early fiction and poetry frequently dealt with such Jewish subjects as the Eastern European shtetl, Jewish life in Poland before the advent of the Nazis, the Holocaust, and family relationships and memories. "Yahrzeit" takes its title from the Jewish memorial ceremony for the dead and invokes the memory of her immigrant grandfather, while "May Levine" is based on the figure of her grandmother. While both poems recall members of the poet's family, each does so in order to expound upon larger, more universal issues. Schaeffer was born in Brooklyn, New York. She earned a doctorate in English from the University of Chicago, and—since 1974—has been a member of the faculty at Brooklyn College of the City University of New York.

Yahrzeit

Grandfather, we come to you now
For the coins on your eyes.
The trolleys have run into the ground
And we are in a dark town
Where the sky is purple, and the buildings are black.
Flowers are blackening before each door.

Your grave keeps announcing your name
Like a butler, but you
Stay alive in a small store of your own
And though we arrange your memories like wares
Above your narrow shelf of grass
Your fist stays closed against us, and above us
The sky is wearing its many-colored coat
And we are cold in our skins.

At eight, you sold clothes from town to town
Pushing your wheelbarrow like a belly.
The sky was your roof, full of holes.
You took the clouds with you, attached
Like balloons to your wrists and your knees.
Everyone tried to cheat you, but you grew up
Like a cactus in sand. *You were born old,*
Your daughter said. You packed up your family
Like others pack clothes, and came here to live.

You came to live among the cut-glass swans,
The palms, the rockers in shade
And the swing on the porch: the children in school,
And the children in satin, and the chopped liver duck.

Your children grew taller than trees. Then, we said,
You were not wise.
Keeping records in your black book,

Reckoning the sins and the shames,
The insults and blunders, charging us tax.
We said you could not trust.
Then night closed you in like the lids of your book.
Now you live in the weddings, bar mitzvahs,
The photograph rooms—elegant; while we
Are dressed in the tents of our innocence,
Tattered, like cloth.

Angels stand on tiptoe above these stones.
Father of us all, you were wiser than most.
You kept your many colored coat
And watched the children grow.
Abraham, grandfather, we come to you now
For the coins on your eyes
And you give us more:
You wore
Your coat of many colors under the many colored sky
And wore it well, and wore it long,
And did not die.

May Levine

Grandmother, the same hot night you died
Our house burned down.
Sweet cynic ghost, it did.
Before that, we sat round
Our Aunt's old table.
You were the sugar stirring in our tea,
The pattern on our plates.

That night, my mother had a dream.
In the Bedford-Stuyvesant brownstone house,
She stood in the white closet.
Red saucers were stacked on red plates.
One was cracked. She frowned.
Her grandmother, braids coiled
And fastened with a diamond clip,
Said not to worry that May was late;
Coffee and cake would keep.
Uncle Bill said the same; Manny too.
My mother woke and smiled.
The next morning she frowned to see
What her dream meant.
All, all were dead.
The shades, the beloved shades
Were welcoming the newly dead.

May Levine,
I did not dream, but coming home
I saw the steps to my attic room
Burned and blackened. The rail was gone.
Grandmother, while we were children
We never knew that fire burned,
Much less consumed.

Your petalled hands soothed our wounds,
such dolls, such songs,
We burned, but not for long.
Grandmother, Grandmother, childish, at last
You became a doll to us.
They have put you back in your box.
Now you fall from me
Like childhood's petals,
Hot crimson tulips,
You leave your warmth.
We never knew you scorched till you burned up.

Now I am the one who wakes to watch
In the watchful night.
Asbestos of my youth, cold ghost,
I would see you rest.
In the next room my mother stirs.
House of my childhood, drawbridge to this,
Again through dark corridors
You go first.

Irena Klepfisz (b. 1941)

Irena Klepfisz was born in Warsaw, Poland. Although her father was killed in the Warsaw Ghetto uprising, she and her mother managed to escape and live out the war, hiding among Polish peasants. In 1946 they emigrated to Sweden and in 1949 to New York. She attended City College of the City University of New York and earned a Ph.D. in English from the University of Chicago. Klepfisz's poetry is shaped by the forces that have dominated her life: her experiences as a child Holocaust survivor and as an American Jewish immigrant. "Death Camp," "Perspectives on the Second World War," and Dedications from "*Bashert*" (which she translates from the Yiddish as "inevitable") are all moving accounts of those events. Klepfisz's writing also reflects her struggle to preserve Yiddish culture and language, as for example her use of Yiddish in Dedications from "*Bashert*," "Fradel Schtok," and "*Der mames shabosim*/My Mother's Sabbath Days." The poems reprinted here are from *A Few Words in the Mother Tongue: Poems Selected and New 1971–1990* (1990).

Death Camp

when they took us   to the shower   i saw
the rebitsin   her sagging breasts   sparse
pubic hairs   i knew   and remembered
the old rebe   and turned   my eyes away
i could still hear   her advice   a woman
with a husband   a scholar

when they turned   on the gas   i smelled
it   first   coming at me   pressed myself
hard to the wall   crying   rebitsin   rebitsin
i am here with you   and the advice you gave me
i screamed   into the wall   as the blood burst from
my lungs   cracking   her nails in women's flesh   i watched
her capsize   beneath me   my blood in her mouth   i screamed

when they dragged my body   into the oven   i burned
slowly at first   i could smell my own flesh   and could
hear   them grunt   with the weight of the rebitsin
and they flung   her on top   of me   and i could smell
her hair burning   against my stomach

when i pressed through   the chimney
it was sunny   and clear   my smoke
was distinct   i rose quiet   left her
beneath

rebitsin (Yiddish)—Rabbi's wife.

Perspectives on the Second World War

it is a terror
in the closet   her knees
are limp   eyes straining to see
every object glows with a
private halo   pulling down
her skirt   the trickle
of urine along her thigh and calf
she wipes it carelessly with her hand
biting her lips she fixates on
pebbles and rusty nails along
the path to the truck   it is an oblivion
seen in matter-of-fact gestures
wiping the child's nose with her fingers
she says   blow   his eyes shine   as she
feels the pressure of the doorknob   palms
wet slipping out of her grasp   she whispers
not now   not yet   we've been so careful
he's a good child   just a little more time
she pleads with them   we will not be
careless anymore   this time the knob falls
into the glare of lights   voices scream
orders she does not understand   but obeys
blow   she tells him pulling down her skirt
and wiping his nose with her fingers   later
it is still over   has been over
since the knob slipped from her hand
like the wet fish that jumped while she tried
to scale it   later after the not yet
not now   the walk nude across the yard
she glimpses the meaning of the order
allows her eyes to widen for one
moment and see the path   it is a coldness

never before felt or imagined   she clutches
her hands tearing at her thighs   wailing
to the others she tries to lean on them
to explain the mistake   the small error
nothing is irrevocable   she screams   nothing
to them trying to lean   they push her away
and her hands cup the knob   for a better hold
to keep out the light   her world is cement
stone   iron

                    ii
listening to conversations   over brandy
i am always amazed at their certainty
about the past   how it could have been
different   could have been   turned around
with what ease   they transport themselves
to another time/place   taking the comfort
confidence of an after dinner drink

              it would be too impolite
of me to say   my mother hid with me
for two years among ignorant peasants   who
would have turned us in   almost at once   had
they known who we were   who would have watched
with glee while we were carted off   even though
grandad had bounced me on his knees and fed me
from his own spoon   and my mother is a frightened
woman

              it would be too impolite
to say   you do not know yourselves   you do not know
others

DEDICATIONS FROM *Bashert*

These words are dedicated to those who died

These words are dedicated to those who died
because they had no love and felt alone in the world
because they were afraid to be alone and tried to stick it out
because they could not ask
because they were shunned
because they were sick and their bodies could not resist the
disease
because they played it safe
because they had no connections
because they had no faith
because they felt they did not belong and wanted to die

These words are dedicated to those who died
because they were loners and liked it
because they acquired friends and drew others to them
because they took risks
because they were stubborn and refused to give up
because they asked for too much

These words are dedicated to those who died
because a card was lost and a number was skipped
because a bed was denied
because a place was filled and no other place was left

These words are dedicated to those who died
because someone did not follow through
because someone was overworked and forgot
because someone left everything to God

ba-shert (Yiddish)—inevitable, (pre)destined.

because someone was late
because someone did not arrive at all
because someone told them to wait and they just couldn't any
longer

These words are dedicated to those who died
because death is a punishment
because death is a reward
because death is the final rest
because death is eternal rage

These words are dedicated to those who died

Bashert

These words are dedicated to those who survived

These words are dedicated to those who survived
because their second grade teacher gave them books
because they did not draw attention to themselves and got lost
in the shuffle
because they knew someone who knew someone else who could
help them and bumped into them on a corner on a Thursday
afternoon
because they played it safe
because they were lucky

These words are dedicated to those who survived
because they knew how to cut corners
because they drew attention to themselves and always got
picked
because they took risks
because they had no principles and were hard

These words are dedicated to those who survived
because they refused to give up and defied statistics
because they had faith and trusted in God

because they expected the worst and were always prepared
because they were angry
because they could ask
because they mooched off others and saved their strength
because they endured humiliation
because they turned the other cheek
because they looked the other way

These words are dedicated to those who survived
because life is a wilderness and they were savage
because life is an awakening and they were alert
because life is a flowering and they blossomed
because life is a struggle and they struggled
because life is a gift and they were free to accept it

These words are dedicated to those who survived

Bashert

Fradel Schtok

Yiddish writer. B. 1890 in Skale, Galicia. Emigrated to New York in 1907.
Became known when she introduced the sonnet form into Yiddish poetry.
Author of *Erzeylungen* (Stories) in 1919, a collection in Yiddish. Switched to
English and published *For Musicians Only* in 1927. Institutionalized and
died in a sanitarium around 1930.

Language is the only homeland.
　　　　　　　—*Czeslow Milosz*

They make it sound easy: some disjointed
sentences a few allusions to
mankind.   But for me it was not
so simple   more like   trying
to cover the distance   from here
to the corner or between two sounds.

Think of it: *heym* and *home* the meaning
the same   of course   exactly
but the shift in vowel   was the ocean
in which I drowned.

I tried. I did   try.
First held with Yiddish   but you
know   it's hard. You write   *gas*
and *street*   echoes back
No resonance. And—let's face it—
memory falters.
You try to keep track of the difference
like *got* and *god*   or *hoyz* and *house*
but they blur   and you start using
alley   when you mean *gesele*   or *avenue*
when it's a *bulevar*.

And before you know it
you're on   some alien path
standing   before a brick   house

the doorframe   slightly familiar.
Still   you can't place it
exactly.   Passers-by   stop.
Concerned   they speak   but you've
heard   all this   before   the vowels
shifting   up and down   the subtle
change   in the guttural sounds
and now   it's nothing more
nothing   more   than   babble.
And so   you accept it.
You're lost.   This time   you really
don't know   where you are.

Land or sea   the house floats before you.
Perhaps you once sat   at that window
and it was home   and looked out
on that *street* or *gesele*.   Perhaps
it was a dead end   perhaps a short cut.
Perhaps not.
A movement by the door.   They stand there
beckoning   mouths open and close:
Come in! Come in!   I understood   it was
a welcome.   *A dank! A dank!*
I said   till I heard the lock
snap   behind me.

Der mames shabosim/
My Mother's Sabbath Days

Inspired by Vella Grade in Chaim Grade's memoir

Bay undz is es geven andersh.   I knew nothing
of the 613 *mitsves*   which did not bind me   nor
of the 3 which did   though I am sure my grandmother
Rikla Perczykow knew them all   and I have a vague
image   of her covering her eyes   and swaying.

Shoshana   Różka   Lodzia   Mamma Lo   and more recently
Rose   in short: my mother   in all her reincarnations
did not pass on   such things.
She'd given them up   even before she'd ever claimed them.
She was more modern   and besides   there were other matters
to teach   so by age 11   *kh'bin shoyn geven a brenendike sotsyalistke*
I was a passionate socialist   impatient   so impatient
to grow   into my knowledge   never guessing
there was no choice   for work   and rest   wrestled
in every human life   with work   inevitably
the unbeatable winner.

So for us it was different. *Erev shabes*   was plain   *fraytik*
or more precisely: *piontek.*   I remember   summer evenings
I'd wait for her at the Mosholu stop of the Lexington line.
Bright heat and light   at 6 o'clock.   She was full
of tales   of Miss Kant   the designer   a career woman
longing for home and family   in love with a handsome pilot
of Scottie   the model   who married smart   a wealthy buyer

Bay undz iz es geven andersh (Yiddish)—At our house it was different.

mitsves (Yiddish)—obligatory good deeds required of Jewish men (613) and women (3).

Erev shabes (Yiddish)—Friday night, Sabbath eve.

fraytik (Yiddish)—Friday.

piontek (Polish)—Friday.

376

and now sat brazenly chic   in a reform synagogue.
I listened   eager   to understand these widow tales   of romance
amid the rush   of each season's showing   and once   even
saw   on a page of the *Times*   a mannequin   dressed in
the very gown   Mamma Lo had made.

All the way up Jerome Avenue   we'd walk   past the Jewish deli
where we never ate   (what was the point if you could make it at home?)
past the pizza place   where occasionally   while shopping   she'd buy me
a slice   past the outdoor groceries   fruit stands   fabric   shoes
lingerie   and stationery stores—till Gun Hill Road   and Jade Gardens.
Perhaps I knew it was *treyf*.   She certainly did
but was not concerned.   We'd order   the salty wonton soup
chow mein   or pepper steak   and though she mocked the food
she never resisted.
It was Friday.   The shop was closed.   We'd eat dinner and like the rich
lean leisurely back in our booth.   I didn't know it was *erev shabes*.
Still—she rested.

treyf (Yiddish)—non-kosher.

Louise Glück (b. 1943)

One of America's foremost poets, Louise Glück was born in New York and was mostly self-educated, attending poetry workshops whenever possible at Columbia University. She has published nine volumes of poetry, including *The Wild Iris*, which was awarded the Pulitzer Prize in 1992, and *Meadowlands*, which appeared in 1996. She has taught at a number of institutions, including Goddard College, the University of North Carolina, Columbia University, and Williams College. Although Jewish concerns and memory do not dominate her work, Glück's more personal poems often reflect her interest in biblical sources, her family's history, and spiritual belief. In "The Gift," Glück addresses "Lord" directly, asking protection for her young son. "Day Without Night" is a personal and detailed investigation of the story of Moses, while in "Legend" the poet writes of her grandfather, an immigrant from Hungary who wanders lost and alone in the New World.

The Gift

Lord, You may not recognize me
speaking for someone else.
I have a son. He is
so little, so ignorant.
He likes to stand
at the screen door, calling
oggie, oggie, entering
language, and sometimes
a dog will stop and come up
the walk, perhaps
accidentally. May he believe
this is not an accident?
At the screen
welcoming each beast
in love's name, Your emissary.

Day Without Night

The angel of god pushed the child's hand
away from the jewels, toward the burning coal.

1

The image
of truth is fire: it mounts
the fortress of heaven.

Have you never felt
its obvious power?
Even a child
is capable of this joy.

Apparently,
a like sun
burns in hell, It *is* hell,
day without night.

2

It was as though Pharaoh's daughter
had brought home a lion cub
and for a few weeks
passed it off as a cat.
You did not press this woman.
She said she came upon
a child in the rushes;
each time she told the story,
her handmaidens recreated
their interminable chorus of sighs.
It had to be:
A little prince. A little lion cub.

3

And then with almost no encouragement
a sign came: for awhile
the child is like
a grandson to Pharaoh.
Then he squirms; on Pharaoh's lap
he reaches for the crown of Egypt—

4

So Pharaoh set before the child
two trays, one of rubies, one of burning embers:

*Light of my heart, the world
is set before you:
fire on either side, fire
without alternative—*

5

It was like a magic act: all you saw
was the child move; the same hand that took
such active interest in
the wealth of Egypt showed
this sudden preference for a pile of coal.
You never saw the actual angel.
And to complete the act,
the child maimed himself—
And a cry arose,
almost as though a person
were in hell,
where there is nothing to do
but see—

6

Moses
lay in the rushes:
he could see
only in one direction,
his perspective being

narrowed by the basket.
What he saw
was great light, like
a wing hovering.
And god said to him,
"You can be the favored one,
the one who tastes fire
and cannot speak,
or you can die now
and let the others
stay in Egypt: tell them
it was better to die in Egypt,
better to litter the river
with your corpse, than face
a new world."

7

It was as though a soul emerged,
independent of the angel,
a conscious being choosing
not to enter paradise—
at the same time, the true
sun was setting.
As it touched the water
by necessity the mirrored sun rose
to meet it from
the depths of the river:
Then the cry ended.
Or was hidden
in the stammering
of the redeemer—

8

The context
of truth is darkness: it sweeps
the deserts of Israel.

Are you taken in
by lights, by illusions?

Here is your path to god,
who has no name, whose hand
is invisible: a trick
of moonlight on the dark water.

Legend

My father's father came
to New York from Dhlua:
one misfortune followed another.
In Hungary, a scholar, a man of property.
Then failure: an immigrant
rolling cigars in a cold basement.

He was like Joseph in Egypt.
At night, he walked the city;
spray of the harbor
turned to tears on his face.

Tears of grief for Dhlua—forty houses,
a few cows grazing the rich meadows—

Though the great soul is said to be
a star, a beacon,
what it resembles better is a diamond:
in the whole world there is nothing
hard enough to change it.

Unfortunate being, have you ceased to feel
the grandeur of the world
that, like a heavy weight, shaped
the soul of my grandfather?

From the factory, like sad birds his dreams
flew to Dhlua, grasping in their beaks
as from moist earth in which a man could see
the shape of his own footprint,
scattered images, loose bits of the village;
and as he packed the leaves, so within his soul

this weight compressed scraps of Dhlua
into principles, abstractions
worthy of the challenge of bondage:

in such a world, to scorn
privilege, to love
reason and justice, always
to speak the truth—

which has been
the salvation of our people
since to speak the truth gives
the illusion of freedom.

Enid Shomer (b. 1944)

Born in Washington, D.C., Enid Shomer was educated at Wellesley College and the University of Miami. She is the author of a prize-winning collection of short stories and five volumes of poetry, including *This Close to the Earth* (1992) and *Black Drum* (1997). Shomer has taught at the University of Miami, the University of Florida, Ohio State University, and Florida State University. Her poetry reveals a strong commitment to issues surrounding her American Jewish identity: her role as a woman and a Jew, the moral consequences of being a second-generation Holocaust survivor, the psychological bond between American Jews and Israel, and her own religious beliefs. "From the Wailing Wall" records Shomer's impressions of the remaining Western Wall of the Second Temple, one of Israel's most sacred monuments. In "Freestyle, on the First of Tishri" (the first of Tishri is the Jewish New Year), she invents her own metaphor for renewal and rebirth, while in "Shards" she speaks of death, mourning, and loss. "Refusing the Call" is dedicated to the novelist Henry Roth and explores his curious, nearly fifty-year silence.

From the Wailing Wall

It's an ordinary rock
without a single elegant edge,
a dolt of a rock
unlike the arrowheads
we've found in streams,
those nimbly chinked blades
that cleave the light
with one purpose.
This rock hoards shadows
in its pocked surface.
We place it next to our other books
as if it were the fossil
record of prayer,
an unsplit geode
with ancient words
glittering at its core.

Soon the bit of rubble rules
the house, paring all our goods
down to mannerisms, ploys.
It is the weed in the garden
of history, what must be swept
again and again from doorsills,
the part of the outside
that keeps wanting in.
It is the muscle of the land.
If there is another world
this is its scaffolding—
what comes to hand
from the hard earth
for building or throwing
under our blue
curfew, the sky.

Freestyle, on the First of Tishri

The metaphor here is the pool, regular
and deep as the tradition itself. First I float,
still and buoyant in what I don't
accept. Then I shatter the surface, a scholar
dissecting text not to destroy but to enrich,
a farmer plowing and disking the earth
before planting. On land, I forget breath's
noisy ball bearings, the flutter kick's
fringes blazing like tangible will. I imagine
that faith is nothing but a grudging promise
of repetition, like these laps, until this
continual splash in the mind begins—
not with grievance or prayer
but as gasp, a momentary bargain struck with the air.

Shards

Inside the strict pine coffin
he is wrapped
in a cotton sheet
and over the three vanities—
the eyes and mouth—
potsherds have been placed.
All night a vigilant Jew
sat by the body
while a candle ate
into the dark
and his feet grew rigid
pointing to Jerusalem.
Now we cover him

with tidewater clay.
To slow us down,
to remind us that grief
is a difficult labor, we dig
at first with shovels
turned over, a trickle
of red dirt fine
as hourglass sand.
Then we are permitted
grunting shovelfuls, stabs
that match the cries

of the mourners who watch
from unsteady chairs
as we spade respect
onto the *aron*,
Hebrew for coffin, for clothes closet,
wardrobe, chest of drawers,

that one word conveying
what we hope against:
that nothing can contain us,
that wood itself
is only soil haunting
the above-ground world,

ghosts in solid form.
It is right that burial
begin at the face
with earth baked
into something like a memory
of itself,
so that his humanness
can be taken away from us,
so we will not picture him
about to blink or speak,
so we may begin the leveling
with small rubble.

Refusing the Call

For Henry Roth, author of *Call It Sleep*

It's said you spoke once and then chose silence,
a waterfowl farm in Maine. Did the loft
of snow and feathers white out the violence
of the Lower East Side? The Maine coast sifts
light, explains horizons, while the city stirs
strange magic in a child: a patch of sun that creeps
between the tenements, the ruby flare
of rosary beads. Once you saw high voltage leap
between train tracks and feared it was the word
of God. He chose you, but you called it *sleep*.
In Maine, touched by their sameness, you killed the birds
yourself. I imagine you saw portents seep
from the runnels of bloody snow, that the cambered
blade felt heavy in your hand as slumber.

PART IV

A WORLD

ABOVE

SUFFERING

Philip Schultz (b. 1945)

Born in Rochester, New York, Philip Schultz, the author of *Like Wings* (1978) and *Deep Within the Ravine* (1984), frequently addresses Jewish concerns in his work. His father, a Russian immigrant who died when Schultz was eighteen, dominates many of his poems, as for instance, "For My Father." Other poems explore his Jewish upbringing, Israel, the immigrant experience, and contemporary American Jewish culture. Moreover, both Schultz's language and his particular combination of humor and despair are reminiscent of Yiddish literature. "For the Wandering Jews" and "The Bar Mitzvah" are typical of his successful blending of pathos, humor, and keen psychological insight. Schultz was educated at the University of Louisville, San Francisco State University, and the University of Iowa. He has taught poetry and creative writing at Kalamazoo College, the University of Massachusetts, and New York University.

For the Wandering Jews

This room is reserved for wandering Jews.
Around me, in other rooms, suitcases whine
like animals shut up for the night.

My guardian angel, Stein, fears sleeping twice
in the same bed. Constancy brings Cossacks in the dark, he thinks.
You don't explain fear to fear. Despair has no ears, but teeth.

In the next room I hear a woman's laughter
& press my hand to the wall. Car lights burn
my flesh to a glass transparency.

My father was born in Novo-Nikolayevka, Ekaterinoslav Guberniya.
Like him, I wear my forehead high, have quick eyes, a belly laugh.
Miles unfold in the palm of my hand.

Across some thousand back yards his stone
roots him to the earth like a stake. Alone in bed,
I feel his blood wander through my veins.

As a boy I would spend whole nights at the fair
running up the fun house's spinning barrel toward its magical top,
where I believed I would be beyond harm, at last.

How I would break my body to be free of it,
night after night, all summer long, this boy climbing
the sky's turning side, against all odds,

as though to be one with time,
going always somewhere where no one had been before,
my arms banging at my sides like wings.

The Bar Mitzvah

King for the night! the rabbi cried.
My pockets heavy with savings bonds, I stole kisses
from every woman old enough to recognize what was starting.
Oh we bunny-hopped round mountains of chopped liver
& sliced cakes big as Buffalo. Uncle Hy explained success:
Mexican Hat Dance with the best! Uncle Lou showed
his war wounds & Aunt Becky pulled me close: "A word
to the near-wise. Responsibility's the road to happiness.
Life's not all corn on the cob, darlink!" Later, I pulled
Susan into a back room. But she turned away. "We'd only
hate ourselves in the morning," she sighed. So I went
up to the roof & tightroped the ledge & threw up
my first whisky eight floors down onto Uncle Herb's new Buick.
Downstairs my father counted our loot in the empty hall
while my mother stared at her emerald gown as I whirled
an eighty-four-year-old girl between tables, her braids bouncing!
Round & round we went, the room swaying without stop.
Suddenly it was Russia in her eyes & everything about to begin.
Myself a man for the rest of my life!

For My Father

Samuel Schultz, 1903–1963

Spring we went into the heat of lilacs
& his black eyes got big as onions & his fat lower lip
hung like a bumper & he'd rub his chin's hard fur on my cheek
& tell stories: he first saw America from his father's arms
& his father said here he could have anything if he wanted it
with all his life & he boiled soap in his back yard & sold it door to
     door
& invented clothespins shaped like fingers & cigarette lighters
that played *Stars & Stripes* when the lid snapped open.

Mornings he lugged candy into factories
& his vending machines turned peanuts into pennies
my mother counted on the kitchen table & nights he came home
tripping on his laces & fell asleep over dinner & one night
he carried me outside & said only God knew what God had up His
     sleeve
& a man only knew what he wanted & he wanted a big white house
with a porch so high he could see all the way back to Russia
& the black moon turned on the axis of his eye & his breath
filled the red summer air with the whisky of first light.

The morning his heart stopped I borrowed money to bury him
& his eyes still look at me out of mirrors & I hear him kicking
the coalburner to life & can taste the peanut salt on his hands
& his advice on lifting heavy boxes helps with the books I lug town to
     town
& I still count thunder's distance in heartbeats as he taught me & one
     day
I watched the sun's great rose open over the ocean as I swayed on the
     bow
of the Staten Island Ferry & I was his father's age when he arrived

with one borrowed suit & such appetite for invention & the bridges
were mountains & the buildings gold & the sky lifted backward
like a dancer & her red hair fanning the horizon & my eyes burning
in a thousand windows & the whole Atlantic breaking at my feet.

Marcia Falk (b. 1946)

Widely known as a translator of biblical verse, Marcia Falk is herself an accomplished poet. She was born in New York City and was educated at Brandeis and Stanford universities. She has taught English and Hebrew at Stanford and the State University of New York at Binghamton, among other institutions. Her acclaimed translation of The Song of Songs was published in 1977. *The Book of Blessings: New Jewish Prayers for Daily Life, the Sabbath, and the New Moon Festival*, a compendium of blessings and prayers (in non-gender specific language), as well as original poems, appeared in 1996. The poems which follow are typical of Falk's own poetry, in which she combines her commitment to both Judaism and feminism. "Shulamit in Her Dreams" is based on the only female figure in The Song of Songs. "Sabbath Morning" presents a series of dreamlike images reminiscent of a Chagall painting, while the sadly evocative "Home for Winter" creates a more realistic picture of domestic love and longing.

Shulamit in Her Dreams

Day and night she dances,
between the suns
she dreams

By day she is the moon
turning
on the underside of earth

At night she is the windmill
waving
above the city walls

Dusk, she is
Shulamit

As she turns
the warriors chant her praises,
her thighs spin like jugs
on the potter's wheel,
her belly is round
with promise

Everywhere she moves
she captures
kings in the moats
of her eyes,
worlds in the locks
of her hair

Day and night she dances,
between the suns
she dreams

Home for Winter

Late Sabbath afternoon, remembering—
Father leaving through the snow for shul
to hear the final reading and the prayers,
mumbled cacophony in ten-part tune;
while here, Mama and I would sit and watch
the evening sky close down, unveil three stars
that marked the end to Shabbes. And between

the first three to appear and all the rest,
while Father, walking, bore the new week home
with spices in his pockets, light between
his fingers, sanctifying the mundane,
we knew a time suspended out of time,
not Shabbes, not yet week, and ours alone.

Then window turned to mirror by the night
would catch our eyes in accidental glance,
holding us there; and turning, she would ask
if I would spend the evening here at home.
Other things her eyes alone would ask:
Where would I be next winter? In whose home
and through what windows would I watch for stars?

Unspoken questions—how they echo through
the rooms of later weeks and later years,
for silence is a presence we still share,
and even under distant skies we trace
those same ascending paths of early stars.
Mama, if I knew—but you know better

where our stars gather, on what tangent curves
they bend their light, and where they congregate
in threes this Sabbath waiting, waiting for night.

Sabbath Morning

In the green and yellow grass of the broad field
fringed by greening trees,
leaves flapping,
birds talking and flapping,
a young girl disappears.
She lies down in her bright shirt
into the soft green grass
and disappears.

Later, the girl rises from her bed in the grass,
lifting her head above the white-topped stalks of clover.
She rises and walks off,
wading down into the field,
which waves around her like a lake—
so that soon she imagines she is sailing on a summer lake,
her body light as a sail in the fresh cold breeze.

All this is seen by the woman who sits on the roof.
She sits on the sun-warmed roof
and watches the tree-ringed field rock and sway
around the bobbing head of a girl wading through the weeds.

This is the picture the woman sees:
field, girl, bluejay, trees.
No matter what happens outside of this,
the girl will always be part of this.

Then, for a tiny instant,
the woman is weightless in the galaxy
which floats around her, blue and indifferent
and fierce as the sea.

Albert Goldbarth (b. 1948)

Born in Chicago, Illinois, Albert Goldbarth received his undergraduate education at the University of Illinois, Chicago Circle, and an M.F.A. degree from the University of Iowa. He is the author of more than a dozen volumes of poetry. While his early work tended to be experimental and surrealistic (*Opticks: A Poem in Seven Sections*, 1974), and his middle work somewhat philosophical and complex (*Original Light: New and Selected Poems 1973–1983*), his recent poetry is more personal, realistic, and narrative (*Across the Layers: Poems Old and New*, 1993; *The Gods*, 1993; and *Adventures in Ancient Egypt*, 1996), as well as more apt to explore the ramifications of his Jewish heritage. "Steerage," "Gallery," and "A World Above Suffering" imaginatively re-create the experiences of his immigrant grandparents, while "*Shoyn Fergéssin*: 'I've Forgotten' in Yiddish" recalls the tradition of Yiddish immigrant humor.

Gallery

When my grandfather stepped from the boat
they gave him a choice of paintings to enter. "This one,"
he said by a nod of his head. Why not?—for weeks
in the bodystink quarters of steerage,
the lice had run as freely as milk through his crevices,
and the only food was saltbread softened in engine water,
but here, in *The Boating Party* by Renoir, it's spring,
the light is floral, even cloth and skin
are really petals in this light, the glass
the wine is in is alive in this light, the men are easy
in speaking with women (he noticed, oh especially,
the women), their mutual fascination is another flower
filling the air, and the clusters of fruits
looked as shining to him as an orchestra's brass section
—when he peeked around the corner of the painting, in fact,
he saw a grouse was simmering in peppered cream
and that settled it, he sat down at a nearby table,
listening to the bright and empty talk, his shy eyes
staring at his waiting plate. A server appeared
and left. On my grandfather's plate was a boiled potato,
only that. But he was starving, so he ate it. He ate it
indelicately, with an almost sexual fervor, and then
looked up to see the family around him,
with their corded hands, with their faces like worn-out shoes,
were eating theirs, just that, with a root tea. He
was in Van Gogh's *The Potato Eaters*. The room
was as dark as the tea. Outside, the wind was a punishing switch.
The talk was hushed and raw and familiar,
he was at home here, he was at home in the broken
light of the hanging oil lamp. When the meal was done,
he stepped out into the lane, he breathed the country dark in
hungrily, then walked. He needed a wife.

He needed a future. What did he see ahead,
when he squinted? He would barely understand
that man in Edward Hopper's *Nighthawks*,
on a distant corner, some depleted 3 A.M.,
was his son—who slides the dime for his java
over the counter, slants his hat, then heads out into streetlight
from the diner's unrelenting angles and planes.
He's lonely. It's 1942. He'd love to meet my mother,
someone humming a hot little tune
and pretty as a picture.

Steerage

. . . inferior below-decks accommodations on a ship: by extension, the whole of a certain kind of immigration as the poor experienced it

By now, the satchel's leather has reclaimed its living redolence,
it riles at the hasp, and reaching inside it is entering
up past the wrist in the vault of an animal body. Here

they are, in the various tea and fecal colors
of early photography: my grandparents, carrying everything
Europe crammed in a single bag. This

bag. Clumsily held on his shoulder, like a hod, perhaps
to ease an earlier posture. Waiting. One of the first of the lines,
I think—the oily air of the ship's pit still on their faces: it

may be the only thing reproduced here in the original hue.
So now this satchel has its miniature replica floating inside
its belly: a strange idea, vaguely canopic,

soul-like, or homuncular—eldritch, at least. They're
eldritch too, on the dock in their Cracow woolens: little
people, 3, 4 inches, yes, look: I can hold them in my palm

like in the stories. The wee folk. The thumblings. Everywhere,
these old ones, the root ones, have their stories, and
gain strength as the dusk along the woods duff deepens:

menehunes, filing through gates of Hawaiian guava, mango,
for a moment their eyes like budding fruit
the moon lights in the lavish branches; brownies,

kaukases, domovniks, pukys (our Puck) . . . the global
elvish, faces fresh as a thimble-diameter of cream
or puckered like overbathed toes. The nisse, the deive,

the forthright English sprite . . . with their credos,
their language, and their acorn-color aprons or radiant
cobweb negligees . . . every night, through the portals, from their

great ancientdom, into the settlements we've made
the planet's governing order. Darkness
is their steerage; and in it they enter that order,

comprehending or not, however best they can. We
all do. I remember (I was maybe 5, I barely came up
to the bathroom doorknob) tumult over my father's

failed attempts at happily sorting family business
in the files of City Hall. Some long, grandparently
problem, I guess now: rights to property, or citizenship,

who knows? I watched the man who fed me,
flung me, beat the neighbor hound away, walk
dwindling into a building the size of an ocean liner and

walk out hours later looking simply used up. Because
we're little—people born into a giant's land
of bureaucratic backrooms and, beyond it, the universe

stacking matter and antimatter—we have these secret
handshakes, satchels of family heirlooms, private songs . . .
whatever it takes to personalize and console. He

was shaving. I stood by the bathroom door and watched
him suds the mug, then tauten the grain of his neck.
He didn't know I was there. He whistled,

that tune *his* father whistled. Maybe it made the whole damn
day wash away. I think I could whistle it too, a goofy
old world melody—by which we mean there are some of us who

have heard a music that's not of this world.

Shoyn Fergéssin: *"I've Forgotten" in Yiddish*

But now it's the Yiddish itself I'm forgetting;
it's back on the wharf, in a grimed-over jar
we can barely see into. What's this: is it a cameo brooch,
the bride's profile eaten-at by pickle-brine; or
is it a slice of radish? This is a tooth,
yes? We can turn that jar in the sun all day and
not be able to read it. There's a label, with a name
in black script dancing just beyond arm's reach.

* * *

A woman is weeping. what did he *do*? he asks
the noncommittal stars, the dark and rhythmic water,
even the slimy pilings. This is a wharf,
in summer. He tells her a joke, not that
it does much good. This is my grandfather,
Louie (in English). This is my grandmother, *Rosie*.
1912. They're in each other's arms again by morning
and don't need to say a word.

* * *

We'll find them, like ancient coins or arrowheads.
Now they can only be approximate. Here, washed up
on the beach: a few maxims, song titles, even that joke.
It goes: " 'You're a Jew, how come you have a name
like Sean Ferguson?' He says, 'I was so frightened
when we landed at Ellis Island that I couldn't remember
anything for a minute. So that's what I said. They asked me
my name and I said *I've forgotten.*' "

A World Above Suffering

1

When my grandfather Louie came here, from Chicago,
his phlegm was already marbled with blood.
So here he stayed for a year, in the flat
and unclogged light of the mountains,
and here he healed. He stayed on one year more,
a kind of payment, he helped with the gurneys and the pans,
in Denver, in 1906,
at the Jewish Sanitarium for Consumptives.

2

Even near the giant windows, the air in the ward seemed brown
with institutional viscosity. Outside, though,
on the balconies designed to accommodate hospital beds,
the patients were lined up side-by-side like tiles in a game,
white tiles in sunlight.
                    In the left bed,
Morris Rosenfeld, the "sweatshop poet,"
"the voice of the people," coughing up the bunched threads
of his 15-hour days bent to the hemming machines or the irons
". . . until I was a machine as well," he says, then starts
some quavering lines from one of his poems
of raw-throated grief and indictment.
                    In the bed on the right,
Yehoash (Solomon Bloomgarden), whom they called
"the Jewish Byron"—translator ("Hiawatha,"
even the Koran), lexicographer, diarist, and aspirant
to the gates of the lofty, "singingness" he termed it, and
he cultivated an Orientalist's interest
in the music of Chinese poetry, its willow and plum.

             *   *   *

My grandfather tended to both of their enfeeblements,
the spit-cups and the soiled strips. In the afternoon light
of the balcony, which seemed to hit the three of them uninfluenced
by a single touch of the Earth, he'd listen bemusedly
to their conflicting Yiddish.

3

Today they're reading new poems to each other.
"And this time, Mr. Shakespeares," says the nurse,
then wags her finger, "NO EXCITEMENTS! Louie,
see they shouldn't get heated." Last time, both of them
waxed apoplectic in righteous aesthetic wrath.
"Hokay now," Rosenfeld clears his throat
                                        and
we're back in an attic firetrap shirtwaist work pit,
tethered there by hunger to an 84-hour week, in the heat
that clambers on your naked shoulders pickaback,
in the piles of scrap and mouse-filth past your ankles,
in the insufficient gaslamp, eye wobble, wrist fatigue,
the stitch in the hem and its sister stitch
the razor-edged worm in your side. For this,
twelve dollars a week. For this, with twenty people breathing
thickly in a windowless room, the gaslamp trickling fumes,
the bucket toilet radiating waves of human waste in a corner.
Some of these workers are twelve years old, some in their seventies.
Rosenfeld soars in exhortation, then squinches his spirit down low
in hurt or self-pity, then takes off soaring
explosively again. "The time clock drags me off at dawn
to the corner of Pain and Anguish . . ."
                                        And Yehoash
is moved by this, and by the rocks and birds
his balconymate makes alternately with his gesturing hand.
It would be unfair, saying anything else; Yehoash
is moved, his eyes grow damply alive. But also
his work could be, as Irving Howe would later phrase it,
"willfully distant from any Jewish experience." This
afternoon, he reads lines modeled loosely on
"The Song of Picking Mulberry," "Song of Plucking Cassia,"

"A Fish Trapping Song," "The Cowherd's Song," and
"Song of the Woman Weaving," where, if there's complaint
(". . . the levy of the silk tax comes too early this year . . ."),
labor isn't pain so much
as cause for meditation, under the great, gong Chinese moon,
and weariness isn't more than mist
a white crane sculls obliquely through. He reads
about the Empress Yang-Tse-Fu, and in the Denver air
appear her hundred golden doors, her sapphire-sided palanquin
and honor guard. "And the cherry blossoms
settle on the shore," he ends.
So of course
in a moment they're squabbling, and their normally pale,
whey-blue faces ruddy the color of brick. "Boys!
BOYS!"—the nurse can see it from out on the lawn,
and yells up: "Louie, DO something!" And
my grandfather stands between them,
in their utterly befuddling adjacence, holding out
—ineffectually, for no particular reason
other than chance—a length of bandage gauze: something
like an ancient Egyptian attendant
whose mummies refuse to hold still.

4

That night, my grandfather dreamed.
He was back in Chicago, following
the stink of the tenement twistways.
Here was the cart of herring piled like ingots,
just as he remembered: wavering
in their day's-end aurora . . . Here,
the rubbish mound to the height of a three-floor warehouse
with, as usual, some street kids sledding on greased planks
down its wormy length . . . Everything was real,
more than real. At one corner he saw a woman,
above, in a sixth-floor window, naked from the waist up.
It was an ironing sweatshop—the heat was too much.
Her breasts were small, but drooped with appalling weight
to the six floors of gravity. She was retching. "I don't CARE!

I need the air from the roof!"—then she disappeared from the
window.
Now, in the dream, he saw her sitting at the roof-edge
as the rim of the city turned the burning tulip colors of sunset.
It was cooler here; her breast-flesh pebbled slightly in the air.
The moon came out, the whole of a wheel-of-cheddar moon. She
started singing, it was "The Song of the Hemmer and Ironer":
Near dawn the pigeons stitch the sidewalks.
Later, at noon, the streets of my city are ironed
By the August sun.
Mother, a life is harsh but also beautiful.
Father, the rhythm of the piecework is a red thread
In my wrist. At night I want to unfasten this immense
Bone button in the sky, and see what's on
The other side of the night, if work is required there too.
Let the ladies of the court play their flutes
And peek at the day from behind their fans.
I'm going down into the streets, I'm going
To dance stitch-stitch in the gutters!

* * *

Then he woke. "China,"
he thought—and he would always picture this roof—
"a world above suffering."

* * *

He woke, he washed, he walked into another shift
of pads and ointments. Everything
was ahead of him still. He, who believed so much
was behind already, in merely his getting here . . .
everything was ahead of him still. The caged-up days
in the elevator, wearing the liver-colored-and-gold-braid
organ grinder's monkey outfit, whisking the buyers
of silk kimonos and homburgs to their appropriate floors . . .
the fish store, and the failure of the fish store, and
the dented awl for chipping the pike from its jacketing ice . . .
and Rosie, meeting Rosie, wooing Rosie in the candle-lit dinge,
and sticking with Rosie, over whatever

decades of sexual ardor, scrimping, and piety made their life then . . .
all of it waited for him, in him, was a seed
inside my grandfather as he lathered his hands, then
wheeled his charges into the immediate sun.
Both Rosenfeld and Yehoash would be cured, and off
to their individual destinies. But that would be long after
Louie packed his satchel and took the train away
from the mountain of poems and wetly rumbling lungs.
Enough was enough.

5

Years later, back in Chicago now, he wandered
into Chinatown. Not the tourist version; the actual
squat-in-a-corner thing. He recognized
the ghetto poverty, the open ghetto
furnace of a heart—although the milky smoke
unwinding from the joss sticks wasn't his,
nor the amazing hothouse orchid-like fish
in pails on the peddler carts. A man named Lee Hsün
stopped him, he was so obviously lost.
"Fella, where you from?" He meant
what neighborhood, but my grandfather answered
"From Poland."
                    "Ah—Poland!" And Lee's eyes
widen in admiration.
"Poland! Princesses! Palaces!"

Mark Rudman (b. 1948)

Mark Rudman is the author of more than a dozen books, including poetry, criticism, essays, and translations. *Rider* (1994), from which the selection included here is taken, received the National Book Critics Circle Award. It is an unusual volume: a book-length poem that recreates the author's relationship with his stepfather—a circuit-riding Rabbi in the West. Its form is unconventional as well, consisting of a combination of dialogue, conversational prose, and lyrical verse. It is by turns ironic, funny, elegiac, and sad. Part 5, reprinted here, is a mock-serious dialogue, recounting one of Rudman's formative experiences as a young boy. In addition to *Rider*, Rudman's other volumes of poetry include *By Contraries and Other Poems, 1970–84* (1986), *The Nowhere Steps* (1990), and *The Millennium Hotel* (1996). He was born in New York City, educated at the New School for Social Research and Columbia University, and currently teaches in the writing programs at Columbia and New York University.

Rider

5

What about that girl in first grade? The one who hopped up on her desk
when you walked in the room and exclaimed, "Oh goody, a boy!"

You preferred to play with girls
only you didn't know it then.

One of the girls and a seducer of girls.

Between jump rope and guns I chose guns.

Now I see the low desks and windows
and the radiators lined up along the sills—

You are torn at every moment in time, aren't you?

Nearly.

When will you rest?

*   *   *

You did or didn't play with her?

No. Instead I entered a macho battle
with a boy named Otto Blank. He was the
soi disant leader of the pack and would not
let me play "Wyatt Earp" unless I paid
him a nickel, so I made this wager
with myself that I would swallow my pride
this once to get the hazing over with.

But the next day, when he wanted more, you flew at his throat—

415

and each day, in the half-hour or so after school
in which we waited for
    someone to retrieve us,
we fought, Otto and I—

and he nearly always pinned you down.

But he was two years older, a leap-year birth,
and how well I remembered his second, i.e.,
eighth birthday—

you had to say it—Otto is two!

The class cracked up. He started after me—

And the teacher yelled—

Otto! Sit down right now!

The class tittered.

*Only ten years after the war and the Germans and the Jews were at it
again.*

Huh?

*You don't think Otto knew your stepfather was the local Rabbi? You
don't think he heard anything at home to provoke his . . . animosity.*

No, I don't.

That's why you're you.

But our quarrel started in the first recess after I arrived.

*You arrived in spring. The first grade class had been together all year.
And you, confess, wanted to be Wyatt.*

What happened to the struggle for racial supremacy?

He identified you as a Jew, walking in the door and wanting to take over, to improve the playing conditions at recess.

I thought the role of Wyatt should rotate.

Uh huh.

A little candor here wouldn't hurt; I can see what you're insinuating: out with it! No, don't impeach yourself with the question.

What, you think I don't know that if anyone in the world could have known that Wyatt Earp was Jewish that Sidney would have known? Or how quickly this sort of discovery moves through Rabbinical circuits? The sermons you could milk out of the material . . . ?

Imagine America switching on its television sets in light of the idea that Wyatt Earp—whose cover as a *noirish* hero in expressionist westerns was now blown open by this weekly program "with Hugh O'Brien in the role of Wyatt"—had been a Jew in "real life". . . .

So—another experience undergone in the dark of ignorance. Human ways mystify me. I can see no bottom. If things are the way they are because they are that way, I am driven to embrace chance: as an antidote— at the very least a palliative—against unreason. If things are the way they are for no reason than because they are that way, then nothing is determined. . . .

And the first time I got the best of Otto,
    the very second I had him pinned,
my mother (how did she get there, she didn't drive?)
    arrived at the playground and said,
"Come on, dear, we have to go,"
    and I YELLED—

"in a minute, Mom, I've got Otto
    PINNED—"
        and she—
"No— NOW —"

She didn't know what you'd been going through?

She was unaware, to be frank,
    of the darkness in my soul,
    of the heaviness of the burden I carried,

and carried,
        with no clue as to why—
unaware of the inner resistance I had to overcome
    to be among others
        and not break down,
of the effort it cost me   to live—a day—

No, the woman whose daily fare
is a wish she'd never been born?

Well . . . she's more stoical and more
easily distracted by the idea
that baubles heal; she successfully transferred

her anguish onto objects and their absence—

The jury is out on that one.

Rodger Kamenetz (b. 1950)

Born in Baltimore, Maryland, Rodger Kamenetz was educated at Yale, Johns Hopkins, and Stanford universities. He has published several collections of poems and essays, including *The Missing Jew: New and Selected Poems* (1992), a poetic investigation of Jewish tradition and identity. In that volume, Kamenetz creatively blends disparate aspects of the Jewish experience: family story and ancient history, comic and tragic events, the sacred and the profane. Many of the poems are ironic commentaries on religious or mystical Jewish texts, rendered in distinctly Jewish rhythms and speech patterns ("Why Ten Men?" for example). Others, like "History of the Invisible," encompass the many ramifications of the "huge and murky" history of the Jewish people, as does "This Is the Map," which juxtaposes various languages to illustrate the long and eclectic history of anti-Semitism. "The Missing Jew" is dedicated to the writer Louis Daniel Brodsky and addresses the ambiguities and ironies of Jewish religious observance. Kamenetz teaches English and creative writing at Louisiana State University in Baton Rouge.

History of the Invisible

I

The invisible is stronger than the visible.
The desert subtracted so many objects
there was nothing left but the wind.
Like all good ideas, God was stolen.
The Jews being superior thieves
removed all the markings.

The history of my family is
the history of breezes.
And the exodus, the getaway:
my grandfathers, one carrying
a barber pole, the other
a tailor's needle.

II

Jews do not come from heaven
they come from Russia.
With green eyes and olive skin.
Jews do not go to heaven
they go to Baltimore.

They do not come from heaven
because heaven is always
in the back of their minds.
They don't want to think about
heaven any more
it's too much trouble.

III

God was stolen by the Jews
from an old Egyptian. My grandfather
with his sack on his back

carried God in steerage to America.
In the beards of rebbes
in loaves of challa
God was smuggled
into America.

But when they assembled the pieces
there wasn't enough
God in America
to fill the empty spaces:
too much desert
too many opportunities.
The Jews went about their business
because they forgot God was
looking, and they dropped
the pieces all over the place
a little here, a little there
the sweepers have too much
work to do, there are
only a few sweepers and they stand
with their brooms
looking for God in the dust.

IV

The dead are with you when you try
to write history—it cheers them up.
Most of time is so gloomy and slow
but in history time moves with a lilt.
My grandfather on his boat to
America stood on the deck to
get some fresh air. A sailor
knocked him on the head with a bat
and stole his sack. There was
nothing inside it but rags.

V

The Jews' history was huge and murky
no room for it anywhere in Europe.
If only the Jews could inherit Texas
it might be big enough to hold their past.

The Jews who went out West
wore cowboy hats
like Cousin Dan from Oklahoma
who showed up
at my grandfather's funeral
by uncanny instinct
in his cowboy hat and boots
and just sat in the living room
while we stared.

It is amazing how the land
will transform a man's face:
Cousin Dan looked part Cherokee
part fat cat oilman
(he sold buttons).
And he spoke with a twang,
the yarmulke kept falling off
his ten gallon head,
only a cowboy hat
would fit.

VI

Being Jewish is magnetic.
A polarity points us
in the same direction
just as all synagogues
have a praying wall facing east.
So that around a Jew, even if
he doesn't know he's a Jew,
there's a disturbance in the air,
something has cut across
his spiritual field,

someone is interfering
with the regular broadcast
to insert a special message.

Because what 5000 years
would sound like is
a lot of Jews killed
for no particular reason
over and over
in an insistent rhythm
that beats under ordinary time
sending shocks everywhere.
Any time a metaphor
gets out of hand
more Jews are killed
to restore the general complacency.

Why Ten Men?

Why ten men?
So there will be a minyan, said Reb Abram.

Ten commandments, said Reb Basho
a man to obey each one.

Ten fingers, said Reb Basho ben Basho
to point in ten directions.

To make two fists, said Reb Basho his grandson.

Ten footstools, said Reb Carlo.

Ten cocktail waitresses, said Reb Devo.

Ten doorways, said Reb Ephraim.

Ten disagreements, ten scourges
said ten rabbis all together.

So the souls would be gathered in one skein
and form a knot to grab a world by.

This all agreed on.

The Missing Jew

For Louis Daniel Brodsky

In the heart of the heart
we have searched for him.
Everywhere we shine a light
the missing Jew wears
a tallis of shadows.
He quotes elliptical scripture
knows syllables missing from Torah.

But where is the missing Jew?
He disobeys every law
he violates every precept
he has memorized them
so he will know exactly
how to avoid them.

We search for him, raising
the dust in which he hides.
He loves it, he laughs.
If we knock on his door
he whispers a stubborn
commandment and we flinch.

The missing Jew has opened a store
sells milk and meat, pork and oysters
carefully obeys the laws of the land.
He owns what he knows.
How can we find him?

The missing Jew is faster than history
he disobeys the laws of time
he interprets himself into the present
hides himself in an explanation.

He scrapes Torah from his palate
rabbis mingle their voices in his
his blood quotes pilpul
in the veins of his neck
his penis wears a yarmulke of sweat
his thighbone full of midrash
yet his feet never know
which path to take.

The Hebrew letters
swing violent arms
their sharp black legs
scythe the air
spelling his hidden name.

This Is the Map

Judenrein.
Jew free.
Pas de juifs.
Defense de juifer.
No Jews allowed.
No dogs or Jews.
This word Jew
an insult in itself.

Get used to the sound:
Jaws work up and down
saying Jew.

The word Jew, from Judah
hence Judaism, in German
juden, yiddish, yid
juif, en anglais:

I am a Jew.
You are a Jew.
He, she, it is a Jew.

It is a Jew.
Watch it walk.
Welcome, Jew!
That sounds strange.
Welcome to our land.
Our land.

Edward Hirsch (b. 1950)

Edward Hirsch is the author of five collections of poetry, including *Wild Gratitude* (1986), *The Night Parade* (1989), and *Earthly Measures* (1994). He was born in Chicago, Illinois, attended Grinnell College, and earned a doctorate from the University of Pennsylvania. Since 1982, he has taught creative writing at the University of Houston. Hirsch's poems frequently emphasize his Jewish roots: sometimes through minor references, often through retelling of family history or of his early years in Chicago, and occasionally through dramatization of the history of Jewish suffering. In "Ancient Signs" Hirsch creates a memorable image of his grandfather and his early life in Latvia; in "My Grandfather's Poems," he remembers and identifies with his grandfather's "lost, unhappy" Yiddish language poems. In "Paul Celan: A Grave and Mysterious Sentence," the poet exhibits a different sort of collective memory, as well as a personal identification with the poet Celan.

Ancient Signs

In memory of Oscar Ginsburg, 1894–1958

He loved statues with broken noses,
  the flaking white bodies of birches
after disease had set in,
    the memory of peasants
    kneeling at garish, hand-carved altars.

He loved old women washing laundry
  by the river, coolly slapping the
bedsheets senseless on the stones.
    It was sixty years later
    and yet he still couldn't forget them.

And he was still ashamed of the damp
  bodies of men's shirts filling the wind,
flapping about like chickens
    at the signs of hard weather.
    Only a woman's hands could calm them.

My grandfather loved thunderstorms.
  He loved to see the restless weaving
of trees and all the small shrubs
    kneeling down like penitents.
    As a child, in southern Latvia,

he used to run through the streets shouting
  while the ominous clouds moved slowly
across the dark horizon
    like a large foreign army
    coming to liberate the village.

My grandfather used to stand calmly
  by the open window during storms.

He said that he could see lightning
        searching the empty rooftops,
    rifling the windows for his body.

    He said that rain is an ancient sign
    of the sky's sadness. And he said
that he could feel the wind trying
        to lift him into its arms,
        trying to carry him home again.

Paul Celan: A Grave and Mysterious Sentence

Paris, 1948

It's daybreak and I wish I could believe
In a rain that will wash away the morning
That is just about to rise behind the smokestacks
On the other side of the river, other side
Of nightfall. I wish I could forget the slab
Of darkness that always fails, the memories
That flood through the window in a murky light.

But now it is too late. Already the day
Is a bowl of thick smoke filling up the sky
And swallowing the river, covering the buildings
With a sickly, yellow film of sperm and milk.
Soon the streets will be awash with little bright
Patches of oblivion on their way to school,
Dark briefcases of oblivion on their way to work.

Soon my small apartment will be white and solemn
Like a blank page held up to a blank wall,
A message whispered into a vacant closet. But
This is a message which no one else remembers
Because it is stark and German, like the silence,
Like the white fire of daybreak that is burning
Inside my throat. If only I could stamp it out!

But think of smoke and ashes. An ominous string
Of railway cars scrawled with a dull pencil
Across the horizon at dawn. A girl in pigtails
Saying, "Soon you are going to be erased."
Imagine thrusting your head into a well
And crying for help in the wrong language,
Or a deaf mute shouting into an empty field.

So don't talk to me about flowers, those blind
Faces of the dead thrust up out of the ground
In bright purples and blues, oranges and reds.
And don't talk to me about the gold leaves
Which the trees are shedding like an extra skin:
They are handkerchiefs pressed over the mouths
Of the dead to keep them quiet. It's true:

Once I believed in a house asleep, a childhood
Asleep. Once I believed in a mother dreaming
About a pair of giant iron wings growing
Painfully out of the shoulders of the roof
And lifting us into away-from-here-and-beyond.
Once I even believed in a father calling out
In the dark, restless and untransfigured.

But what did we know then about the smoke
That was already beginning to pulse from trains,
To char our foreheads, to transform their bodies
Into two ghosts billowing from a huge oven?
What did we know about a single gray strand
Of barbed wire knotted slowly and tightly
Around their necks? We didn't know anything then.

And now here is a grave and mysterious sentence
Finally written down, carried out long ago:
At last I have discovered that the darkness
Is a solitary night train carrying my parents
Across a field of dead stumps and wildflowers
Before disappearing on the far horizon,
Leaving nothing much in its earthly wake

But a stranger standing at the window
Suddenly trying to forget his childhood,
To forget a black trail of smoke
Slowly unraveling in the distance
Like the victory-flag of death, to forget
The slate clarity of another day
Forever breaking behind the smokestacks.

My Grandfather's Poems

I remember that he wrote them backwards,
In Yiddish, in tiny, slanting, bird-like lines
That seemed to rise and climb off the page
In a flurry of winged letters, mysterious signs.

Scrupulously he copied them out
On the inside covers of his favorite books
While my sister and I romped through the house
Acting like cops and robbers, cowboys and crooks,

Whooping, shouting, and gunning each other down
In the hallway between rooms, mimicking fright,
Staggering from wall to bloody wall before
Collapsing in wild giggles at his feet.

Always he managed to quiet us again,
Kissing us each on the upper part of the arm,
Tucking us in. . . . We never said prayers,
But later I could hear him in the next room

Talking to himself in a low, tearing whisper—
All I could fathom was a haunted sound
Like a rushing of waves in the distance,
Or the whoosh of treetops in the back yard.

For years I feel asleep to the rhythm
Of my grandfather's voice rising and falling,
Filling my head with his lost, unhappy poems:
Those faint wingbeats, that hushed singing.

Robin Becker (b. 1951)

Born in Philadelphia, Pennsylvania, and educated at Boston University, Robin Becker is the author of four collections of poetry. Both Becker's parents were children of Russian Jewish immigrants, and Yiddish—as well as English—was spoken by her family as she was growing up. Becker's poetry is influenced by her family history (especially the suicide of her sister), her Jewish background, and her lesbian-feminist orientation. Although emotional and expressive, her poems are rarely self-indulgent. Becker often employs references to Jewish history, ritual, or her Yiddish-speaking grandmother as metaphors for her present life and as a means of unlocking her own sense of isolation. Although her allusions to Jewishness in both "Spiritual Morning" and "Yom Kippur, Taos, New Mexico" are brief, they are essential to understanding the speaker's emotional state. The title of "The Crypto-Jews" refers to medieval Spanish and Portuguese Jews who, while publicly converting to Catholicism, secretly remained faithful to Judaism. Becker teaches in the writing program at Pennsylvania State University.

Grief

It is the kindness of the rabbi I remember now, nine months
after my sister's death. After the funeral, he took me aside
and said, *Call me when your lover arrives: we'll meet at the cemetery
and hold our own service.* The next day we buried her again.

Then it was summer, and I stood, a Jew among the Catholics
of Florence, dropping my lire into the tin box
with the mourners in Santa Maria Novella. My lover watched,
estranged, and I could not explain why I needed to leave the bright

piazzas, climb the steep steps to San Miniato al Monte and walk
beside the dim paintings, down the long naves, past the spectacular
tombs, to light candle after candle in Santo Spirito, Santa Maria
del Carmine, Santa Croce. I paused on a bridge over the Arno

and considered the way Italy resembled a vast cemetery,
generations buried beneath the marble floors of every church.
Like an island in the Venetian Lagoon, her life was
a place I visited by boat, changed each time I arrived on shore.

Now I dream her face, the color of a Bellini masterpiece,
painted when he was old and saw his dead against the dawn
light, blameless, cold. Already the grieving gather the candles
and clothing they need for the seasons of mourning, naming

themselves lover, mother, father, friend, brother, sister.

The Crypto-Jews

This summer, reading the history of the Jews of Spain,
I learned Fra Alfonso listed "holding philosophical discussions"
as a Jewish crime. I think of the loud fights
between me and my father when he would scream that only a Jew
could love another Jew. I love the sad proud history
of expulsion and wandering, the Moorish synagogue walled
in the Venetian ghetto, persistence of study and text.
If we are the old Christ-killers on the handles of walking sticks,
we've walked the earth as calves, owls, and scorpions.
In New Mexico, the descendants of Spanish *conversos* come forth
to confess: tombstones in the yard carved with Stars of David,
no milk with meat, generations raised without pork.
What could it mean, this Hebrew script,
in grandmother's Catholic hand? Oh, New World, we drift
from eviction to eviction, go underground,
emerge in a bark on a canal, minister to kings, adapt to extreme
weather, peddle our goods and die into the future.

Spiritual Morning

I am as virtuous as a rabbinical student
after my morning run, God in the body awake, God
of the May apple and wild ginger. Even the little
stiff hands of the whistle pig reach
toward me in death's perfection. Once,
in Katmandu at dawn, I watched a monk in a saffron robe
brush his teeth on the roof of a temple and spit—
and from his mouth flew peach and azure birds
fluttering in the milky sweetness of the air.

This morning of Pennsylvania
woodchuck and wild geranium, I grasp the
connection among all sentient beings and feel
communion with the wretched of all species and the dead.
The orange swallowtail looping overhead, for example,
is really my old grandmother, back to remind me
to learn Yiddish, the only international language.
I'd like her to sit on my finger
so we could talk face-to-face, but she flies
out of sight, shouting, *Big talker! Don't run on busy streets!*

Yom Kippur, Taos, New Mexico

I've expanded like the swollen door in summer
        to fit my own dimensions. Your loneliness

is a letter I read and put away, a daily reminder
        in the cry of the magpie that I am

still capable of inflicting pain
        at this distance.

Like a painting, our talk is dense with description,
        half-truths, landscapes, phrases layered

with a patina over time. When she came into my life
        I didn't hesitate.

Or is that only how it seems now, looking back?
        Or is that only how you accuse me, looking back?

Long ago, this desert was an inland sea. In the mountains
        you can still find shells.

It's these strange divagations I've come to love: midday sun
        on pink escarpments; dusk on gray sandstone;

toe-and-finger holes along the three hundred and fifty-seven foot
        climb to Acoma Pueblo, where the spirit

of the dead hovers about its earthly home
        four days, before the prayer sticks drive it away.

Today all good Jews collect their crimes like old clothes
        to be washed and given to the poor.

I remember how my father held his father around the shoulders
    as they walked to the old synagogue in Philadelphia.

"We're almost there, Pop," he said. "A few more blocks."
    I want to tell you that we, too, are almost there,

for someone has mapped this autumn field with meaning, and any day
    October, brooding in me, will open to reveal

our names—inscribed or absent—
    among the dry thistles and spent weeds.

Alan Shapiro (b. 1952)

Alan Shapiro is the author of five books of poetry, including *Happy Hour* (1987), *Covenant* (1991), and *Mixed Company* (1996). Shapiro writes in a plain, almost conversational style, which is especially well suited for his poems that explore personal experience and such themes as religious and familial continuity within a secular, contemporary culture. Many of his poems are written in the first person and recall autobiographical detail in order to examine the emotional and psychological undercurrents of each situation. In "On the Eve of the Warsaw Uprising," which is only indirectly about the Warsaw uprising, Shapiro remembers an early, family Passover seder. Both "Mezuzah" and "A Christmas Story" are personal narratives that function as religious allegories. Similarly, "The Basement" employs a particularly memorable figure from the poet's youth as a guidepost for understanding Jewish identity and one's relationship to recent Jewish history. Shapiro was born in Boston, Massachusetts, and educated at Brandeis University. He is professor of English and creative writing at the University of North Carolina at Greensboro.

On the Eve of the Warsaw Uprising

At the end of the Passover service, a cup of wine is set aside for the prophet Elijah. The messenger of God, he is appointed to herald the era of the messiah.

Elijah come in glorious state
For thy glad tidings long we wait.
Ah me, ah me, when cometh he?
Hush! In good time cometh he.

My uncle said, "This is Elijah's wine."
Till then I mimicked listening, wide-eyed
with piety, while underneath the table
I kicked my brother back for kicking me.
The bitter herbs and the unleavened bread
that my uncle said were meant to make me feel
the brick and mortar, and the hurrying
between the walls of water that wind held back—
to me meant only an eternity
of waiting while he prayed, before a meal.

But when that wine was poured, the door left open,
waiting seemed almost holy: a worshipper,
the candle flame bowed in the sudden draft.
And for a moment I thought I'd behold
Elijah's glad lips bend out of the dark
to brighten and drink up into His Light
the Red Sea in the glass
      that never parted.
For soon my uncle closed the door when we
grew cold, and the flame straightened. "Where was Elijah?"
Nobody in the room had ever asked.

And now I think, knowing what I know,
if anyone had ever come to us,
he could have come only to keep watch
and not to drink; to look upon the glass,

seeing within the wine, as from across
the whole of night, the small flame still as God;
someone who would have known the numberless
doors that have been opened, to be closed;
the numberless who watched till they became
the shimmer in the wine he looked upon.

Mezuzah

A small case containing a parchment scroll on which a portion of Deuter-
onomy is written, attesting to God's everlasting love. It is said whoever breaks
open the Mezuzah and removes the sacred scroll will incur God's everlast-
ing retribution.

Though unable to imagine
how harm could fit in there,
in that tiny case,
I thought I knew enough
to stay afraid.
                    But once,
moving through the quiet house,
I thought, if I can't hear
my own steps, how can God?
And in the laundry room,
by the dryer humming out its heat,
the thick air,
itself, a kind of linen
covering me, unseen,
unnoticed, I knelt down,
and all I was supposed to fear
I crushed
              with my mother's iron.
The little parchment, speckled
with marks too small to read,
fell out . . .
              and nothing happened:
only the washer jerked
into its spin, and made me wait
a little longer
for my blood to turn to salt,
for my hands to wither,
                              for pain.
But nothing happened.
                              And later,

playing with my friends, I knew
there was no mark of Cain
upon my forehead, no
lightning come to split me
like a tree.
        Only something else,
from then on,
wouldn't go away, kept me
up late at night, damaging
my prayers, till even they no longer tamed
the dark
world of my room:
I knew God's wrath, all right,
His retribution coiled,
forever,
in my questioning.

A Christmas Story

And the Lord said to Moses, "When you go back to Egypt, see that you do
before Pharaoh all the miracles which I have put in your power; but I will
harden his heart, so that he will not let the people go."

—EXODUS 4:21

It wasn't only envy but also a vague desire
to make amends, to glorify the baby Jesus
with my friend Charlie (who said the Jews had killed him)

that made me sneak into my parents' bedroom
Christmas morning before anyone was awake
to phone Charlie about all the presents

I hadn't received, the tree we didn't have.
Quietly as Santa (whom we must have also killed)
I took the phone down from my father's bedside table

and slipped under the bed into the cramped dark
of springs all intricately crossed and swollen
against me where my father slept. A long time

I lay there cradling the phone; I dialed
when either parent shifted or snored, afraid
that they somehow would answer at the other end;

or hear Charlie's father yelling "Charlie make it quick"
and the forbidden prayer I whispered to him then
of every toy I had ever owned, or seen,

imagining that he imagined all of them right here
under a tree like his, and not the stark menorah,
our stunted version, with its nine thin candles

solemn as school, or the inkstand and underwear—
more chores than gifts—which I received for Chanukah.
No, it was Christmas here under my parents' bed,

445

it was His manger, and His death was as far from me
as I was from my own house carolling a holy
inventory to my friend. Then he was gone.

The springs became cold law against me as I was hauled
out clinging to the receiver like a hooked fish
to where my father waited, stern as the candles,

fisher of Jews: you want to be a goy, he said,
be a goy, and sent me to my room for the whole day
where it was Chanukah. And I was more a Jew

the more I pictured to myself all of the presents
I had seen at Charlie's house the day before,
a king's treasure, from which the tree ascended

in a pyramid of flames and glittering angels.
On my bare walls, all day, I had to build it
higher and brighter, as though it were a burden

I could not put down, could never escape—
driven to build it all day by a heart
the God of my father, the Lord our God, kept hardening.

The Basement

How many years, decades, since I'd even thought of Gary
when my mother told me on the phone the other night,
in passing, that he'd been thrown in jail for kiting checks,
and that this on top of all the other heartache Gary's mother
had from him, the busted marriage, the drug problems,
had sent her to an early grave. But it wasn't Gary's mother
I thought of as I listened but the basement where we spent
most of our afternoons one summer, the two of us and Helen,
Helen the only German Jew I knew, who'd come after the war
from someplace else, not Germany (though no one told me where),
to live with them, to be his nanny. He called her Zumzing
because she hardly spoke except to ask, every so often,
can I get you zumzing, Gary, you vant zumzing now?
and whether he wanted anything or not he'd answer,
get me zumzing Zumzing, and laugh, so I'd laugh too.
Helen, though, unmindful of the teasing, or inured to it,
which made it easier to do, would hover over Gary,
her readiness to please him unassailable, yet strangely dour,
joyless, like someone on indefinite probation for some crime
nothing she could ever do could quite make up for.

Whenever he'd ask, she'd get the bottle Gary said
wasn't a bottle but a big cigar. Though eight years old,
he'd nuzzle against her, "smoking," gazing at nothing,
Helen stroking his hair, reminding him, Vee don't tell Mama,
dis just our secret, vee don't tell your mama now,
at which he'd pause, grinning, saying Vee dis, vee dat,
with the cigar held gangster style between his fingers.
It never occurred to me to make fun of him.
He'd look up from the bottle from time to time, and smile,
and seem so certain I'd admire him for this, I couldn't not.
It was as if in going down into the basement

he'd gone beyond the reach of how we usually were,
becoming at the same time both older and younger
than he should have been. It thrilled me, being there
with him, all the rules suspended, making new rules up,
the games he'd want to play so like and unlike
the games I knew that to play them was to feel
myself complicit in the secrets he and Helen shared:

Whoever was "it" would be buried under cushions,
and stay there dead while Helen counted to a hundred.
Then "it" would roar and rise and hunt the other down,
whipping him back into the pit where he'd be buried.
Or with the cushions Helen would wall in a corner of the basement,
and Gary and I would take turns guarding each other, marching
back and forth before the entrance, a rifle on one shoulder,
until the prisoner watching for the slightest lapse
would storm the gate, all of the cushions tumbling
down around us as we wrestled to the floor.

I remember reading of the children in the camps and ghettos,
how in their stubborn urge for pleasure where there was no pleasure
they'd pretend the horrors they were living through:
the bigger ones who got to be the Germans whipping and beating
the smaller ones who were the Jews, to dig their graves,
stage funerals, line each other up, and through it all,
German and Jew together, they would all be laughing.
During the war, wouldn't Helen have been about the age
that we were then? I wonder now what she was seeing, or
wanted to see as she looked on, waiting until the play
got too rough, as it always would, and one of us would cry
before she'd pull us off each other and, hugging Gary
or hurrying to get him out another bottle, ask
in the same flat tone, Now vee do zumzing else now, jah?

My mother didn't know where Helen was now,
or whether she went on living with the family
after Gary dropped out of high school and moved away.
She said it drove his mother crazy, how she spoiled him rotten.

Did Helen mourn the trouble he got into? Or had she
by the time we knew her had her fill of mourning,
her heart by then concerned with other things, things he
unwittingly provided, Gary never more enslaved
than in the license she made him think was his? Could he
have been her plaything too, as much as she was his,
her puppet of a secret brooding on what couldn't be forgotten,
all of her life from the war on (and she was just a girl then)
a mere reprise, a deafening echo chamber?
                                                    And even now
I wonder who's obliging whom when Helen—
after all these years of never being thought of, lost
among the minor people of my personal history—
rises from the dead through small talk to become
my personal link to what I can't imagine.

It almost seems I have my way with her again,
seeing her there in this last scene, down on her knees
surrounded by a chaos of innumerable pieces
of the train set she's saying is like the one she played with
with her papa long ago, an aura of dread and urgency
about her as she hurries to put it all together, working
to keep us down there with her a little longer,
to keep us from going anywhere she wouldn't follow
(did I ever see her leave the house?): all over the basement,
the tracks in curves and straightaways, the signs for Stuttgart,
München, Würzburg, Berlin, the flashing signal lights,
the flagman in the switching yard, black-coated porter at the station,
and beyond it shops, cafés, and houses, a church and school—
the flanged wheels fitted to the tiny rails, and Gary
settled in her lap now, his hands on the black box
easing the levers as she whispers dis one, jah, now dat,
and the cars click forward through that miniature world.
Soon, though, bored, he throws the black box down, and he and I
rampage over everything, stomping and pulling it all apart
while Helen laughs (the only time I ever heard her laugh).

Richard Chess (b. 1953)

Richard Chess was born in Los Angeles, raised in New Jersey, attended Glassboro State College, and earned his doctorate from the University of Florida. He is the Director of the Center for Jewish Studies at the University of North Carolina at Asheville. Chess's poetry reflects his lifelong interest in Jewish history, culture, and theology, as well as his fascination with Jewish mysticism—especially the writings of Isaac Luria, the early sixteenth-century Kabbalist. The title of Chess's first collection of poetry, *Tekiah*, refers to the sound of the Shofar, the ceremonial ram's horn that is blown on Yom Kippur, the Jewish Day of Atonement. "Growing Up in a Jewish Neighborhood" and "Yiddish Poets in America" successfully combine images and experiences from both the New and Old Worlds. "Two and One" strikes a subtle Kabbalistic tone in its use of riddle and proverb, and in its affirmation of religious belief. "No Music," on the other hand, is an ironic portrayal of contemporary Jewish religious observance.

Growing Up in a Jewish Neighborhood

He wants to go
Where no one freezes
When the phone rings

When meat is sliced, he wants
The stench of blood
To concentrate his hunger

Once he saw
His grandmother's breasts
They were sour yellow stars

He wants a crow
That speaks not Yiddish
 But its own ugly language

The seasons enclose him
Like a barbed-wire fence
His name is a button

Stitched to a coat
A style his grandfather in Minsk
Might have worn

At the urinal
Connie Mack Stadium
He wants his penis to signify

Nothing
He wants to reach for the stone
Flashing in the river

Without thinking
Of Aunt Dora
He wants the glass of a broken window

To tell no story
He wants an empty pocket
He wants new shoes

Yiddish Poets in America

The sky above us was silent and empty,
The earth below, silent, empty,
Our pockets were empty,
And our hands, empty, failed to fly.

We heard villages lock their gates,
We heard our language burn in a great fire,
And we urged it, the fire, to take
The tongue of our despair.

From yellow hearts we rescued no poems.
Nor can we purchase poems from the dead
Among whom we live in suburban verses.

Two and One

Two roses I gave the therapist,
One for my thorny soul, one for hers.
Two answers to a step-daughter,
One in the hollow voice of her father.
Two days with an old friend,
One to recover the past,
One to recover from the past.
But I turn to one God only
When I lie down and rise up,
One God at the end of a day
When I empty the pockets,
And at dawn when I fill them again.

A proverb I recalled for my father
The day he confessed he was broke:
Rich man and poor man meet;
The Lord made them both;
He listened patiently.
Two gifts for the bride,
One of this world, one of the world to come.
But I labor to repair one world only
When I walk by the way.

Two coins for the beggar,
Two loaves for the Sabbath
Which ends when three stars open
In the Saturday night sky.
Two parents, neither one on this earth.
Two hands, one with which to give,
One with which to take away.
Two ears with which to hear, O Israel,
The Lord our God, the Lord is One.

No Music

The rabbi tells us music on the Sabbath
is prohibited. No clarinet chuckling
after roast chicken, no accordion
ordering us up on our feet to dance, no fiddle
whose delight can even be felt
in the bones of the deaf among us.
On the Sabbath, the rabbi says, you shall have
no music, recorded or live, other than that
which can be made without instrumentation,
and he strums the air to illustrate how
to play on this day God ceased from creation.
Not to worry, the rabbi instructs us, not to
disturb the strict peace of the sanctuary
we enter on the Sabbath and from which we depart
wedded, once more, to the souls we divorce
and divorce. No gossip, the rabbi implores,
shall pour from the spigots of your mouths,
not on the Sabbath, not on any one of the six
days of the week. But the days leave us weak,
that's why we plead with him to deal with us
mercifully, to give us our *klezmer* and soul, the salve
of Aretha's voice will relieve the pain, the *freylach*
will free us to move back into our bodies, our luxury,
from which we have been exiled too long, our hips,
our buttocks and breasts and the bones of our bones,
but the rabbi says, the rabbi who speaks
from the past where he believes we lived
as our true selves, the red-headed rabbi whose garbled
sermons must make sense to the angels, the freckled
rabbi whose long, muscular legs carry him far
from house to house where he inspects the angles
at which *mezuzahs* are hung, the rabbi says no
music on the Sabbath and don't come late to synagogue.

Judith Baumel (b. 1956)

Judith Baumel's first book of poems, *The Weight of Numbers* (1988), received the prestigious Walt Whitman Award from the American Academy of Poets. Her second collection, *Now*, was published in 1995. In her poetry, Baumel mixes memories of her urban, Jewish upbringing with meditations on earlier, more universal events and places. As the title of her second volume indicates, Baumel's poems explore her fascination with the present moment. But that moment always points to an earlier, more meaningful event, one which evokes complex emotions and thoughts. In "Let Me In," for example, the image of a speeding ambulance recalls the death of the speaker's grandmother. "To the Parents of a Childhood Friend, a Suicide" links images of childhood friendship with death, with Nazi extermination, and ultimately with universal loss. "Samuel" is a first-person account of the poet's early memories of her grandfather. Baumel was born and raised in the Bronx, New York, received an undergraduate degree from Harvard, and earned an M.A. degree from Johns Hopkins University.

Samuel

As soon as I knew all the verses of the Shema
by heart they pushed me to my grandfather where he sat
so I could recite them.
The year before, I'd dropped belly to floor
in my velvet dirndl,
arched, and touched toes to head repeatedly
while the Family Circle admired my gymnastics.
He had just unwrapped the phylacteries;
the slight red depressions crossing his arm
were rising and receding. He was reading the psalms.
I said, "v'awhavtaw ais hashem . . . chirp chirp chirp . . .
polly want a cracker? . . . uv'lecht'chaw baderech,
uv'shawchb'chaw . . ."
All three paragraphs, rapid fire, including,
in the third, kissing, as if a man, my imaginary tallis.
And he nodded, gave no praise or smile,
only the silent shame that this piece of faith
was not performable, that the covered eyes
and whispered declarations come in fear,
humility and concentration. I had made a mistake.
He showed me the cavern I might fall into.
I would fall over and over.
His namesake anointed Saul and warned Saul
of the future history of his devastating pride.
Quiet and diligent in his habits
of which his observance was composed,
my grandfather found prayer like the constant weather
of a mild American June,
no Galician struggle
with the rightness, perfection, presentation,
correction of what the Lord has given.

Just—when He calls: "Here am I."
And when He asks: "I have heard and I will do."
"I accept" simply taken unto peace and unto life.

To the Parents of a Childhood Friend, a Suicide

I. SHELACH LECHA / SEND FOR THYSELF, THAT THEY
   MAY SPY OUT THE LAND OF CANAAN

To have escaped Hitler and come to this.
What were the gifts that remained to give to her?
Necklaces, pearls, small jewels which she returned
a week before her death? What I remember
is how you'd lie mysteriously silent
and still on the couches in your living room,
the plastic covers on chairs, shades brought down.
The dark and constant eerie presence of blue.
In numbers. And your arms: untouchable
as biblical blue dyes whose formula
and sacred color is lost. I can't explain
this time to you, hunched and thin, alive,
but find I wonder if in "those years" you hoped
to forget you ever ate or slept or kissed.

II. MASSEY, BEMIDBAR / THE STAGES OF GOINGS
    FORTH, IN THE WILDERNESS

I often feel I catch a glimpse of her
in the predictable streets or find her shape
approaching me in crowds and want to rush
to her to say, "I knew it was a mistake."
But knew, at home last night, I saw for sure,
through open doors, above a pile of clothes,
Emily's white face. Could recognize
a familiar roundness, bits of straight dark hair,
the downward slant of her reluctant smile,
the weight of sadness sitting underneath
her eyes as if some tiny pebbles sewn

in the bags, at birth, steadied and pulled her face,
which, seen, pulls out to our open eyes
dry and hurt with tears that still won't come.

III.   BERIT MELACH OLAM / AN EVERLASTING COVENANT OF SALT

Her burial was the second-hottest day
ever in the city: a hundred and four.
Only the earth of her open grave seemed cool,
even sweet. The Rabbi told me privately,
"we must remember her in life, not death."
I thought, how wrong, how he could never tell
one child's unrumpled face from a hurt one
in school. I bit my hand and tasted salt.
He'd tell us how conquerors of biblical towns
spread salt on the ruins, a desert. I remembered how
Emily forced an extra punishment
in games of knux. The loser drank two cups
of warm salt water. No matter if she gagged,
or, worse, threw up. She drank it all. At once.

IV.   AKEDAH / THE OFFERING OF ISAAC

Your childhood disappeared when they changed Lemburg
to Lvov. When you left the town for German camps.
And now, once more, when Emily died. Mine too;
we've lost some recent, private history.
It's more than convenient talk to say such things:
the robbery chain-links forever from aunts
she did not know, past nieces who won't know
their aunt, and the children who played with you just drift
into memory from that black unmentioned event.
Unwilling to be a ram's horn to redeem it,
my playmate forced me to repeat your loss.
We're left with nothing. No record of ourselves,
no bible to measure what has passed or changed,
and events become just an emblem or a cause.

Let Me In

What goes on inside those ambulance boxes,
those little worlds of activity negotiating the traffic?
I've always been awkward about pulling to the side,
wedging myself between a pillar of the El
and a van, or too slow to take the shoulder.
For three minutes the ambulance wailed
my grandmother to the hospital less than three blocks away
but across and around the parkway.
"Oy vey," she gasped, fell back
on her bed and became so light my mother
could move her. The year before when she'd fallen
on the way to the bathroom and broken
her ribs, she was impossible to move,
her thick legs splayed, the ulcerous flesh,
the heavy breasts still alive.
But oy vey, and that was it, except
for a technicality machines sustained.
That day my period had come, I was trying
to conceive, and the failure became dating
of the pregnancy I did have.
It wasn't a girl I could name for her
but somehow he was she, somehow, she still there.
The laugh, this boy's clear blue eyes—
they're hers. At least I can believe so.
The ambulance couldn't do anything for her.
Still they go past now, in every one a little story,
a little store window of pain,
there they go, taking someone, no her, her, her.
I pull over, I want to follow them this time,
this time it's she. That's where she's gone, it's she. Let me in.

Jacqueline Osherow (b. 1956)

Jacqueline Osherow is the author of three well-received collections of poetry: *Looking for Angels in New York* (1988), *Conversations with Survivors* (1992), and *With a Moon in Transit* (1996). Osherow's poetry reflects her interest in history, politics, the Old Testament, and recent Jewish history—especially the Holocaust. For Osherow, Nazi extermination defined the horror of the twentieth century as "a fact of life," and much of her poetry seeks to depict and bear witness to that horror. "To Eva," "Song for the Music in the Warsaw Ghetto," and "My Cousin Abe, Paul Antschel and Paul Celan" are all part of Osherow's attempt to convey the events and the significance of the Holocaust through her poetry. (Celan changed his name from Antschel when he settled in France.) In "The Yiddish Muses," she pays homage to the long tradition of Jewish poetry. Osherow was born in Philadelphia, Pennsylvania, and was educated at Radcliffe College and Princeton University, where she received a Ph.D. degree. She teaches English and creative writing at the University of Utah.

The Yiddish Muses

I—unneeded, a poet among Jews—
Growing, like wild grass, from a soil not ours. . . .
In an alien world I sing of the cares
Of men in a desert beneath alien stars.
                              —*Mani Leib* (1883–1953)

They arrive, always, unexpected,
Silent as the glide of angels
On six wings. Only the idea of sound,
Wind that for a moment might be ocean.
I want to catch them, to make something
For them, a city or at least a psalm,
But I have nothing to build it with.
Yiddish is no language for poetry, so homely
On the page, vowels instead of silences.

Unneeded, a poet among Jews,
I end up wandering the streets
With unknown visitors, who speak
In a language round and thick
As pillows squashed against my head.
They are telling dreams, so old,
So corny, dreamed by now in almost
Every language and a few elements:
Wood, stone, even gold, preserved
In cloth with needles and silk thread.

They have left a little dreaming
Everywhere: watery cities, towered cities,
Even in Córdoba, blank with sun, so white
And so unlikely, they left a whole room
Engraved with psalms. Judah Halevi
Left a palace and a family. Tired
Of poetry and dreams, he headed East.

After that, no one is certain.
They say he was trampled by a Turkish horse
As he kissed the earth, arriving in Jerusalem.

You will tell me this is not a pleasant story,
But you know nothing about dreams.
What would have happened if the sun
Had bowed to Joseph? I know for a fact
It would have killed him and any unsuspecting
Bystanders. I suppose we must be patient
Here, at the stony end of the ladder.
Only angels can go up and come back down.

I stay awake nights, though I'd give
Anything to see the curved backs
Of stars, and wonder who needs ladders
With three sets of wings. I watch shadows,
Cast by my Venetian blinds, stretch
Across the ceiling like the tracks
For unknown trains. Can you blame me
If I ride and ride, unneeded as I am
And dangerous, a dreamer among Jews?

The muses burst out laughing, "Some dream."
All morning, in synagogue, they chuckle
As they praise The Name, "Some prize to be a traveler
Among Jews." Still, they manage silence
For the eighteen prayers, establishing that routine
Miracle, reordering of heavens, Jerusalem
Rising like the sun above their heads,
Above, even, the women's section, higher
Than any memory its walls and domes.

To Eva

Born: D.P. camp, Lanzburg, Germany, March 21, 1947
Died: New Jersey, January 9, 1985

As usual, the seasons change too fast.
This year's early balmy spell so leisurely,
Convincing, it tricks even the cautious
White magnolia into opening
And giving up its petals to a sudden
Change of air, to scatter on the ground
Like a thousand schoolgirl hopes to pluck, "he loves me."
Forsythia and crocus, from a distance,
Are confetti, what crowds in Venice
Throw into the air at *Carnivale*
To color streets for two weeks into Lent.
That's what the willow branches look like,
Even close up, or some oriental
Decoration for the year of the dragon,
Dripping long, chartreuse crepe-paper scales.
And I would so much rather be waking
To a sky like the inside of a shell,
The nearly invisible gray-white chambers,
Swirl enfolding swirl in clouds of snow,
Establishing a clear, white, soundless
Distance between place and place, all pale
Until the twisted stretch of branches starts
To darken over bars of rose and gold,
Looking like that kindergarten trick
Of covering a wildly crayoned picture
With a heavy coat of black, then scratching back
The colors with a pin. And I would watch
Those leafless trees even without a sunset,
All those previously well-kept secrets
In the open air, wayward arrows,
Umbrella frames turned inside out in wind.
Commuting, through the thinnest gauze of snow,

I would watch them from the window, knowing what
The world will look like when there is no world,
How its ghosts will haunt the empty space.

And what happened to you was almost
Tolerable on those days. At least
It didn't screech the way it screeches now
Against these garish blossoms floating lies
Up and down the Northeast Corridor,
Until even I am starting to believe them,
Smelling lilac, grabbing crimson beds
Of tulips with the corner of my eye,
Mauve azaleas. For your father, it must
Be like his first, lurid days out of Dachau,
Europe a bizarre, trick continent,
The same names on the signposts of the towns,
On the railway platforms, on the street signs,
The same shops, the same houses, the same doors,
And the people, if anything at all,
Hallucinations. It was spring then, too,
Not that he noticed it, though I would bet
He knew the season two springs later. You
Were the rarest of the rare, a person *born*.
The others must have envied your grandmother
When she got you to fill her empty name.
Now it's back again, with all those hundreds
And hundreds of thousands of unused extras,
In a vast invisible pile, like those
Famous piles of eyeglasses and shoes,
Waiting for the Messiah, I guess,
When the bodies of the dead will rise,
Asking questions of the rabbis among them.
Does the prophecy include the decomposed,
The graveless? Will they come alive as soap
And parchment and blankets or their old selves?
What will happen if the soap's been used,

The parchment printed on? The talmudists
Will work it out in singsong arguments,
Gesturing at blackboards made of air.

What they decide will not apply to you.
You died in better times, you had a service,
A grave, a tombstone, prayers for the dead.
Even the seasons cooperated,
Though, of course, they resumed their schedule
In no time, almost as oblivious
As the railway lines that still persist
In pushing Europe eastward, making stops
That shouldn't exist, bringing mail to them.
You would have thought that they would change the names,
That the earth would turn to salt, or something,
That this spring would at least have declared
Some brief moratorium, not come
So early, at least, so sure of itself,
Dragging cherry blossoms streaked with rain.
Look at them, an Impressionist might have
Painted them. See how they expose
Those frauds for what they were, opportunists,
Taking advantage of a freakish storm
To paint the world as petals smeared with rain,
As if they'd made it up, a new art form
Out of this horrible freak of nature
They catch before the real catastrophe
When everything comes down in heavy wind
And the shaken trees, lost, just stand there,
Thinking this isn't supposed to happen,
Isn't the order of things, unlearning
Everything they know, while, all around,
The spring regains composure, flourishes,
And at their feet the petals mimic snow.

My Cousin Abe, Paul Antschel and Paul Celan

O one, o none, o no one, o you
Where did the way lead when it led nowhere?

Perhaps, like everything, it has its flow and ebb,
The way nowhere, I mean, your brutal question.
Not that you were asking me. You asked no one
But I once eavesdropped on the conversation.
Regards, by the way, from my cousin, Abe;
I'm hoping they will serve as introduction.

Do you remember him? For twelve years your classmate?
A Yiddish speaker, religious, quick at math?
I was telling about his great *lantzman*-poet
And he identified you by your death:
He killed himself? In Paris? In the Seine?
His name is Antschel, Paul Antschel, not Celan.

He even has a picture of your graduation
(You were both dark-haired dreamy-eyed young men).
It's a wonder the photograph survived.
My cousin must have brought it to Japan,
A surprising place to go, once the war began,
But, for a while, his uncle's business thrived,

Import-export, I think it was, coral, pearls.
My mother has a strand of heavy beads
That Abe's wife, Beka, brought to her years later,
Like setting suns erased by wisps of clouds.
Abe must have meant them for his mother or sister
Or perhaps even the shiest of the girls

In matching fur-trimmed muffs and collars and hems
Whom you'd watch dawdling on their way to *shul*
While you were working on your weekly themes.

Abe said no one else could win the prize,
That everything you wrote was something beautiful
And he's a hard man, of little praise.

When I asked him more questions, he grew fierce:
Nice? Sure. We were all nice. Nice. Quiet.
Yes. I saw him daily for twelve years
But what do you ever know about a person?
I would speak in Yiddish, he spoke German;
My family was religious, his was not.

He pointed out some others in the picture:
The one who got to Venezuela to manufacture
Was it textiles? The one who managed to hide,
The one who teaches chemistry in Austria;
He didn't bother to say the rest had died
With his mother, his sister, your parents, in Transnistria . . .

As a child, I never dreamed it was a place,
It seemed to me some sort of fatal curse,
The heaviest among the floating words
I'd always heard but couldn't precisely trace.
Transnistria, it was only uttered in whispers
That lingered, unresolved, like bungled chords.

I later learned that Beka's mother had died
In Transnistria, my grandma's brother's wife.
They'd written back and forth, a charming girl,
So gracefully she'd filled sheaf after sheaf:
How they went out picking berries, mushrooms, sorrel . . .
Perhaps she met your parents on the ride.

How she must've made my grandma long for home
When she described her soups of sorrel and mushrooms,
The brandy she would coax from new, ripe plums
From raspberries, the syrup to sweeten soda,
From gooseberries, the compote, sponge cake, jam,
I suppose you could call Transnistria their coda,

Certainly no more letters ever came
And there was no more anything to long for;
Longing was, itself, a strange taboo
But you couldn't quite help yourself, could you?
All you wanted was one untroubled hour
In the cinema, perhaps, or in a dream

Or wandering, aimless, down adopted boulevards
Oblivious to storefronts, noises, faces,
Trying to piece together shards of words
Scattered over Europe like the scattered beads
Of a thousand trunks of undelivered necklaces,
Bent on mapping out where nowhere leads.

Wherever it is, the way is rich in colors,
Loosely strung with dark pink coral beads,
Littered with fur-trimmed muffs and matching collars,
Crumbs from airy cakes, gooseberry seeds,
Ink stains from a schoolboy's dreaming pen
And pale confetti floating on the Seine

And here is Abe, as he interrupts his wife
Who's describing making brandy out of plums;
To no one in particular he's quoting psalms,
Mumbling about the holiness of life.
What could have happened? He is bruised, distraught,
What could have made him do a thing like that?

Song for the Music in the Warsaw Ghetto

Pity the tune bereft of singers
Pity the tone bereft of chords
Where shall we weep? By which waters?
Pity the song bereft of words

Pity the harps hung on rifles
The unsuspected cunning in each hand
Pity the shrill, bewildered nightingales
How could they sing in that strange land?

Pity the string that has no bow
Pity the flute that has no breath
Pity the rifle's muted solo
Pity its soundless aftermath

Robyn Selman (b. 1959)

Born in New York City, Robyn Selman received an M.F.A. degree from Sarah Lawrence College. Her first collection of poetry, *Directions to My House*, was published in 1995. In her poems, Selman mixes conventional lyrical forms, such as the sonnet, with unconventional rhyme schemes and free verse. Her subjects range from feminism and sexuality to her Jewish family roots. Like Becker, her references to Jewishness are usually succinct but important to an understanding of personality and circumstance. In both "Descent" and "Work Song," Selman recalls events and people from her early life in an effort to explain and illuminate her present state of mind. "For the Field" evokes a mood of sadness and loss, as well as one of invitation and hope.

For the Field

From the seven small windows of my room:
the last of the maple's stars have fallen.

There are new browns to see, ochres and grays.
The rain on the leaves, a minstrel all day.

Come across the field. I wish you would now.
With our dutiful mothers, come across,

with the gold stolen from their cousins' teeth.
I wouldn't ask if I weren't ready.

How is it that six million deaths equal
one atrocity? With our ragged trust,

come across, not my god but my lover.
Our wailing beasts and mirrors in shambles,

with darkness that lights the blue-green numbers,
our lost as many as leaves, come across.

Descent

When I squeeze through the narrow sluice of grief,
dust myself off, sprout new elbows and knees,
if or when I can be in the world again,

I'll see trees on the side of the hill grow thick,
vistas of green instead of barrenness,
when I squeeze through the narrow sluice of grief.

We are two women alone in these thick woods,
one of us more alone than the other.
If or when I can be in the world again,

I'd like to learn the names of birds with you,
I'd like to do some swimming in the nude,
when I've kicked through the narrow sluice of grief.

I was the child who said she didn't need
either parent from that old, old world.
When I could be in the world with them

they were each fifty years older than me
and had grown up wary on the Bowery
where Jews squeezed through a narrow sluice of grief.

My mother's bony fingers frightened me.
I played war. My father bought in quantity.
Before I was in the ruined world with him

he had lost a young wife named Anne.
He never said how. He rarely said *Anne*.
Once he squeezed through the narrow sluice of grief

he married a singer, twenty years younger.
I was born. Bored with it all, she left soon after.
Once my father could be in the world again

he met Ruth, divorced from a salesman.
They were married at sea by a ship's captain
and sailed through a narrow strait of grief.

My father sailed away at sixty-seven.
Ruth knit nine more years of afghans
and never came back to the world again.

I think of the singer I look like, often.
She never comes back again and again.
Once I sigh through the narrow throat of grief

I'll walk with you on Delancey Street.
We'll be with them and yet be rid of them.
You and I together in what world then?
When I squeeze through the narrow sluice of grief.

Work Song

1

A trucker leans on his horn down below.
I'm reading an essay on Latino
immigrants who live four, five to a room
in damp, lightless studio apartments.
They live this way to save every cent—
their goal being a family-owned business.
The caveat: male-only ownership.
Its foundation: Biblical argument.
My father lived in a Grand Street tenement,
his parents and brothers cramped in two beds.
Pulled from school by fourth grade, the boys were sent
to work as schleppers in the garment trade.
The money saved bought a truck for hire.
The three boys who survived became partners.

The three boys who survived became partners.
They grew a tough business, were tough themselves,
hauling textiles from southern cotton mills
to the North where the fabric was patterned,
to the South to be cut and assembled,
then back up North to be tagged and labeled.
My father was proud of his business mind,
edging out his brothers until he died.
Those uncles are still alive in Florida
with their wives. One works afternoons sorting
piece goods. The other took mornings at a
zipper concern in Little Havana.
They say the same thing, though at different times:
Whichever comes first—I'll work or I'll die.

2

My stepmother's mother owned a teahouse on
the New York docks where immigrants
like her, Hungarian-Romanian,
came for tea and black bread barely leavened.
Her husband, well-dressed but indigent,
failed at collecting rents on apartments
which she'd leased to other Europeans.
She didn't believe in banks or mattresses,
so pinned her money beneath her dress hems.
After the late shift, 1936,
her sons went down to the teahouse with picks
and axes. They razed the place, then torched it.
It was for her own good, they insisted.
She was carried off her own premises.

She'd been working since the age of nine when
her mother got TB. Her father also died.
Married and pregnant in her teens, she still
worked a twelve-hour day, six days a week,
at a pedal-driven sewing machine
beside other Jewish minors in an
East Side ladies' foundation factory.
She lost three consecutive unborn children.
Her womb gave way to the constant pumping.
She quit and opened the tea company
which she ran alone until seventy,
when, with her insurance money, the sons
went into business: lumber on Mott Street.
With no work to do, she died in her sleep.

3

My stepmother wished she could die in her sleep.
She'd been married for twenty-nine years to
a slippery life insurance salesman who
left her for a younger, redheaded beautician.
Needing work for the first time and over
fifty, she turned for help to her sister,

Bloomingdales' most cost-conscious bookkeeper,
who got her a job as a comptometer
operator. Years later, still alone,
she met my newly divorced father.
The wife who'd left him left me and my brother.
(*He worked too hard. He was never at home.*)
Older still, tired, but not in love,
she married him and quit her paying job.

She married him and quit her paying job
to be wife and mother to his children.
Like the wife before her who had left him,
none of us saw my father often.
He worked Mon-Sat from eight until ten.
We saw him one day over the weekend
when he slept in a brown living room chair
and we watched from afar like zoo patrons,
awed and careful not to provoke him.
Then some mob toughs who were angry that
he hadn't paid the piper truckman's graft
burned his shipping terminal, his temple.
I saw my father red-eyed and sullen
but couldn't bring myself to welcome him.

4

I couldn't bring myself to welcome her—
the wife who left my father, my birth mother.
She worked at a nightclub frequented by
aspiring wise guys of the underworld
as a part-time singer, part-time call girl.
They divorced by the time I was sixteen
months old. She didn't sue for custody.
Being rid of him meant rid of their baby.
The fruit of her labor and the worker
didn't meet again until I was eighteen,
off from a job I had selling car parts

to mechanics whose names I read off lists.
Calling to sell fan belts, rebuilts, filters,
I heard myself called *cunt*, *snatch*, and *salesbitch*.

To earn my pay I would justify it:
a child still with a child's words, *sticks*
and stones, I'd repeat, as I rhymed my way
through rain-slicked Florida streets toward home,
cash in my pocketed, phone-warmed palm.
She let me try to justify what she
did at a drink-stained Miami table
where I mistook silence for approval.
I used terms like *oppressed* and *class struggle*.
We both knew I knew too little. She said,
Work hard, but forget it at the end of the day.
Her hands swept the air, two brooms in motion.
The check came. We struggled over who would pay.
Rain knifed a work song out of the trade winds.

Credits

Grateful acknowledgment is made for permission to reprint work by the following poets:

JUDITH BAUMEL: "Let Me In." From *Now* by Judith Baumel, copyright © 1995 by Judith Baumel, published by Miami University Press. Reprinted by permission of the author. "Samuel," "To the Parents of a Childhood Friend, a Suicide." From *The Weight of Numbers* by Judith Baumel, copyright © 1986 by Wesleyan University Press. Reprinted by permission of the University Press of New England.

ROBIN BECKER: "The Crypto-Jews," "Spiritual Morning," "Yom Kippur, Taos, New Mexico." From *All-American Girl* by Robin Becker, copyright © 1996 by Robin Becker. Reprinted by permission of the University of Pittsburgh Press. "Grief." From *Giacometti's Dog* by Robin Becker, copyright © 1990 by Robin Becker. Reprinted by permission of the University of Pittsburgh Press.

MARVIN BELL: "The Extermination of the Jews," "Getting Lost in Nazi Germany," "The Israeli Navy." From *New and Selected Poems of Marvin Bell* by Marvin Bell, copyright © 1987 by Marvin Bell, published by Atheneum. Reprinted by permission of the author. "The Book of the Dead Man (#58)." From *Ardor: The Book of the Dead Man, Vol. 2* by Marvin Bell, copyright © 1997 by Marvin Bell, published by Copper Canyon Press. Reprinted by permission of the author.

STEPHEN BERG: "Desnos Reading the Palms of Men on Their Way to the Gas Chambers," "Prayer." From *New and Selected Poems* by Stephen Berg, copyright © 1992 by Stephen Berg. Reprinted by permission of Copper Canyon Press, Port Townsend, Washington.

MAXWELL BODENHEIM: "Old Age." From *Minna and Myself* by Maxwell Bodenheim, copyright © 1918 by Maxwell Bodenheim, published by Pagan Publishing. Reprinted by permission of Jack B. Moore. "Poem to Gentiles."

481

482

485

489

Acknowledgments

I would like to express my gratitude to my colleague Edgar Hirshberg for his perceptive reading of the manuscript and for his helpful recommendations; to my research assistants at the University of South Florida, Linda Sarbo and Joyce Karpay; and to my editor at Beacon Press, Susan Worst, for her support and guidance throughout the development of this project. As always, I am indebted to my wife, Jean Moore, for her suggestions and encouragement.

Subject Index

Index of Poets